3D Game Creation

3D Game Creation

Luke Ahearn

CHARLES
RIVER
MEDIA

Charles River Media, Inc.
Hingham, Massachusetts

Publisher: David F. Pallai
Production: Publishers' Design and Production Services
Printer: InterCity Press, Inc.
Cover Design: The Printed Image

CHARLES RIVER MEDIA, INC.
20 Downer Avenue, Suite 3
Hingham, Massachusetts 02043
781-740-0400
781-740-8816 (FAX)
info@charlesriver.com
www.charlesriver.com

This book is printed on acid-free paper.

Luke Ahearn. *3D Game Creation.*
ISBN: 1-58450-067-0

Library of Congress Cataloging-in-Publication Data

Ahearn, Luke.
      3d game creation / Luke Ahearn.
         p. cm.
      ISBN 1-58450-067-0 (alk. paper)
      1. Computer games—Programming.   2. Computer graphics.
   I. Title: Three d game creation.   II. Title.
   QA76.76.C672 A42 2001
   794.8'151—dc21

                                             2001003450

Printed in the United States of America
01 02 7 6 5 4 3 2 First Edition

For Julie, Ellen, and Cooper.

Contents

10 ADVANCED CONTROL OF ACTIVE OBJECTS 171

18 ASSEMBLING THE FINAL GAME 317

APPENDIX C WHAT'S ON THE CD-ROM 349

Acknowledgments

To Clickteam (www.clickteam.com) for The Games Factory and Install Maker. François Lionet, Yves Lamoureux, and the Games Factory Manual writers: Ian Young, assisted by Philip Chapman, Richard Vanner, and Lee Bamber.

To Pie in the Sky Software (www.pieskysoft.com) for the Pie 3D Game Creation System.

To Jenifer Niles and Dave Pallai of Charles River Media.

Thank you.

Introduction

W elcome to *CyberRookies 3D Game Creation*.

WHAT'S IN THE BOOK

This book provides you with some excellent game systems and tools to introduce you to game design and development in an easy-to-understand manner. When you're comfortable with these systems and concepts, you'll have a good foundation to use as you move on to more complex systems and tools.

Part One: Game Technology and Design

In Part One, we look at what you need to know before you begin to develop games and interactive applications. We walk through the design process, and discuss what equipment you will need for game development.

Game development and *game design* are often confused. Design comes first, and then development. Designing is planning the game, and development is making the game. This distinction is critical, and we will refer to it often. We focus on design in Part One, and then spend a good portion of the rest of the book on development.

Part Two: 2D Game Creation

ON THE CD

In Part Two, we actually make a 2D game using The Games Factory, or TGF. You will find a copy of TGF on the companion CD-ROM that you need to install before we get started. Don't worry if you have trouble installing it; there is a section to walk you through the installation.

TGF is an easy-to-use game creation tool. It represents state-of-the-art animated graphics and sound, multimedia functions, and fabulous game-structuring routines that make it very quick and easy to produce your own games without any programming skills.

HINT!

You can also make slide shows, interactive tests, presentations, and screen savers with the full version of TGF!

With TGF, you can create platform games, maze games, and many other graphic adventures. You don't even have to make the characters, images, and sounds for your games, because TGF has a huge graphics library that contains many different characters and backdrops. After you learn the basics, you can make your own animated characters, backdrops, and even record your own sound effects to make a game that is uniquely yours.

Part Three: 3D Game Creation

In Part Three, we'll actually make a 3D game using The Pie 3D Game Creation System (GCS). The Pie GCS is an integrated software package for nonprogrammers. With this program, the user can create a 3D action game that is comparable to *Doom*, *Wolfenstein 3D*, *Terminator*, and others. The GCS is a DOS application that requires a 386 or better computer and a VGA graphics card. Pie in the Sky designed GCS to be an easy-to-use program for nonprogrammers; therefore, the program is mouse and graphically based.

Since you are probably new to the subject of game development, you should read this book from beginning to end and work through the exercises. You will need to understand the terms and technology reviewed in Part One, and the skills you learn in Part Two are applied in Part Three.

KEEP IN TOUCH

We would love to see the games or other applications you create with the skills you learn here and the tools provided on the CD-ROM. Please send links to your creations to cyber@goldtree.com, and we'll post or link to the best ones.

Game Technology and Design

Your Game Studio

IN THIS CHAPTER
· · · · · · · · · · · · · · · ·

- What Is a Game Development System?
- What Are the Parts of a Game Development System?
- What System Do You Need?
- How to Minimize Your Risk when Buying a Computer

WHAT IS A GAME DEVELOPMENT SYSTEM?
· ·

In short, a game development system is a computer system adequate for developing your game and all of its components. A game development system can range from a low-end, inexpensive machine for simple game productions to a high-end machine that costs thousands of dollars. High-end systems are often linked to a network of other powerful machines, providing increased power to all of the machines on the network.

Determining what type of system you need is like choosing the right tool to solve any type of problem. For instance, if you were driving six children to school, driving in a road race, or driving into combat, you would have to select the appropriate vehicle—a minivan, a racecar, or a Humvee. While a minivan, racecar, and Humvee all have four wheels, they are each designed for very different purposes. The same is true for computers: they are all basically the same piece of equipment, but they can have very different levels of power and functionality. Therefore, the big question is "What will you be doing with your computer?" You may not be able to answer this question just yet, but once you have worked through the book and the different types of tasks you need to do as a game developer, you will.

Hopefully, you already have the basic tools of a game system, but we'll look at the typical components of a good game system and determine which components you may need to add.

SYSTEM AND EQUIPMENT

There are many things to consider when setting up your system, and one of the most important is the system requirement for the applications you will be using. These requirements are usually stated on the box, in ads, or on the home pages of the product and are typically broken down into *minimum* and *recommended*.

WATCHOUT!

Usually the *minimum system requirements* are just that—the bare minimum to run the application. The minimum system usually isn't the most comfortable or usable system for running the application, and it doesn't take into account the other applications you'll probably be running at the same time. Let's say that the minimum RAM requirement for your art application is 16MB, but you plan to run other applications at the same time (and you will as a game developer), such as a level editor, game engine, word processor, or 3D application. There is no doubt that if you have only 32MB of RAM, your system will be severely taxed and run poorly, if at all. The minimum requirements also don't usually take into account the files with which you will be working, so it's better to go for the recommended system setup if you can. So, the more RAM you have or can get, the faster and more efficient you'll be.

Another thing to watch for is recommended hard drive space, usually referred to in gigabytes on newer systems. This is the amount of space you have for the entire hard drive, so although it may sound like a lot, when you start adding programs and creating huge graphic and game files, that space will be used up quickly. Another critical thing to look for is speed. When working with large graphics files, speed is key. Processors are running in the 900-MHz range these days, so the faster you can get, the better.

Now that we've covered a few important things to watch out for, let's talk about specifics. To get started with the projects in the book, you'll need to own a basic computer setup with a few important peripherals.

COMPUTER

We'll assume you have a computer to use for now that is at least a 486 or higher CPU with Windows 95 or 98, 32MB of RAM, and 50MB of hard disk space. It should also have a good monitor, graphics card, Sound-Blaster or compatible sound card, and a mouse or other pointing device. If you don't have a computer, there are great deals to be found these days for a minimal investment (see "Tips for Buying Your Equipment" later in the chapter).

When purchasing or upgrading your system, remember to consider the different applications you will run. The operating system is the place to start. In this book, we'll use Windows 95 or 98, but new systems usually ship with the latest version of Windows or Macintosh's OS. The basic computer system today often has a 17-inch monitor, lots of RAM, and fairly large hard drives. You should have no problem with an off-the-shelf system or a mail order system from a reputable company.

HOW FAST SHOULD MY PROCESSOR BE?

As mentioned earlier, your computer should be as fast as you can afford it to be. The processor is the hardest and most expensive part of a computer to upgrade, so having or getting the fastest chip possible not only makes sense in general, but as a game developer you will be pushing your system harder than most other users, so you'll need the speed. You should have a processor that's at least 200 MHz, or everything will run very slowly.

However, even if your system is not the latest and greatest, you can still design and develop games with a minimal system (described earlier), as long as it can run the applications you are using. You may find yourself waiting a bit longer for applications to open and files to process with a slower machine, but you'll still get it done.

GRAPHIC (VIDEO) CARDS AND 3D CARDS

A graphic (video) card is what allows images to appear on your monitor. A video card usually controls how big the image is on your screen, how much detail it can have, and how many colors are displayed (we discuss the specific elements of an image in Chapter 2, "The Basics of Game Technology").

There are also 3D video cards, or hardware accelerated cards. While most applications require only the drawing of simple pictures such as your Windows desktop, a game or 3D application such as 3ds max needs a lot of help with the intense 3D calculations used to draw 3D scenes. With 3D, the computer is literally building each image as you play or create a game. Many times per second, the 3D application is drawing something new and using a lot of the processor's power. The 3D card is designed to take over these 3D rendering tasks for the computer, in order to free up the processor for other jobs.

RAM (RANDOM ACCESS MEMORY)

RAM means *random access memory* and is measured in megabytes, or MB (or "megs," as some people like to call them). The computer uses RAM as temporary storage for any applications in use. If you have ever been working on a document when your system unexpectedly shut down and you lost the document, you know all about RAM. RAM only functions when the computer is on, so it's a good idea to have a surge protector that will allow your computer to convert to battery power if there is a power failure. Then you have time to save your document and shut down the computer yourself.

How Much RAM Should I Get?

Again, get as much RAM as possible. In general, RAM is the most important thing you can have. It is often the best, cheapest, and easiest thing to upgrade in a computer. More RAM usually makes a more noticeable performance difference than a faster chip does. If you have 16 or 32MB of RAM and a fairly decent chip (at this point, a P200 is pretty minimal but fairly decent), then going to 120MB of RAM or more will be cheaper than buying a new computer, and you will see a huge performance boost.

OTHER PERIPHERALS

The other peripherals you need are pretty standard on most computers: a *modem* for accessing the Internet, a *zip drive* for backing up and transferring large files, and a *sound system*. Advanced peripherals that you may want to have eventually if you get into more complex game development or content creation could include the items discussed in the following sections.

SCANNER

A scanner basically works like a copy machine. You lay a document on the glass plate, close the cover, and scan it. A scanner converts your flat document or image into a digital image that can be manipulated in the computer as described in the next chapter. This can be very useful for creating game art or Web site art or simply getting standard photographs into the computer.

WATCHOUT!

Remember, you need permission to use other people's images and art. If you didn't create it yourself, someone else did.

DIGITAL CAMERA

A digital camera works like a traditional camera, but instead of film, you get a digital image such as the scanner produces. The major difference is that a scanner is good for high-resolution scans of flat images, while a digital camera is great for real-life 3D image captures. For example, if you want to add a cracked stone driveway to a scene in your game, you can take a picture of one with a digital camera and import it. With the scanner, you can only scan what already exists.

HIGH-SPEED INTERNET ACCESS

Most computers still come with a 56K modem. This is adequate for most uses, but if you are serious, you should try to get high-speed Internet access. The Internet is such a valuable resource, especially to game developers, that it is worth the investment: you'll be downloading some huge images, game demos, sound files, development tools, and animations. You can see in Table 1.1 that download times vary according to the access device.

TABLE 1.1   Download Time Comparisons for a 3.75MB File

Modem	Min:Sec
14.4 Kbps dial-up modem	35:33
28.8 Kbps dial-up modem	17:47
33.6 Kbps dial-up modem	15:14
56 Kbps dial-up modem	09:09
1.5 Mbps ADSL	00:20

CD-ROM BURNER

A CD-ROM burner is almost a necessity now, and many new systems have one. When you start serious game creation, you will want to back up your files for safety. In addition, if you want to share your game with others, it's easier to put it on a CD-ROM than on 50 floppy disks. There are other large-capacity storage disks such as the 250MB disks and removable drives that hold many gigabytes of information, but the 100MB Zip and the CD-ROM are the most common.

- A floppy disk holds 1.3MB of data. You can erase and recopy data on a floppy.
- A zip disk holds 100MB of data. You can erase and recopy data on a zip disk. There are also 250MB zip disks, but they can't be read on 100MB drives, so keep that in mind.
- A CD-ROM holds 650MB of data. On some burners, you can rewrite data. You can also burn multi-session CDs that allow the laying down of more data to empty parts of the disk. Usually you can write data only once.

There are also drives that operate like a zip drive and have larger data capacity, such as 250MB or more. Many companies are working on other types and sizes of storage, and a Boulder, Colorado company is working on a 500MB optical disk that is about one inch square. They are write-only disks, like CDs (so you can't reuse them), and will cost about five dollars each.

DIGITAL ART PEN OR DIGITIZER

The artist especially will like the digital art pen. This pen-like device allows you to draw more naturally into the computer by drawing on a "pad" rather than using a mouse.

These pads range from very inexpensive (about $50 at present) to several thousand dollars. On one end of the spectrum are small tablets that are good for recording a signature, and on the other, there are tablets coming on the market that are actually a combination tablet and monitor. With the Wacom PL series of tablet you can draw directly onto the monitor. This removes the sensation many artists cannot adjust to—drawing on a block of plastic and having to look up at the screen to see the results.

When buying a tablet, consider the following.

- Are you paying for the company or brand name or the quality of the product?
- What will you use the tablet for? Getting a digital signature requires the smallest and least expensive of the tablets, so you don't need to spend a lot of money.
- Touching up photos and artwork may require a more sensitive and accurate tablet, but not a large one.
- The largest tablets are good for creating art (drawing and sketching) directly into the computer, but many artists still prefer to do their sketches on paper and then scan them in.

A GOOD CHAIR

Buy a comfortable chair; you will be doing a lot of sitting.

TIPS FOR BUYING YOUR EQUIPMENT

- **Use a credit card.** If you don't have your own credit card, find someone to do this for you, especially when buying online. If you pay with cash or check and have a problem with your system, it may be more difficult to get a refund. With a credit card, you have the credit card company and the Fair Credit Billing Act behind you. This rule allows you 60 days to report a billing error or vendor dispute.
- **Understand what you are paying for.** Avoid the "under a thousand dollars" computers unless you *really* know what you are getting into. Often, these systems don't include everything you need, and you'll end up spending more than you wanted to for the complete system. Read the fine print and know exactly what's included in the price. Some reputable vendors to work with include Dell, Gateway, Micron, and Compaq. Expect to pay around $1500 to $2000 for a

computer with a good assortment of peripherals and software. It is also a good idea to purchase the extended warranty—you'll definitely use it.

- **Protect everything!** Buy the CD-ROM burner and zip drives. Try to back up data daily to a zip (or another computer). And monthly to a CD-ROM. You can *never* be too safe. Buy a battery-supported surge protector. The surge protector allows you plenty of time to save your work and shut down your computer if the power goes out. It's worth the investment. Of course, the best protection during thunderstorms is to turn your computer off and unplug it.
- **Research.** Above all, learn about computers for yourself. If possible, try the applications you expect to run on a few systems first. See how those systems handle massive graphic files and huge levels. Also remember that most people are very biased about their own systems, so be careful when asking for opinions.

Once you have assembled your game development system and have it up and running, you will have made a huge step toward becoming a game developer. The next step is to learn the basic building blocks of a game: sights and sounds.

ACTIVITIES

1. Look at the system you are currently using. List what you have—chip type (in terms of MHz), RAM, hard drive size, and so forth. Compare the cost of buying a new computer to upgrading select components. Remember, upgrading your RAM and buying a really good 3D card may cost only a few hundred dollars and may be your best investment. If you end up spending more than a few hundred dollars, you may want to consider buying a new system. In addition, even if you buy a new system, you may be able to save some money if you have a good monitor, sound system, or other component that you don't need to upgrade.

2. Decide what you want to do with your computer. List the games and applications you want to run, and find their minimum and recommend system requirements. Build your dream system based on the things you really want to do.

3. If you don't have a computer system at your disposal, or if your system can't run your games and applications, look into using the systems available at schools, libraries, and clubs. Remember to honor the rules of the organization.

SUMMARY
• • • • • • • • •

In this chapter, we discussed the game development system. As you determine which applications you will be running, you'll also determine what type of system you need. In addition, as you think about the types of activities you want to do (game development, graphics, programming), you'll figure out which peripherals you need to add. Once you've considered all of these issues, you'll be ready to upgrade or buy your system.

The Basics of Game Technology

IN THIS CHAPTER

• Adding Visual Components to Your Games
• Using Sound in Your Games for Atmosphere and Effect

In order to make games, you need to learn, and eventually master, the fundamental elements of sight, sound, and interactivity. Although interactivity (the ability to interact with a computer while playing a game) is important, the basics of interactivity are dependent on the type of game and the application you are using to develop it. We will learn about interactivity later in the book as we create different types of games, so we'll concentrate on the core building blocks that exist in virtually all games: sights and sounds.

Let's begin by breaking a game down to its most fundamental level. Once you understand these fundamentals, you can apply them to many areas beyond game development, including graphic design, Web layout, and almost all types of interactive computing.

SIGHTS

Sights are the things you see on the screen. In any type of production, whether a Web site or a game, sights are the first thing you see, and are usually determined by a number of people—the designer, producer, art director, and others. Even in your own game creation efforts, you'll need to wear several hats and think like a designer, producer, and artist. The sights you use in your games are called *assets* and can be in two dimensions or three dimensions. (We'll discuss the differences between 2D and 3D shortly.) All of the assets you create for your game should fit the interests of your intended audience, and they should work with the technology you'll be using. Thinking about your intended audience is part of marketing your game and is an important issue, especially if you want to publish your game, but we'll talk about marketing much later in the book. Before we go into any of these areas, however, let's do a quick review of computer games and technology.

HINT!

Assets are primary components of the game, its images, and sounds.

IN THE BEGINNING

The very first computers did not have graphics; they only displayed "text"—letters and numbers. However, games were still created on these primitive machines, and once the first graphics cards were available, the colorful games we see today were created. It can be argued that games have pushed the development of the computer because "gamers" demand (and are willing to pay for) faster chips, better video cards, and better sound.

However, even as the technology advanced, it was common for artists to be the programmers because it was still technically demanding to get even rudimentary art into a computer format. Today (thanks to the gods of digital art), the technology has advanced so far that traditional artists have been able to make the transition to digital art quite effectively. They still need to understand the technology underlying the art program so that they can understand how to make different formats compatible, adapt screen sizes, and adjust for color limitations. However, today's software has made it much more accessible for the non-programmer, which brings us to the beginning of the creation process and the tools you'll use.

GETTING STARTED

To create assets, you need to use a variety of tools and techniques. The first step is to sketch your ideas on paper or mock them up on a computer. Some of the tools used are 2D "paint programs" (such as Microsoft Paint) that work only with flat images, 3D programs that allow you to build and render objects that look lit and solid (such as 3ds max or Animation: Master), and even digital photographs and scans. To use these tools effectively, however, you need to understand the basic principles behind them, so let's start by looking at the different types of assets.

2D ART ASSETS

Two-dimensional, or 2D, art is a *flat image with no depth*. You can find the 2D assets in a game in practically every aspect because almost all assets begin in 2D.

Menu screens. Look at the toolbar in your word processor, browser, or even your favorite game, and you will see 2D art.

Credit screens. Screens that list the people who created the game often contain art such as logos, images, and even fonts or special letters from the product, people, and company they represent.

Logos for companies, products, and services. Logos can be simple letters, 2D masterpieces, or fully rendered 3D scenes. Look around on the Net and you will see logos that range from clip art to actual pieces of art such as a Monet painting. They are created in different styles based on the type of company and the image it wants to portray.

User interfaces. User interfaces (such as Internet Explorer or Microsoft Word's menu bars) are broken down into background images, buttons, cursors, and other art objects a user must click on or interact with.

In games. The 2D sights or assets include the textures on the walls, the floors, the characters, the vehicles, the weapons, the environment, and so forth, all of which have 2D art in them.

Now that you know what types of things are considered 2D, let's look at the difference between 2D and 3D art.

3D ART

Three-dimensional, or 3D, art includes all of the sights and art that show depth and look three dimensional, as illustrated in Figure 2.1. Although you can portray depth in 2D, you cannot explore it as you can in a 3D cube, which can actually be rotated and viewed in 3D.

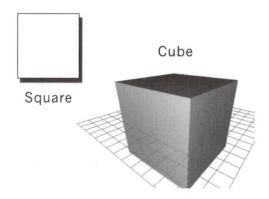

FIGURE 2.1   A square is 2D, and a cube is 3D.

The three dimensions are described as *XYZ* coordinates. Yes, this is the Cartesian coordinate system that you learned about in algebra. In fact, making a game requires many of the subjects you might have wondered why you needed to learn, including geometry, physics, reading and writing. (If you are an aspiring game developer, getting a good education is the best thing you can do to advance your chances of achieving that goal.) The Cartesian coordinate system defines X as a *horizontal line* (or axis), Y as a *vertical line*, and Z as the distance backward and forward that gives the figure depth (see Figures 2.2 and 2.3).

HINT!

A 2D figure only has the X- and Y-axes. A 3D figure has X-, Y-, and Z-axes.

That was a brief and very simple explanation of 3D art. We focus on 2D art, because you must have a solid understanding of 2D technology

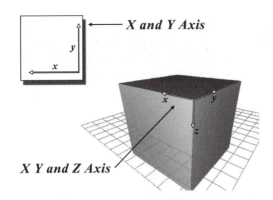

FIGURE 2.2   The Cartesian coordinate system. The X-axis, Y-axis, and Z-axis.

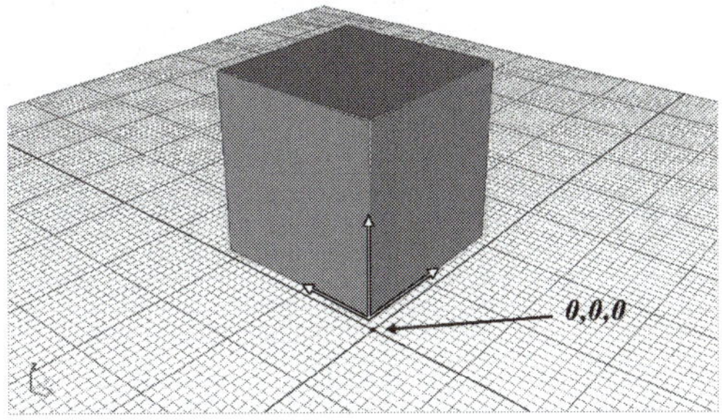

FIGURE 2.3   A cube and the *XYZ* value of its location in space.

before you can move up to working in 3D. For example, a great deal of 2D work must be done before a 3D model makes it into a game. Typically, the developer starts with 2D sketches of the art, models, scenes, and story that will be used for the game. Even in the 3D production stage, one of the most important aspects of 3D is applying 2D textures to the models. A *texture* is simply a picture of what the image should look like applied to a 3D model. Take a treasure chest, for example. The 3D model of the chest is simply a six-sided cube, but when you apply pictures of wood planks, brass hinges, and a keyhole to the model, it looks like an actual treasure chest. The pictures of the planks and hinges are the textures. Let's go ahead and look further into what makes up a graphic image.

THE PIXEL

To begin, let's look at the most fundamental of fundamentals—the most basic element of an image—the pixel, or "picture element." A *pixel* is a colored dot on the screen, and computer images are made up of many pixels arranged in rows and columns. See Figure 2.4 for an illustration of a pixel. No matter how big and fancy a computer image is, or what has been done to it, it is still a group of pixels.

Once an image is saved to the computer, the maximum detail is set and cannot be increased, so a great deal of time is spent making the images right before finalizing them. The image can be enlarged and the number of pixels increased by a mathematical process called *interpolation,* which is illustrated in Figures 2.5 and 2.6. However, this does not increase the detail; it simply adds extra pixels to smooth the transition between the

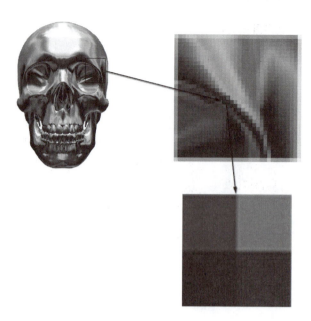

FIGURE 2.4   A pixel is the smallest unit of a computer image made up of colored dots.

original pixels. Look at our fish, for example. Making the image bigger will not add detail; it simply makes the pixels bigger and fuzzier.

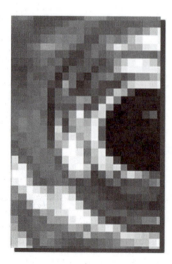

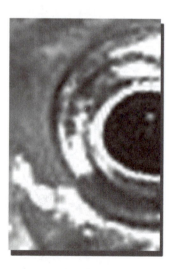

FIGURE 2.5   Here is an area of the fish image before enlarging.

FIGURE 2.6   Here is the same area enlarged with pixels *interpolated.*

RESOLUTION

Resolution is the actual number of pixels displayed in an image, or Width x Height.

HINT!

You've probably heard of dpi, or *dots per inch*. This refers to the number of pixels per inch in an image. A typical computer monitor displays 75 to 90 dpi. A printed image usually needs to be 300 dpi or more if it is to look good in print.

Some of the most common screen resolutions are 320x200, 640x480, 800x600, and 1024x768.

For example an 800x600 resolution means that your screen will be 800 pixels wide (horizontal) and 600 pixels high (vertical). See the examples in Figures 2.7, 2.8, and 2.9.

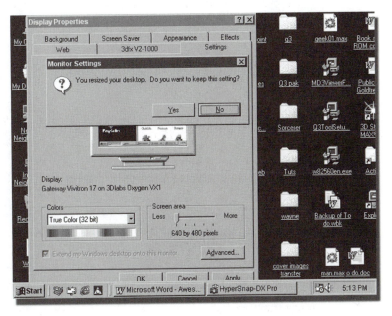

FIGURE 2.7   Windows desktop at 640x480 dots per inch.

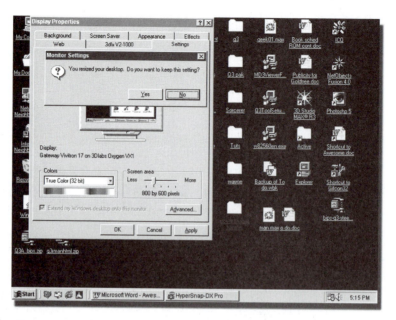

FIGURE 2.8   Windows desktop at 800x600 dots per inch.

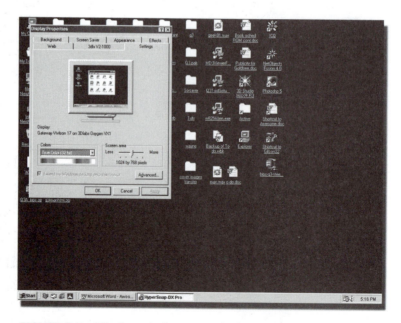

FIGURE 2.9   Windows desktop at 1024x768 dots per inch.

ASPECT RATIO

Another important component of resolution is *aspect ratio*, or the ratio of the pixel's width to the pixel's height. This is important because not all pixels are square.

In 640x480, 800x600, and 1024x768 modes, the aspect ratio is 1:1, or 1, meaning that the pixels are perfectly square.

In 320x200, the aspect ratio is 1.21:1, or .82, meaning that the pixels are higher than they are wide.

If you create an image in 320x200 mode and display it in 640x480, it will appear slightly squashed, since the pixels are about 20 percent shorter. See Figures 2.10 and 2.11 and notice the distortion in the image.

Image created by Nick Marks 1999-2000

FIGURE 2.10   Here is an image created at 320x200 dots per inch.

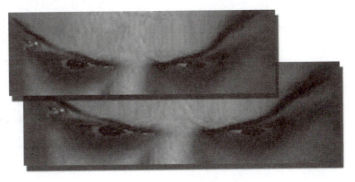

Image created by Nick Marks 1999-2000

FIGURE 2.11   Here is the same image displayed in 640x480 mode.

COLORS

When working with games, you need to understand how color works in the computer. You will have to have precise control over your colors in some situations in order to achieve certain effects. This is especially true in games and Web sites because certain scenes or characters may require a very specific color selection to be realistic and consistent. It's a good idea to keep a list of the colors you are using and the details about them while creating your game. That way, your character's clothes, the backgrounds, and overall color theme won't suddenly change because you can't remember the color selections. There are two major value categories for color: RGB and CMYK. These are very important to understand, so let's discuss them now.

RGB

An RGB value is the mixture of red, green, and blue used to make other colors. You might remember mixing red and yellow paint to make orange in your art classes.

HINT!

To open "Paint" on a computer running Windows, go to Start | Programs | Accessories | Paint.

ON THE CD

To see this more clearly, open an art program such as Paint. Within the program select Colors | Edit Colors | Define Custom Colors. Here you'll see a chart that lets you set the color scheme. Red, green, and blue are all set at 0, but if you change it to 255,0,0, you'll get all red and no green or blue. In Figures 2.12 through 2.16, you can see the RGB values of the color and (even though the images are in 0,0,0 and 255, 255, 255—excuse me, black and white) the position of the marker in the color palette. (You can see all of these images in color on the companion CD-ROM, so be sure to refer to them.)

Red = 0
Green = 0
Blue = 0

Red = 255
Green = 255
Blue = 255

Figure 2.12   The RGB color palette for black.

Figure 2.13   The RGB color palette for white.

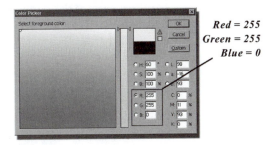

Red = 255
Green = 0
Blue = 0

Red = 255
Green = 255
Blue = 0

Figure 2.14   The RGB color palette for red.

Figure 2.15   The RGB color palette for yellow.

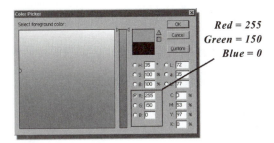

Red = 255
Green = 150
Blue = 0

Figure 2.16   The RGB color palette for orange.

HINT!

CMYK is a mode used by traditional printing processes, and stands for *cyan, magenta, yellow,* and *black*. You will almost *never* use CMYK color in game and computer content creation and will deal in RGB or indexed color, but it's good to know the term.

NUMBER OF COLORS

A graphics card can display a certain number of colors: 16, 256, thousands, and millions (see Figures 2.17 through 2.20).

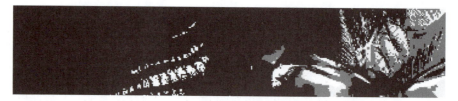

FIGURE 2.17   An image in 16 colors; see the CD for the color version.

FIGURE 2.18   An image in 256 colors; see the CD for the color version.

FIGURE 2.19   An image in thousands of colors; see the CD for the color version.

FIGURE 2.20   An image in millions of colors; see the CD for the color version.

The number of colors is called *color depth* and describes how many colors can be displayed on your screen simultaneously. Color depth is described in terms of bits, and refers to the amount of memory used to represent a single pixel. The most common values are 8-, 16-, 24-, and 32-bit color. The number of bits corresponds to the range of colors that can be displayed.

True-color (24-bit color) is capable of displaying 16.8 million colors for each pixel on the screen at the same time. The human eye cannot distinguish the difference between that many colors.

High-color displays only 32,000 or 64,000 colors—but still a very impressive range of colors and enough for most work.

256-color is the most limited in colors. It stores its color information in a palette. Each palette can be set to any of thousands or millions of different color values, but the screen can't show more than 256 different colors at once. Some games still use these because, like resolution, more colors mean more data pumped to the screen. Therefore, if you can get away with only 256 colors, you can render (or draw) the game pictures to the screen faster. More recently, games have started to use thousands of colors as the hardware permits.

HINT!

The word *render* is used in games, especially real-time 3D games, as the computer and software literally renders or builds an image instantly based on where you are in the 3D world; hence the term *interactive*. In a movie, you watch each frame as the moviemaker created it, and the frame is unchangeable. In a 3D game, you control how each frame looks by where you choose to go in the world and what you do once you're in that world. Each frame of your gaming experience is made for you "on the fly," or as your experience is happening.

256 PALETTES EXPLAINED

Each pixel can have a numerical value from 0 to 255 (a total of 256!). The screen knows where to get the color from, but it doesn't know the color. Figure 2.21 shows the 256-color palette.

So, follow me here. Say you have a picture and open the color palette to have a look. If you note that a certain color is assigned to the number-

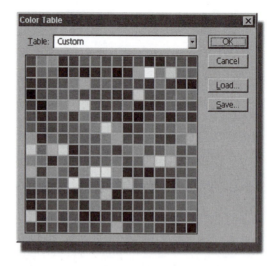

FIGURE 2.21   A 256-color palette. You can only see shades of gray here, but those squares are 256 different colors.

three place on the color palette, and then decide to reassign another color to the number-three position, your image will now display that new color where the original color used to be.

WATCHOUT!

Even if you have that original color in the palette, it will not be displayed where the number-three position is being displayed. What this means is that a computer can't distinguish color because it only sees numbers. You will have to be aware of this when working on the game tutorials later. In Figures 2.22 and 2.23, you can see how changing one color can affect the image.

You can see color versions of these images on the CD-ROM.

FIGURE 2.22   A 256-color image.

FIGURE 2.23   The same image after changing the palette colors. The computer sees the number, not the color.

Now that we understand the basics of images, we can move on to the basics of manipulating images.

MANIPULATING IMAGES

During the development of your game you will have to manipulate images in order to get them to fit your needs. The basics of image manipulation are similar to the text editing you may have done in your word processor. Commands such as Cut, Copy, and Paste are common. We will also look at Skew, Rotate, Resize, Crop, and Flip.

Cut. If you cut an image, you remove it from the scene, but don't worry; if you change your mind, you can paste it back in or undo your action.

Copy. Copy does not alter your image but creates a copy in the memory of your computer that you can paste in somewhere else, as shown in Figure 2.24.

Copy   Paste   Cut

FIGURE 2.24 Cutting and copying sections of an image. Note that copying does not affect the image.

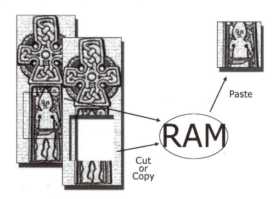

Paste

Cut or Copy

FIGURE 2.25 Pasting a section of an image.

Paste. As mentioned earlier, after cutting or copying an image, you can paste it somewhere else, as shown in Figure 2.25.

Skew. Some image manipulation programs allow you to skew (slant, deform, or distort) an image, as shown in Figure 2.26.

Rotate. Rotating is pretty self-explanatory. You can free rotate an image or rotate it precisely a certain amount, as shown in Figure 2.27.

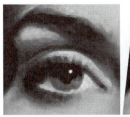

FIGURE 2.26   Skewing an image.   **FIGURE 2.27**   Rotating an image.

Resize. Resizing an image is useful, but be careful: any severe manipulation of an image degrades it, and resizing does a lot of damage (see Figure 2.28).

WATCHOUT!

If you reduce an image and then enlarge it again, you will seriously degrade it. This is because you are enlarging a small image, and degradation takes place going down or up in size (see Figures 2.29 and 2.30).

Crop. Cropping actually cuts an image smaller to a defined area, as shown in Figures 2.31 and 2.32.

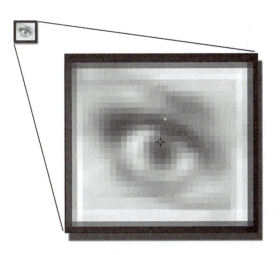

FIGURE 2.28   A smaller image blown up—pixel rip.

FIGURE 2.29   An image reduced.

Image created by Jennifer Meyer 1999-2000

FIGURE 2.30   The same image as in Figure 29 enlarged to its original size. Notice what this has done.

FIGURE 2.31   Cropping an image, and the crop outline.

Flip—horizontal and vertical. You can flip images horizontally and vertically (see Figures 2.33 through 2.35).

Image created by Jennifer Meyer 1999-2000

The image

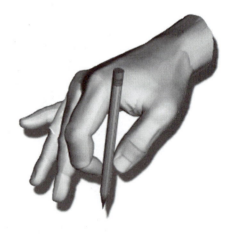

FIGURE 2.32   The image cropped. Everything outside the crop outline is now gone.

FIGURE 2.33   The image.

Flipped horizontally   *Flipped vertically*

FIGURE 2.34   The image flipped horizontally.   **FIGURE 2.35**   The image flipped vertically.

ADVANCED IMAGING

Now let's look at some of the more advanced ways to manipulate 2D images.

Sprites

A *sprite* is a graphic image that can move within a larger image. They're small pictures of things that move around, such as characters, buttons, and other items in your games. Sprites can be animated as well. Notice that the sprite image in Figure 2.36 has a solid border around it, and in Figure 2.37, the solid part is not seen.

Sprite animation is done just like cartoon animation. A series of images is played in sequence to make it appear that a character is walking or a logo is spinning, for example. Figures 2.38 and 2.39 are examples of sprite frames.

FIGURE 2.36   A sprite image. Notice the solid part surrounding the image.

FIGURE 2.37   A sprite image in a game. Notice that the solid part is not displayed (you can see the background).

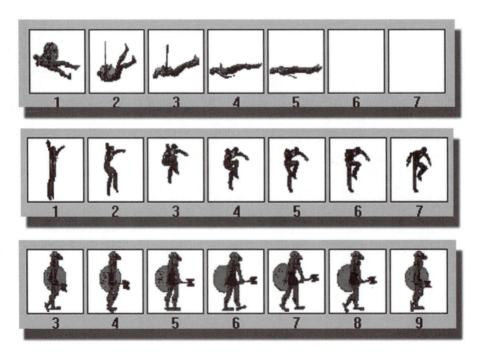

FIGURE 2.38   A series of sprite images for a game animation.

FIGURE 2.39   A series of sprite images for a spinning logo.

MASKING

A *mask* is a special image that is used to "hide" portions of another image. A mask works like a stencil. Since an image is square or rectangular, the mask allows the edges to be any shape as it renders the masked portions invisible, as shown in Figures 2.40 through 2.42.

FIGURE 2.40   An image of a ghost.

FIGURE 2.41   The mask for the ghost image.

FIGURE 2.42   The mask and image combined in a scene.

COLOR MASKING

Masking can also be achieved by dedicating a specific color to be rendered as clear or transparent. This color is usually an ugly green or purple that most likely will not be used any other time in the game art.

Palette or Positional Masking

Finally, some games use a specific position on the color palette to determine what color will not render or will be clear. Remember, the computer cannot see color, it sees only numbers. This method for masking has the computer looking at the position on the palette, not the color, to determine transparency.

Usually, the last color place on the palette is used, so instead of rendering a certain color as transparent, it will render whatever color is in the designated position of the color palette as clear.

OPACITY

Images can also be displayed in games as opaque, halfway between solid and clear (like our ghost image). Looking at each pixel in the image and the pixel directly under it, and then creating a new pixel that is a blended value of the original pixels creates the opacity effect (see Figures 2.43 and 2.44).

FIGURE 2.43   The masked ghost image with opacity set at 50 percent.

FIGURE 2.44   A close-up of the ghost image.

ANTI-ALIASING

Look closely at a computer-generated image. Wait! Don't boot up your system, just look at Figures 2.45 through 2.47. See those jagged edges on the letters? Those are actually the pixels we have been talking about. They look jagged because they are made from a solid color, but if you used various shades of that color and gradually blended the edge color with the background color, you would make the transition between the colors appear smooth from a distance. This is similar to opacity, but the technique is called *anti-aliasing*. This is also why more colors look better

FIGURE 2.45 An image with no anti-aliasing.

FIGURE 2.46 An image with anti-aliasing.

FIGURE 2.47 A close-up of both images' edges.

in an image because you can blend them more gradually. This is also why high resolution (more pixels) makes an image look better: the blending is smoother between pixels.

GRAPHIC FORMATS

Graphic images are stored in different formats (JPG, BMP, TIFF, etc.), depending on how they will be used. In business, they may be in a certain format for technical support reasons, product design limitations, competitive issues, or security concerns. However, the main reason depends on the quality needed and the usefulness of the format for the user. Image formats such as BMPs or TIFFs are quite large because they retain much of the image data. Other formats, such as JPGs, actually compress the image by stripping out data to create a smaller file. Still others, such as GIFs, degrade the image so it is really small and easy to use, particularly on Web sites. Figures 2.48 and 2.49 show two versions of an image. The degradation is not bad (see Figure 2.50), considering that the file size of the BMP is almost 20 times the size of the JPG image.

The specifics you need to know about graphics formats are discussed later in this book and in the documentation of any applications with which you will be working, but you should now have a good under-

FIGURE 2.48   This 640x480 image is in the BMP format and is 900K.

FIGURE 2.49   This 640x480 image is a compressed JPEG and is only 40K.

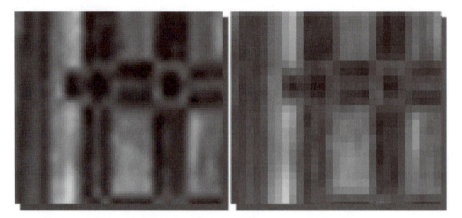

FIGURE 2.50   A close-up of the same area of both images.

standing of the general terminology. Let's move on to a quick overview of the second key game building block: sound.

SOUND

Sound and music can be very important to a game, especially for atmospheric reasons. You can really get immersed in a game with the lights off and the sound turned up. Sounds and different types of music set and change the mood constantly. Think of any game you've played and try to remember all the different types of sounds and music in it. Hundreds, right? That's because sound can deliver messages to the players about what's coming up or what just happened. If you couldn't hear the sounds in the game, it would be a lot more difficult to play. Therefore, when you're designing your own games, remember that the quality of your game and the overall level of satisfaction it will generate depend a lot on your sounds.

While graphics draw you into a scene, the sound in the background has a mental effect on a player that can never be accomplished with graphics alone. Think about your favorite games—it's the shooting, hissing, squealing, and screaming that gets your adrenaline going, not the scenes or characters. That's because we can reproduce sounds on a computer much better than we can visuals. We can make an effect that sounds like the roar of a real lion, but the image of the lion doesn't always look totally realistic.

When playing games, you can be part of the game visually because you can see into another world through that tiny window of your computer or TV, but you don't really feel immersed in the world until you add the sounds. When you hear that world surrounding you (in the dark), then you are immersed.

A good example of sound effectiveness is the movie *Jaws*. Who can forget the terror the music added to the scenes in that movie—DUNT DUNT DUNT DUNT CHOMP! In terms of games, *Trespasser* has powerful sound effects. The sounds make the game incredibly tense and scary. I turned the sound off to play (didn't want to scare the dog) and started laughing. Without sound, the game just looked like a game and was not nearly as involving or tense. Puppetlike raptors stumbled about and floated like balloons. The tension was gone.

You can try this as well. Turn on your favorite game or movie, and watch or play it with and without the sound to analyze what is happening. Consciously pull out the sound effects, ambient noises, and music that make the game or movie feel the way it does.

It's clear that sound can reinforce a physical feeling and can actually create a physical sensation. Sound can be important even in the menu buttons. Have you ever hit a rollover button with your speakers all the way up? You actually feel it roll! Having quality sound in your game will add a lot of production value. It's sort of like the principle of slamming the car door to see if has a good solid *thunk* when you shut it. If it does, you think the car must be safe and well built, right?

ACTIVITIES

1. Load your favorite computer game and stop it during play. Look closely at the image, and chances are you will see the pixels we discussed earlier. Depending on the computer you are using, the pixels will be large and easy to see, or very small—that is resolution.

2. This activity works best with a newer first-person shooter game such as *Quake* (v.1, 2, or 3), *Unreal,* or other games like that. Turn the sound off and play the game. Although you may get killed more easily because you can't hear the enemies out of your range of vision, you will also see more in terms of what is really being displayed. *Trespasser,* as mentioned, is a great example of how much sound and music can affect a game experience.

3. Similar to Activity 2, you can also watch you favorite action movies with the sound off and on. You will see the major effect sound has on these movies. Without the sound, they have much less impact and excitement.

SUMMARY

In this chapter, you gained an understanding of the basics of game technology. Now that you are familiar with the building blocks of a game, you are almost ready to start developing one. Before you go running off into unexplored territory, however, let's look at some of the facts and fables that surround game design and development. It is important that you are not hindered by some of the misinformation you may have heard about game creation.

Game Design and Development

IN THIS CHAPTER

- What Is Game Development and Design, and What Is the Difference between the Two?
- What Makes a Great Game?
- How to Ensure That Your Game Creation Is Successful
- How to Plan Your Game Development

WHAT ARE GAME DEVELOPMENT AND DESIGN?

The difference between design and development is this: design is the planning of the game, and development is the actual creation of the game. Although design may be part of development, design must always happen first. Distinct things happen during design and development, and the following sections provide a brief outline of each.

DESIGN

- The genre (or type) of the game is chosen.
- The game is designed.
  - A storyline is written.
  - Characters are created and sketched.

- All the vehicles, props, scenes, levels, and so on are conceived.
- Different plots are developed for the various outcomes.
- The core team of artists, modelers, and programmers is assembled.
- The schedule and budget are formulated.

DEVELOPMENT

- Programmers begin coding the intricate details of the game.
- Artists sketch and create all of the images and scenes for the game.
- Level designers build the worlds (the different levels of the game you journey through).

HINT!

Although it is clear how different design and development are, they're often confused because much of the information available (especially on the Internet) isn't necessarily correct. However, many newsgroups and discussion forums have members who will help you out no matter who you are. There is a list of links in Appendix B.

SIFTING THROUGH THE INFORMATION

WATCHOUT!

Be wary of any statements such as, "This is the only way to do it," or "You have to create all of your assets first." Everyone has his or her own design style, so you need to find what works best for you.

As you'll discover, everyone has his or her own opinion. Some people insist that you must write the entire game story first, others say you have to draw all the characters first, and still others suggest coding it completely using placeholder assets and then hiring your artist. Obviously, they can't all be right, so how you use the information you gather really depends on what type of game you are creating and which tools you're using. All of these factors determine what you need to do for your particular game, and they will help you focus your information searches on the Internet.

While you are searching the Internet for ideas and instruction, you'll have to learn to sift through good and bad advice. It's easy to become overwhelmed or discouraged, so when getting advice on design or development, ask yourself who is writing the information. Did they ever make a game? If they have, how long ago and in what situation? What types of games do they like and develop?

The constructive critics tell you the good and the bad while providing examples and comparisons to other games, adding a lot of validity to what they are saying. They will be open-minded, and they debate controversial issues fairly. These debates are often where true progress comes from, so seek these people out if you would like someone to beta test your game and provide an objective opinion. These are the people who will help you improve your game.

Now that you have a general idea about what design and development are and how to use information you gather from the Internet, let's move on to what makes a game great.

WHAT MAKES A GAME GREAT?

When you go hunting for information on game design, the first thing you will probably come across are those Top Ten lists (or any number) of "Things You Must Have in a Game," or "What Is a Game," or "The x Elements of a Successful Game," and so on. These never tell the whole story, because the most important thing in a game isn't always the *same* thing.

Games are like films and novels in many ways. For a film to be successful, does it always have great special effects, the biggest budget, or the biggest star? No. A movie can be successful at the box office for many reasons, including these.

- It has a top star, such as Arnold Schwarzenegger or Julia Roberts.
- The director or producer is someone like Steven Spielberg or George Lucas.
- It's based on a unique idea, like *The Blair Witch Project*.
- It includes a popular character, like James Bond.
- It is based on a great book, like *Jurassic Park*.
- It has great special effects, like *Jurassic Park*.
- It has dinosaurs, like . . .

You get the idea. There are many different reasons why people go to see films, which include but are not limited to word of mouth, a good story, awesome effects, a great soundtrack, and so forth. Movies also fail, even if they have all the "right" elements. Remember *The Last Action Hero*? It had Arnold, a huge budget, great special effects—the works—but it still bombed.

The same is true for a computer game: it can be successful for a variety of reasons, including these.

- It has a top developer, like John Carmack of id software or Sid Meier of Civilization fame.
- The producer is a successful company, like G.O.D., Activision, or Nintendo.
- The story on which the game is based is a unique idea, like *Deer Hunter*.
- It includes a well-known character, like Lara Croft or Duke Nukem.
- It is based on a great book, like *Jurassic Park*.
- It has great special effects, like *Jurassic Park*.
- It has dinosaurs, like . . .

There are plenty of examples of successful games with some or all of these things, and there are just as many that had all the right elements but failed. *Trespasser* is a game that should have been successful, but it didn't sell well and wasn't reviewed positively by the critics.

What *Trespasser* had going for it:

- A *very* hot license—*Jurassic Park*! (A license means that you have licensed content from a popular movie, television show, cartoon, or other commercial enterprise, and that you will pay them a percentage of the royalties or a flat fee to use the content.)
- Top stars performing the voices—Minnie Driver and Richard Attenborough.
- A top producer—DreamWorks Interactive.
- A unique idea.
- A very talented design and development team.
- A huge marketing and publicity campaign.

It definitely had all the right stuff.

WHAT HAPPENED TO *TRESPASSER*?

Even though the game had a first-rate team, who should be applauded for doing what people are always asking for—trying something different—the critics and reviewers on sites like Gamasutra.com say that what caused *Trespasser* to fail was basically that not enough up-front design was present. Other critics have similar things to say.

- "Developers weren't allowed to develop their ideas properly."
- "*Trespasser* never had a proper design spec. Our experiences on *Trespasser* made it clear that it is worse to not have a design spec at all, than to have one that becomes out of date and is frequently rewritten."
- "Design didn't set the direction for all other development of the game, and no amount of programming or art could save it."

As you can see from these comments, *Trespasser*'s team was put in a difficult situation because they were not able to complete the necessary design phase or redesign when they needed to—they had to compromise and find quick solutions, not necessarily the best ones. The point here is that even with all the right features, games or movies like *Trespasser* and *The Last Action Hero* can go sour. On the other hand, there will always be games and movies that don't seem to have all the right elements yet become blockbusters, such as *Deer Hunter* and *The Blair Witch Project*.

So, is there any magical list of what makes a good game? No! What makes a game great are the developers and designers, having all the right elements, a vision, and the people who can implement it. If you're creating a game for yourself, your friends, or maybe even for a company, your ideas, vision, and ability to pull it together successfully is what will make your game great. Before you even begin on a game, you need to consider your strengths and weaknesses, the tools you have available, and your overall goals for the game. Will they work together to fulfill the vision for the game?

To better understand these questions, think about some top-selling authors. It is interesting that many didn't set out to be writers.

- John Grisham was an attorney who turned to writing legal thrillers.
- Ann Rule was a crime reporter for years in Seattle; now she writes crime fiction and nonfiction.
- Michael Crichton, a former M.D., writes high-tech and medical thrillers.
- Jeff Deaver was an attorney.
- Stephen King started writing at a young age and wrote consistently for years. His work was rejected numerous times, but he still kept writing.

The list goes on and on. You'll also notice in life that many people combine a previous career with a new one, or even a hobby with a career, and come out with a successful product or business. Therefore, you should expand your abilities as a game developer and designer by playing games, reading books, going to movies, and educating yourself in a variety of areas. The key is to go for what you are interested in. Creating a small production that is done well and is enjoyable to work on is more fun than trying to develop a "blockbuster" that is never completed and leaves you frustrated. What makes a great game is satisfying the audience you define.

Therefore, think about your own strengths and weaknesses, the type of game you want to create, and the technology you have available, and let's talk about how to ensure that it all works together.

DESIGN YOUR GAME AS A PRODUCT TO SELL

It doesn't usually occur to most people when they begin to design and develop games that a game is actually a product. They certainly realize it when they see game advertisements in magazines, or when they pay for games at the store, but when working on their own creations, they often don't look at it as a product. This brings us to the only golden rule of successful game design: games, no matter how small, are products that are created to be played by a specific audience. Now, when we say "product," we don't necessarily mean your goal is to sell it to a mass audience. What we are referring to is the fact that you have to follow the design and development process: come up with a design plan before you even start the game. That's the most important step for any product.

Even if all you're doing is a simple screen saver for a company that hired you, you still have a little planning to do. You have to acquire the assets, learn the applications you'll use, and assemble and test the screen saver. After all that, you may discover that the client doesn't like the colors, certain assets you used require trademark or copyright notices on them, or someone found that you misspelled a word. Every time you find an error or problem, you have to go back in, redo it, and then reinstall for the users. Consequently, something that you considered a small job in the beginning suddenly turns into a lot of work. If you had handled the job as if it was a real product, you would have gone through a testing and beta phase where you had others view it and try it for you. You probably would have caught those mistakes and maybe even been able to expand the usefulness of the screen saver.

Great ideas often come by having an objective tester try out your products. In the case of the screen saver, the simple suggestion of adding the telephone number or Web address to the screen image might allow the company to offer the screen saver for download to its customers, who in turn would know how to contact the company more easily.

If you keep all of these things in mind, even for the games you're creating for yourself, you'll save a lot of reworking and undoing. Think about your game as a product, and remember to consider who you're designing it for, even if it's you.

DESIGNING A GAME FOR AN AUDIENCE

A game designer is like an architect. A designer must have a basic working knowledge of all aspects of making a game, including all of the technical aspects (art, programming, sound, and game play issues) and the business issues (marketing, budgets, and schedules). Designers need to know who their audience is and what type of game they're creating. Even when you're designing for your own use, you should think about these things, and always ask yourself, "For whom am I creating this?"

If you're creating a game just for fun or to learn the basics of the tools, for example, then you can do it however you like. (You'll be using the tutorials in the next section to gain a working knowledge of everything we've discussed so far, and how to use TGF and other game development technology.)

If it is for pure enjoyment, you can ignore the marketing and business aspects of game design. Go wild with your creativity. Make a game that you and your friends will enjoy.

If you are designing a game that you want to sell, get published, or give away in a professional capacity, then you need to start learning about the marketing and distribution of a game.

Ultimately, a game is designed for someone—you, your friends, or a large group of people. Your design will be determined by what you intend to do with the game. Are you designing a screen saver for your business? If so, what will your customers like and what can they handle technologically? If you intend to sell your game, how will you distribute it, and to whom? These are some of the things you will have to consider if you are thinking about creating a commercial game, so let's go over them briefly for those of you who are leaning in this direction.

DETERMINING YOUR AUDIENCE

When you start to consider your audience, be realistic. You're not going to be able to create the next *Quake* or *Doom*—well, at least not for a while—so work on a project that you have the skills and technology to create. To help you focus your ideas more, let's look at the game market and how it is broken down.

THE GAME MARKET

IDSA's fourth annual *Video and PC Game Industry Trends Survey* reports that more women are playing games than ever. Thirty-five percent of console game players and more than 43 percent of PC gamers are women.

Contrary to the popular belief that games are only for kids, 9 out of 10 of all purchasers of video game software are over 18 years of age. The genres (we'll talk about these in Chapter 4, "Game Genres") of interactive games are as diverse as those who play them. The survey suggests that Americans are most likely to purchase the following types of PC games:

1. Puzzle/board/card/learning games.
2. Action games and strategy games.
3. Driving/racing and adventure/role play-games.

Entertainment software users are well educated. Three-quarters (74 percent) have attended some college, earned bachelor's degrees, or completed postgraduate work.

More than half (51.2 percent) of households that have both a PC and dedicated game console earn more than $50,000 a year.

All of this information basically tells you that you don't have to make *Quake 3* to make money. You can make all types of games at a variety of technical levels—there is plenty of room for new games and interactive products.

Quite simply, you need to sift through all the game development information that you'll come across, then decide which audience you want to focus on and what type of game you want to create, and then you can create your design and get to work on the development. It might seem daunting now, but if you work through this book and continue to practice, you have a great chance of being successful.

GAME ELEMENTS

Now we are down to the elements of a game. We could have just listed them up front, but it is really important that you understand your game idea, who the audience is, and what resources you have available, so that you can be realistic about what you can include in your game. You also have to include all the *needed* elements in your game. We emphasize *needed* because many designers throw in all the elements of a game they can think of. The proper parts of a game are not at issue here; what will make a game successful is. Therefore, really think about your game and make sure you include everything that is needed—and nothing that is not.

ELEMENT ONE: GAME GENRE

We will look at specific game genres or "types" in Chapter 4 in detail, but here is a short list of game types. In the book *Game Architecture and Design,* genres are defined in their most basic sense and can be broken down into about seven types.

- **Action**—lots of frantic button pushing.
- **Adventure**—the story matters.
- **Strategy**—nontrivial choices.
- **Simulation**—optimization exercises.
- **Puzzle**—hard analytical thinking.
- **Toys**—software you just have fun with.
- **Educational**—learning by doing.

This is a good start for our design decisions and will greatly simplify the other decisions. What basic genre you develop will determine the focus on technology, art, content, and research.

ELEMENT TWO: GAME IDEA

You are now ready to write down your game idea. A game idea is written first to convey your game idea to others, so everyone understands what the game is in a broad sense. Even if you are making a game on a very small scale, you should still get into the habit of writing down your ideas and documenting the development of your title. This will give you a focus that will benefit your title, and the practice will clarify your thoughts and clear the way for new thoughts to bubble up.

ELEMENT THREE: TECHNOLOGY

The game platform and the technology needed to play the game. You should know what the system requirements for your final game will be.

Will it require a fast computer? When you are finished making it, will it fit on a disk, or will you need to burn CD-ROMs?

ELEMENT FOUR: AUDIENCE

Who did you develop the game for, and why?

Did you get audience input? What were their suggestions?

Look at the previous sections dealing with game design and the audience?

ELEMENT FIVE: A PLAN

If you don't spend the time planning your game, you'll probably end up wasting a lot of your time, talent, and resources. Be patient, and go through the process the right way; it'll pay off in the end.

Try to come up with a plan like the following before you begin to create your game.

   I. Brief description of the game idea
- A) Game title
- B) Game genre
- C) Brief story description
- D) If applicable, main character or units description (including general actions)
- E) Brief description of settings and scenarios
- F) Overall look of the game
- G) General computer AI description
- H) Minimum/recommended hardware specs
- I) List of necessary development tools

  II. Characters/units in the game—Describe the characters in the game.

 III. Level description—Describe each area of the game in detail.

ACTIVITIES

1. List your strengths and weaknesses as a developer, and gear your game development activities toward those strengths.
2. List your favorite games and see what their strong points are. Is it the company, genre, characters, special effects, or some other feature that held your interest?

3. What types of games do you like to play? List them.

4. Go through the "Game Elements" section and fill in the blanks pertaining to your game idea.

SUMMARY

In this chapter, we discussed some of the confusion surrounding game development. We learned to look at the sources of information we may get. We also looked at various aspects of what may make a great game, and why it may not always be the same thing. Finally, we looked at the most important aspect of game development: the audience for whom you are developing your game. In the next chapter we review the different types of games (genres) in more detail.

Game Genres

IN THIS CHAPTER
••••••••••••••••

- How Games Are Organized into Genres for the Retail Store

Genre is a French word meaning a style or format that is applied to books, films, and even computer games. It means that the game or book relates to a certain subject, theme, or setting. As you will see, the concept of genre in computer games starts simple and gets rather complex, which is why we have an entire chapter dedicated to it. There are a lot of reasons why classifying a computer game is difficult. In computer games, many factors create various genre hybrids and combinations. Game such as *Hit Man*, *Half-Life*, and *Deus Ex* combine the genre of the first-person shooter with the role-playing game. Things are also moving so fast that there is barely time for a consensus on how genres should be divided and labeled.

GAME GENRES
••••••••••••

Let's look at the many genres, sub-genres, and hybrids of computer games. You'll need to know the genre of your game before you design it, but if you have an idea for a game, it probably fits into one of the categories listed next.

MAZE GAME

Maze games have been around almost longer than any other genre. These are the very familiar games such as *Pac Man* and *Ms. Pac Man*. Maze games are simply that: you run around a maze, and usually you eat or gather something while being chased by something. Maze games started in 2D with an overhead view of the maze.

It's hard to imagine, but many of the modern high-tech, full-blown 3D games are simply the player being brought into the universe of the 2D maze. We still chase, are chased, gather power, and die in a maze. We tried our hands at a maze game once, as shown in Figure 4.1.

FIGURE 4.1   *Snack-Man* was not received well by any audience.

BOARD GAME

When traditional family games such as *Monopoly*, *Clue*, or *Sorry* are recreated on the computer, they retain their original genre classification of "board game." This is usually done just like the original game with no innovation in game play or original use of technology, other than to make the game function as it does using a board. Initially, the challenge of getting the artificial intelligence to play the game was enough to keep the developers busy, so new innovations in art and game play had to wait.

More recently, board games have been elevated in the computer world from straight copies of their 2D ancestors to more interesting 3D versions. These newer games sport a 3D look, as the pieces can move, and have animated scenes at victory and defeat points during the game.

CARD GAME

Card games such as *Solitaire, Poker, Hearts,* and *Strip Poker* are often loaded on computers at the factory; these are a huge genre. As with board games, these titles have so far seen little innovation. *Hardwood Hearts* by Silver Creek Entertainment is a card game (Figure 4.2) that is showing some really cool innovations, such as multiplayer modes and custom decks.

FIGURE 4.2   A screen shot of the innovative *Hardwood Hearts*. A demo can be downloaded at www.silvercrk.com.

BATTLE CARD GAME

Battle card games came about with the *Magic: The Gathering* craze, which spawned such card games as *Spellfire, Legends of the Five Rings,* and *Poke-*

mon. Battle card games play very much like traditional card games, only with interesting pictures and an emphasis on being "collectible." Naturally, the decks are open ended and if you buy more cards, you will become more powerful. The move to the computer for the genre has been much like the traditional card game's move to the computer.

QUIZ GAME

Quiz games are popular, especially online, and TGF (The Games Factory) makes them easy. Games like *You Don't Know Jack*, *Jeopardy*, and *Trivia Wars* are some of the biggest in this genre. The logic behind these so-called multiple-choice games is rather easy (since all you do is display a question and three or four answers); the hard part is in researching and organizing the content—the questions and answers. Figure 4.3 shows the typical quiz game interface.

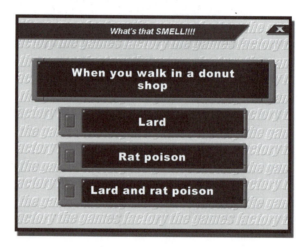

FIGURE 4.3   Trivia game in TGF, *What's That Smell?*

PUZZLE GAME

Games such as *Tetris* and *Dr. Mario* usually show pieces falling from the top of the screen that you have to line up and fit together in the most efficient manner—before they hit bottom. Your goal is to close up the open spaces between the pieces. The pieces become more complex and fall faster as the game progresses.

SHOOT 'EM UP

Examples of shoot 'em ups include *Space Invaders, Asteroids, Sinistar, Space Battle*, and the original *Space War*. (In Part Two of this book, we make a shoot 'em up game). These are the 2D games where you're in a spaceship and you shoot things before they hit you—aliens, missiles, and so forth. *Cosmic Battle* is a typical shoot 'em up and is shown in Figure 4.4.

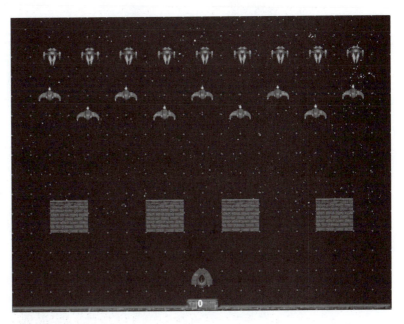

FIGURE 4.4   *Cosmic Battle*, a shoot 'em up you can make with The Game Factory.

SIDE SCROLLER

Side scrollers usually have the hero running along platforms and jumping from one platform to the next while trying not to fall into lava or get hit by projectiles. Side scrollers are what made id software big (remember Commander Keen, *Invasion of the Vorticons*?) The original *Duke Nukem, Prince of Persia 1*, and *Zeb* are all side scrollers. *Zeb*, coincidentally, was made with The Games Factory. Figure 4.5 shows a typical side scroller interface.

FIGURE 4.5   *Zeb* is a side scroller made with The Games Factory.

FIGHTING GAME

There are many fighting games—*Street Fighter 2, Samurai Showdown, Martial Champion, Virtual Fighter, Killer Instinct, Battle Arena Toshinden, Smash Brothers*, and *Kung Fu* (Figure 4.6). Fighting games started with a flat 2D

FIGURE 4.6   *Kung Fu* is a fighting game made with The Games Factory.

interface and now feature full 3D arenas and animated characters. The focus in a fighting game is the endless fighting motions and special moves you can use against your opponent.

RACING GAME

Racing games are centered on the concept of driving at high speeds around different tracks. *Wipeout, Destruction Derby, Mario Kart*, and *South Park Derby*—to name a few—are all racing games. There were 2D racing games made with a scrolling road and the "sprite" of the car moving over the surface. With the explosion of the Color GameBoy, these games are making a comeback.

FLIGHT SIM

A flight simulator (sim) attempts to simulate real flying conditions by giving you control over such things as steering, fuel, wind speed, and the flaps and wings of your craft. A sim will respond with the same limits as a real vehicle, as opposed to a simpler flying game where you just fly and don't have as much to think about. *Wing Commander, X-Wing*, and *The Microsoft Flight Simulator* are all flight sims. In games such as *Terminal Velocity*, antiaircraft guns add excitement. Figure 4.7 is screen shot from a flight sim.

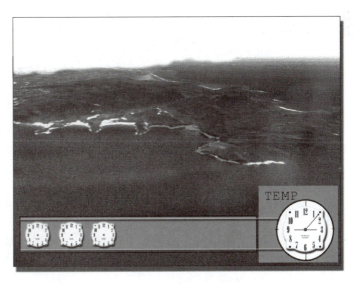

FIGURE 4.7   A flight sim mockup for a game company.

TURN-BASED STRATEGY GAME

In games such as *Breach, Paladin, Empire, Civilization, Stellar Conflict*, and *Master of Orion*, individual players make decisions, and the game progresses as each person takes his or her turn. As with chess, with additional practice, more strategic thought and planning go into your game.

REAL-TIME STRATEGY GAME

Populous, Command and Conquer, Warcraft, and *Syndicate* are a few popular real-time strategy games. In these games, you don't have forever to take your turn before the next person takes his or hers. The faster player can make many moves in a short period. These games are like sims in that you are usually overseeing a large battle and the building of towns and outposts. Resource management is important, such as the amount of gold you can get in *Warcraft* before you run out and can build no more.

SIM

Sim City, Sim Earth, Sim Ant—Sim Everything. You run a simulation of a town, world, or ant colony making decisions and managing resources. These are often called "God games," because you are playing the part of God in the game world.

HINT!

 First and *third person* refer to the point of view of the player. For example, in literature we have first-person novels ("I shot the rocket") and third-person novels ("She shot the rocket"). In gaming, we have points of view as well.

FIRST-PERSON SHOOTER, OR FPS

Castle Wolfenstein 3D, Doom, Duke Nukem', Quake, Dark Forces, and *Sorcerer* are all famous FPS games. The focus of an FPS is usually technology and atmosphere. These games attempt to put you into the action as you are literally looking out of the eyes of the character, seeing and hearing what the character sees or hears. As you can see in Figure 4.8, the point of view is that of a person on the street.

FIGURE 4.8   Screen shot from *Sorcerer*, a first-person 3D game.

FIRST-PERSON 3D VEHICLE BASED

These games are much like the first-person shooter, except the first-person vehicle-based shooter has you in a vehicle that may be a tank, ship, or giant robot. This genre is more similar to a FPS shooter than a racing game because you are not simply driving as fast as you can to cross a finish line, your goals are more similar to the FPS—kill or be killed. Examples of vehicle-based shooters are *Descent*, *Dead Reckoning*, and *Cylindrix*. You can see a screen shot of a vehicle-based shooter in Figure 4.9.

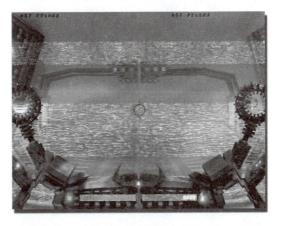

FIGURE 4.9   Screen shot from *Dead Reckoning*, a first-person 3D vehicle-based game.

THIRD-PERSON 3D

Tomb Raider, Dark Vengeance, Deathtrap Dungeon, RUNE, and *Fighting Force* are all third-person 3D games. Although there are games where you can switch from first- to third-person perspective, most games are designed primarily to be one or the other. *Tomb Raider* in first person is not as much fun, as it is designed around seeing Lara Croft jump, roll, and tumble. In first person, you would not see these acrobatics. Figure 4.10 shows a third-person game. Notice that you can see the spell effects (the protection circle) when in third-person mode. Likewise, when playing a first-person shooter (like *Quake 3 Arena*), you depend on speed and accuracy in battle in order to win, which is the point of the game. If you were able to play *Quake 3* in third-person mode, you would "die" often since you would not be able to run, aim, and shoot as quickly.

FIGURE 4.10   Screen shot from *Sorcerer* in third-person mode.

ROLE-PLAYING GAME, OR RPG

Wizardry, Ultima, NetHack, Dungeon Hack, Might and Magic, and *Daggerfall* are all RPGs. These games are focused on the emulation of the traditional pen and paper games where you play against characters that have a lot of data attached, such as health, intelligence, strength, and areas of knowledge or skill. RPGs are like a simulation of an adventure.

ADVENTURE GAME

Zork, Hitchhiker's Guide to the Galaxy, and *King's Quest* are all adventure games. In an adventure game, you walk around a lot and try to fulfill a quest or unravel a mystery. You typically collect information and items; battle is light and not the focus of this game type.

INTERACTIVE MOVIE

Interactive movies are full motion videos (FMVs) like *MYST* and *RIVEN*. Full-motion games require a lot of art, animation, or video production and precious little of anything else; there is simply no room for it as FMV is a limiting genre at present. In FMV, you mostly watch a movie and then select what portion of the movie you watch next, kind of like a computerized version of the "choose your own adventure" books.

OTHER GENRES

Educational and edutainment. Some games or interactive products fall under this genre that seem to be categorized by the intention of the product over the content or technology. A first-person game would be an edutainment title if its intention were to educate and entertain, like a quiz game. These games provide instruction and information, attempting to make learning fun, whereas the educational is straightforward learning. *"Where in the World Is Carmen San Diego?* and *Math Blaster* fit these genres.

Sports. This is a popular selling genre all by itself, although the label doesn't always convey the technology, game play, interface, or other aspects of the game: it's just about sports. In other words, a fiction thriller that takes place at a football game may be called a Sports Thriller, and an inspirational, nonfiction book with a sports theme may be called self-help/sports. However, in games they don't bother to put Quiz Game/Sports or Quiz Game/Football or Third Person Football Simulation—they're all lumped under sports.

Screen savers / desktop toys. Although screen savers and desktop toys are not games (and not even very interactive, for that matter), these products are generally entertaining and are classified with games and interactive products. These are fairly lucrative products that you can make with The Games Factory, like the screen saver in Figure 4.11 for a local company's Web site.

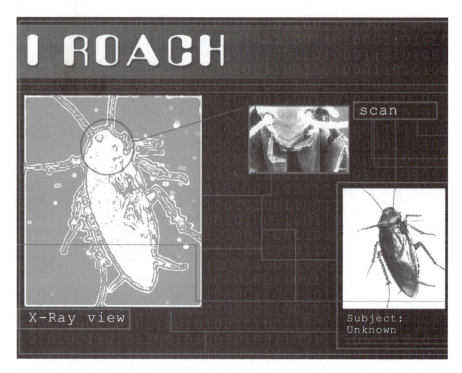

FIGURE 4.11 *Swarming Roaches* is a screen saver Goldtree made for a local Web site as a novelty giveaway.

GENRE MADNESS

Even with all these genre breakouts, there are still other games that cross over and combine with the genres we mentioned. Generally, a good game will have elements of the other genres (puzzle solving in a 3D game for example). We also see genre breakouts where technology permits; for example, many fighting games started out as side scrollers for the 2D platform, and eventually evolved into 3D shooters or 3D games. *Duke Nukem'* is a good example. Duke's evolution from 2D to 3D can be seen in Figures 4.12 through 4.14.

Keep genre in mind when designing your title; it is the first step in communicating your vision to all involved. Once you have a clear idea of your game—"it is a first-person adventure game with shades of military simulation"—you can proceed to describe it in visual terms on paper, eventually breaking it down into the elements that will comprise the "game plan." Once you are at that point, we can move on to the next chapter to look at the elements of design.

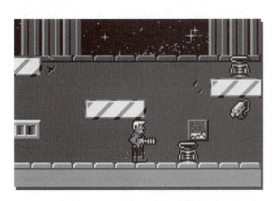

FIGURE 4.12   The original 2D side scroller
Duke Nukem'.

FIGURE 4.13   The first 3D *Duke Nukem'*.

FIGURE 4.14   The latest *Duke Nukem'* using the
Unreal Engine.

ACTIVITIES

There is only one activity for this chapter, but it will take you a few hours to
complete. Go to the local game store and look at the genres of all the games
on display. You can also do this on the Internet; however, a big part of this
activity is seeing how computer games are physically handled in a retail
store and being able to examine their boxes. Look at how prominent the

genre of the game is in the advertising and packaging. Notice that sometimes you cannot tell much about a game simply from its genre. As the game industry becomes more complex, the technology advances, and as developers push the limits of game design, the term *3D* or *action* says less and less about a title on the shelf. At the end of this activity, you should be well aware of the complexity of genres in game development.

SUMMARY

In this chapter, we saw how computer games are organized into genres. This is primarily for the retail channel (the stores where you buy them), but it is also very helpful in communicating your ideas to other individuals as to what your game is about and what it is like to play.

Introduction to The Games Factory

IN THIS CHAPTER
•••••••••••••••

- Working with The Games Factory
- Saving Your Games
- Working with the Event Editor

In the following chapters, we will actually create a game step by step. It will be exciting to see your creations come to life on the computer screen as we work through the tutorials.

Once you go through the process of making a 2D game, you have the basis that you need to go further into game development. Much of what you learn here will apply to more complex applications and tools later. You will find it easier to pick up new software and tools and learn them after learning one application.

We will be using The Games Factory (TGF), thanks to the wonderful people at Clickteam (see Figure 5.1).

Figure 5.1 Clickteam makes The Games Factory, Install Maker, and other fine products. Please visit them at www.clickteam.com.

WATCHOUT!

Important tutorial setup instruction: Please copy the three files on the companion CD-ROM (in the samplegames\tgflibs folder) to the TGF Library Folder on your hard drive. If you did a default installation, the folder will be C:\GFactory\Libs. **Do not copy the folder itself**, just the three files inside the folder.

Once you are comfortable with TGF, you will be able to use it to produce games and interactive applications with ease. TGF is a very powerful 2D game creation package. It contains state-of-the-art animation tools, sound tools, multimedia functions, and fabulous game structuring routines that make it very easy to produce your own games—with no programming.

HINT!

You can also make slide shows, interactive tests, presentations, and screen savers with TGF.

We will start by installing and getting familiar with the major areas of TGF. Make sure the companion CD-ROM is in the drive of your computer. On it is a copy of TGF.

WHAT'S ON THE CD-ROM

 You will find both 32- and 16-bit versions of TGF on the companion CD-ROM. If you are running Windows 3.1 or Windows NT, you need the 16-bit version; all other operating systems should use the 32-bit version.

OPERATING SYSTEMS

Windows 95 and 98 users can install the 32-bit version of The Games Factory on their machines. To do this, simply double-click the My Computer icon on your Windows desktop. Click the button next to the My Computer text box, and select the CD-ROM icon from the drop-down list. Look down the list for the folder that contains the 16-bit or 32-bit version you are installing.

Double-click this file to start the installation.

Windows 3.x users can use the 16-bit version of The Games Factory, GFCR16.exe.

HINT!

 The installation procedure is very similar for both the 16-bit and 32-bit versions.

During the installation, you will be given the choice to install the unregistered, home, or pro version (see Figures 5.2 and 5.3). You should install the *unregistered version*. This is a normal unregistered version of TGF, but as a special contribution to this book, Clickteam has removed the time limit. You can use TGF as long as you like, but you will see a startup screen each time you start TGF. You cannot save stand-alone games, screen savers, or Internet applications, but you can save the GAM file that is readable by TGF.

The unregistered version allows you to save your creations as GAM (.gam) files. Anyone wishing to play your game needs to have TGF installed on his or her computer to load and run the GAM files.

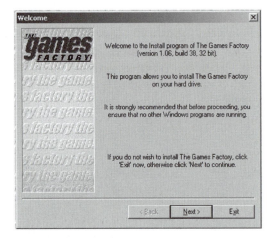

Figure 5.2 The welcome screen.

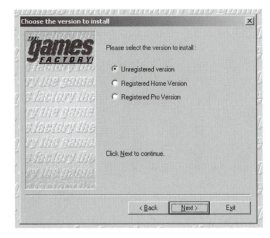

Figure 5.3 Unless you are a registered owner of TGF, select the unregistered option.

WHAT IF I WANT TO SAVE STAND-ALONE GAMES, SCREEN SAVERS, AND INTERNET APPLICATIONS?

ON THE CD

You will have to surf on over to the Clickteam site (www.clickteam .com) and register TGF. You will buy a registration code that will allow you to run either the registered home version or the pro version. We included these files on the CD to save you the download. All you have to do is reinstall TGF, select the proper registered version from the menu during installation, and enter the registration code, as shown in Figure 5.4.

Figure 5.4 The Registration Code window during installation.

HINT!

The registered versions of TGF are home and pro. Both can save stand-alone games, screen savers, and Internet applications, but

• The home version saves stand-alone applications that have an end screen: *games produced with the Home Version cannot be sold for profit.*

• The pro version saves stand-alone applications that have no end screen: *games made with the Pro Version can be sold for profit.*

ON THE CD

We'll assume that you selected the unregistered version on the CD.

After this choice is made, TGF will install itself onto your system and ask if you want to read the README file. It would be a good idea to do so. Click Finish at the bottom of the screen when you are ready to move on.

If you need to, the next screen asks if you want to install either Video for Windows or a QuickTime video driver for showing AVI and QuickTime-compatible video clips. Unless you want to install one of the drivers, click Next. The next screen asks you to type in your full name. When you have done so, click Next.

At the top of the next screen are two tick boxes, one for the 16-bit version and one for the 32-bit version. If you are running Windows 95/98 on your machine, you can install the 32-bit version. The tick box will be filled already. If you are running Windows 3.x, the 16-bit tick box will be filled.

For 32-bit (Windows 95 and 98) users, there is a tick box for Direct X, which is Microsoft's own graphics driver. Unless you specifically don't want to install Direct X, check the box. If you experience problems using Direct X, you should change the graphics driver.

For 16-bit (Windows 3.x) users, there is a tick box for Win G, which is Microsoft's own graphics driver.

At the bottom of this screen is the filename that The Games Factory will use. Unless you specifically want to enter a different name, click Next. You will then be told that the directory does not already exist, and you will be asked if you want to create it. Click OK to proceed. Now wait while The Games Factory installs. When installation is complete, click Return to Windows to return to Windows. Now you can double-click The Games Factory icon to run the program.

HINT!

As mentioned previously, you MUST copy the three tutorial files from the CD-ROM that are located in the samplegames\tgflibs folder onto the TGF Library Folder, now installed on your hard drive. (If you did a default installation, the folder will be called C:\GFactory\Libs.) DO NOT copy the folder itself, just the three files in the folder.

GETTING STARTED WITH TGF

TGF is centered on three main editing screens that allow you to control the three main parts of your game.

- **The Storyboard Editor** is the screen that allows you to decide the order of the levels in the game.
- **The Level Editor** allows you to decide which characters, backgrounds, and objects to put in your level, and how to animate them.
- **The Event Editor** allows you to assign the actions and responses that will make your game come alive.

HINT!

Some of the functions overlap, so look out for the Handy Hints along the way. You can easily move from one editor screen to the next by clicking the Editor icons in the toolbar at the top of each editor screen. Don't worry if you cannot remember what each one looks like. As you move the mouse pointer over the icons, a text balloon will appear underneath the mouse pointer telling you what each one is. Following is a brief description of the functions of each of the editor screens. These functions are described in more detail in the chapters of the user's manual relating to them.

STORYBOARD EDITOR

Most games are comprised of several levels. The Storyboard Editor screen allows you to add levels to your game, copy levels, and change the order of the levels by moving them around. This is also where you decide on the size of your playing area, add and edit professional-looking fades to each level, and assign passwords to enter each level (see Figure 5.5).

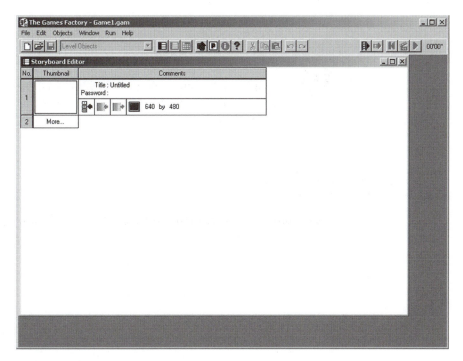

Figure 5.5   The Storyboard Editor.

HINT!

Until you have created a level, the only way to move out of the Storyboard Editor screen is by clicking in the Thumbnail with the right mouse button, and selecting the "Edit this level" option.

LEVEL EDITOR

The Level Editor (see Figure 5.6) is the initial "blank page" for each of your levels. It displays your play area and is where you put background objects and the main characters of your game. You generally access this screen from the Storyboard Editor screen.

From this screen, you have access to the libraries of all the different objects that you can use in your game. This is also where you can create your own animated objects, text, and other object types. Basically, all the objects that you want to play with have to be placed on this screen first before you can start manipulating them. It is also here that you change the animation and movement of objects and change the basic setup of all your objects.

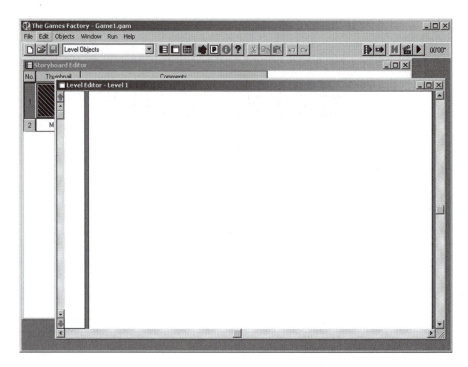

Figure 5.6   The Level Editor.

You will frequently find that before you can manipulate an object from the Event Editor, you must make sure that it is set up correctly on this screen.

EVENT EDITOR

The Event Editor is where your game will really come to life. The actions you assign here are called *interactivity*. Once you become experienced with The Games Factory, you will find that this editor is where you will spend most of your time. It is here that you decide all the events in your game.

The Event Editor (see Figure 5.7) is set up like a spreadsheet, in which you can assign relationships to each object in your game. This setup makes game building easier, because you can see what happens in your game. Examples of the game play you can build are aliens colliding with a spaceship and the main character collecting a power-up or getting hit by a missile. You can also set a time limit or assign a sound event. You

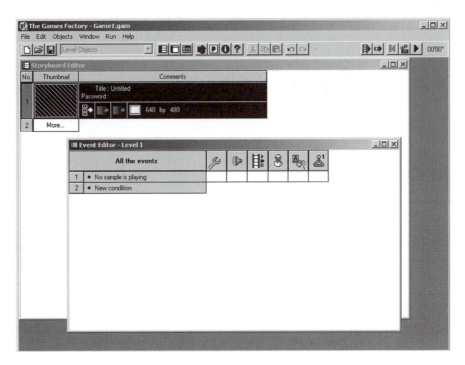

Figure 5.7   The Event Editor.

can create an explosion, destroy an object, add to the score, subtract a life, or even add complicated events such as changing the direction of a character or randomly moving object.

That was the quick tour of TGF. We saw that a game is built in TGF in three stages. First, you lay out the flow of your game in the Storyboard Editor, then you lay out your level and its objects in the Level Editor, and finally, you use the Event Editor to assign relationships and behaviors to your objects.

For the next chapter, you will want to have TGF installed and running if possible, since we will be digging deeper into The Games Factory.

ON THE CD
. . . .

As mentioned previously, you MUST copy the three tutorial files from the CD-ROM that are located in the samplegames\tgflibs folder onto the TGF LIBRARY FOLDER, now installed on your hard drive. (If you did a default installation, the folder will be called C:\GFactory\Libs.) DO NOT copy the folder itself, just the three files in the folder.

If you do not copy the three files into the proper folder, you will not be able to use the sample game tutorials with TGF software!

ACTIVITIES

As an activity for this chapter, make sure that The Games Factory is installed and running properly. Before we move on and start making games in The Games Factory, it would be wise to turn off your computer, restart it, and make sure that The Games Factory runs properly.

SUMMARY

In this chapter, we introduced The Games Factory, including how to download it onto your computer, how to save your game files, and how to create storyboards and events. It's important to copy the tutorial files as described in this chapter, or you won't be able to use TGF. Let's move on and make some games!

2D Game Creation

Behind the Scenes at The Games Factory

IN THIS CHAPTER

- Loading a New Game
- Creating Levels
- Mastering the Event Editor

We will now take you step by step through the process used to construct a very basic shoot 'em up game. I named my retro-creation *Cosmic Battle* (see Figure 6.1), my own version of *Space Invaders*. You will see that, with TGF, we can do a lot more than the original *Space Invaders* could.

Cosmic Battle will show you the basics of creating games with TGF. Those basics will go a long way in game development since many of the procedures you will be using for this game are basic to all games. With this tutorial, you will learn the different functions of the Editor screens and how they relate to each other.

HINT!

We will be dealing with the actual interactivity of a game, an aspect not touched on in Part One. You will see how integrated the interactivity aspect of a game is with the specific application you are using.

FIGURE 6.1 *Cosmic Battle*, a retro-creation using TGF, inspired by *Space Invaders*.

Although *Cosmic Battle* is a very basic game, you will be introduced to a set of interactive behaviors that you will be able to add to and expand on. You can make any game as complex as you like by adding levels, monsters, behaviors, and additional complexity by changing the movement, sounds, power-ups, scoring, and so forth.

HINT!

Retro gaming is still rather popular. People still love to play *Pac Man*, *Asteroids*, *Space Invaders*, and other older games. Many can be found online in the form of Java applets that can play in your Web browser window. A great site for this is http://spaceinvaders.retrogames.com.

LOADING COSMIC BATTLE

Select Open from the File menu at the top of the main screen in TGF, and look for the sample game folder on the CD-ROM.

Open the sample game folder, and look for the battle.gam file, as shown in Figure 6.2. Open this file.

Notice as you are searching for the file that TGF has a thumbnail preview of the gam file (see Figure 6.3).

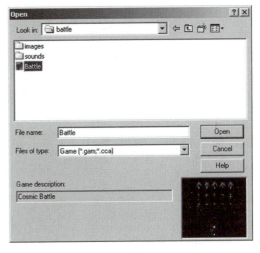

FIGURE 6.2   Opening the battle.gam file.

FIGURE 6.3   Opening the battle.gam file. Notice the thumbnail of your game in the lower right-hand corner.

COSMIC BATTLE—THE STORYBOARD EDITOR

Once you have loaded the *Cosmic Battle* game, you will be presented with a Storyboard Editor screen, as shown in Figure 6.4.

Starting from the top of the screen, we will describe the various features of the Storyboard Editor screen.

Note that many of the features are the same for all of the Editor screens, but what they actually perform on each Editor screen can be quite different. Therefore, you may want to get used to looking at what screen you are in before clicking buttons.

At the top right of the main TGF window are the standard window manipulation icons: minimize (maximize), restore, and exit. By clicking these you can control the window size or close the application. This is mentioned here since the different editors also have their own set of

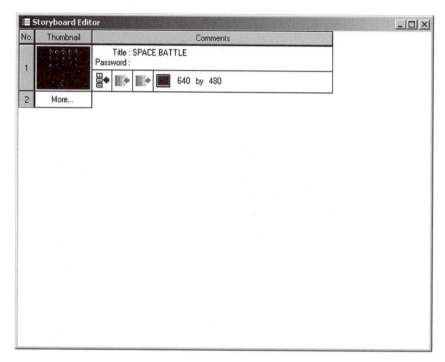

FIGURE 6.4 The *Cosmic Battle* Storyboard Editor.

window manipulation icons, and you could accidentally close the entire TGF when all you really want to do is close a specific editor.

At the very top of the screen is the Games Factory header bar. This displays the current game name—in this case, "battle.gam." Next to this is the name of the current Editor screen, "Storyboard Editor." Below this is the pull-down menu bar. From here you can save your games, change the size of the screen, change preferences, access the Help pages, and customize your display.

Below the menu bar is The Games Factory toolbar (see Figure 6.5). From here you can very quickly and easily move around the Editor screens by clicking their icons. You can also save games, cut and paste objects or events, and conduct test runs of your games.

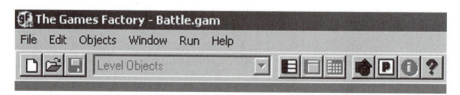

FIGURE 6.5 Toolbar icons.

LEVELS

Each level is displayed as a *thumbnail*, or very small screen shot, on the main window area of the Storyboard Editor. By default, the thumbnail is displayed immediately next to the number of the corresponding level, as shown in Figure 6.6.

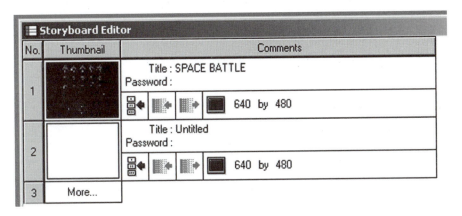

FIGURE 6.6   Close-up of the Storyboard Editor's level window.

Next to the thumbnail are the comments for that level; these include the title of the level and the password. To change these, simply click the text that you want to change with the left mouse button. You can then edit or add a title or password.

Underneath the comments are several buttons, as shown in Figures 6.7 through 6.10.

Figure 6.7 shows the multimedia level buttons, which is what all your levels will be by default because they all contain multimedia—sound and

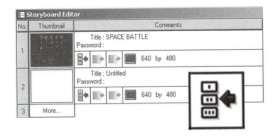

FIGURE 6.7   The multimedia level button.

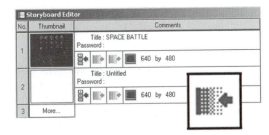

FIGURE 6.8   Fade-in transition button.

images. If you were to make your level an animation frame, this icon would change.

You can add a fade-in transition to your level by using the icon in Figure 6.8. A fade-in is when the scene transitions from black to the game level.

You can add a fade-out transition to your level using the icon shown in Figure 6.9. This is the opposite of the fade-in.

You can select the size of your play area by using the button shown in Figure 6.10. The play area can be much larger than the screen size, if you want. Then you can scroll around it using the standard Windows scroll-bars in the window frames.

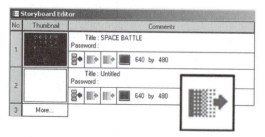

FIGURE 6.9   Fade-out transition button.

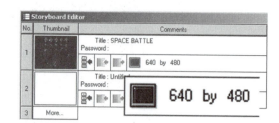

FIGURE 6.10   Play area size button.

SCREEN SIZE

By clicking the numbers, you can enter your own screen sizes via the keyboard. By clicking the Monitor icon, you can pick one of the default (common or standard) monitor sizes. *Cosmic Battle* is set at 640x480, which is a standard monitor size, and will allow the game to play faster than a larger screen size will.

Now that you have a general idea of what all the different features are on the Storyboard Editor, let's look at how we can put all the objects on the screen. Any questions you may have about the Storyboard Editor will be answered soon and in more detail.

COSMIC BATTLE—THE LEVEL EDITOR

If you are just opening the *Cosmic Battle* file, right-click inside the thumb-nail on the Storyboard Editor to get the pop-up menu. Select Edit the level | Level Editor. This will take you to the Level Editor.

HINT!

If you open a new file at this point and then open the Level Editor, you will be presented with a white, empty screen. When you open the battle.gam file, you see the screen as it looks in the game (see Figure 6.11). You will also see several items to the left in a vertical row. In the next chapter, we will look at getting those items into the editor.

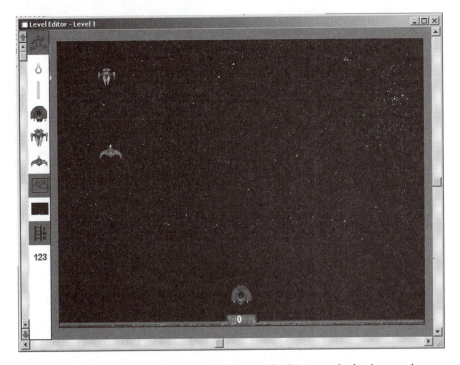

FIGURE 6.11   The *Cosmic Battle* Level Editor, with objects and a background.

After you have been in the Level Editor or the Event Editor, and using the thumbnail from the Storyboard Editor, all you have to do is click the icons on the toolbar to move through the different Editor screens in the future.

Now that you are in the Level Editor, you will notice that the toolbar at the top of the main window is exactly the same as on the Storyboard Editor screen, only now you can access the "object libraries" via the Level Objects window in the toolbar, as shown in Figure 6.12. Notice also that you can see all of the objects that have been used to create *Cosmic Battle* in their own Object window on the left-hand side of the screen.

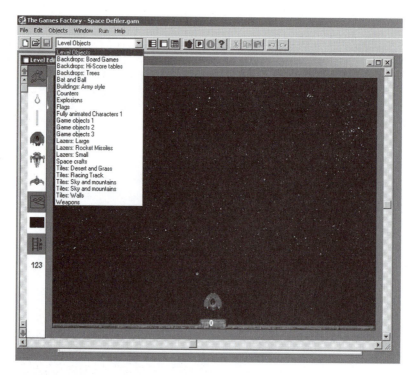

FIGURE 6.12   The Level Objects pull-down menu.

WATCHOUT!

When there are MANY objects in a level, not all of the objects will fit inside that window, so there is a scroll bar to look through them. Scroll the object libraries now.

You will find many premade items that you can use. Notice that as you select a library, it appears in the left-hand vertical window of the Level Editor. When you change libraries by clicking in the Level Objects pull-down menu, all the items go away, unless you have used one. If so, that item is retained. Don't worry, by selecting the library from the list again, the items will return.

HINT!

You can also make the window a "movable window" using the Objects | "Display objects in a movable window" option from the menu bar at the top of the screen. This will allow you to move the windows so you can see the other windows on your desktop.

If you move your mouse pointer over the objects in the object window, a "handy hint" will show you the name of each object, as shown in Figure 6.13. You can now select one of the objects with the left mouse button and place it anywhere on the screen. Try it now—*just don't save the file! If you do, you will overwrite the file.*

FIGURE 6.13   Handy hint balloon over objects in the Level Editor.

WATCHOUT!

If you had fun placing objects all over the level screen, select them with the left mouse button and use the Delete key to erase them. You must do this before you continue, or *you will change the contents of the other Editor screens.* If that happens, what you see will no longer correlate with the contents of this book.

Try moving the mouse pointer over the objects that have already been placed on the screen. You can move them around by clicking them with the left mouse button, and drag them around by holding down the left mouse button. Now, go to the scroll bars at the side of the screen, and try moving around the play area using them. You will notice that there is a gray area, which is the edge of the play area. Any objects placed here will *not be shown* on the screen when you play your game. However, it can be a useful "holding area" for placing objects in a level, which you can later move on to the play area by using the Event Editor.

Now let's look at the menu options for each object. Different types of objects have different menus. Press the right mouse button when you have the mouse pointer over the backdrop object, as shown in Figure 6.14. Look through all the different options, but don't change anything. Now, try it over any of the other objects on the screen. We will be using these menus in a later tutorial. Now that we've had a quick tour around The Games Factory's basic features, let's look at how the game plays!

To be sure that you have made no changes to the game, simply reload the game. To do this:

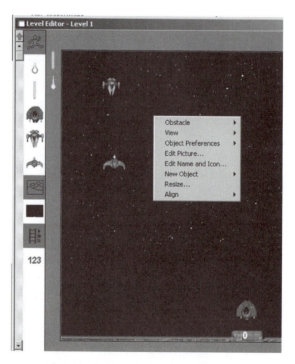

FIGURE 6.14   Right-mouse menu over space backdrop.

1. Click the File menu at the top of the screen.

2. Select the "Open" option.

3. Reload *Cosmic Battle*.

4. Right-click in the thumbnail.

5. Select and open the Level Editor.

Look at the top right of the toolbar. There are several buttons there that control the testing of your game. For now, we are just going to use the Play/Pause buttons and the Restart button, as shown in Figure 6.15.

The controls for the game are the Left/Right (arrow keys), and fire is the Ctrl key.

Now click the Play button. To stop the action, click it again. *When you want to finish playing, be sure to use the Restart button to reset everything.*

Pause

Restart   Play

FIGURE 6.15   The Play/Pause buttons and the Restart button.

COSMIC BATTLE—THE EVENT EDITOR

To get into the Event Editor, simply click the icon on the toolbar at the top of the screen. You should now see a screen that looks like Figure 6.16.

You decide upon the action and strategy of your game in the Event Editor. This is where you add sound and explosions, move on to the next level, display Hi Score tables—the list is almost endless.

We will look more specifically at how to change and edit the events and actions in the Event Editor in the next chapter. Right now, we will be familiarizing you with the logic of the Event Editor.

In addition to the menu bar and toolbar, the Event Editor basically consists of one horizontal line. At first, this line looks like the first line of

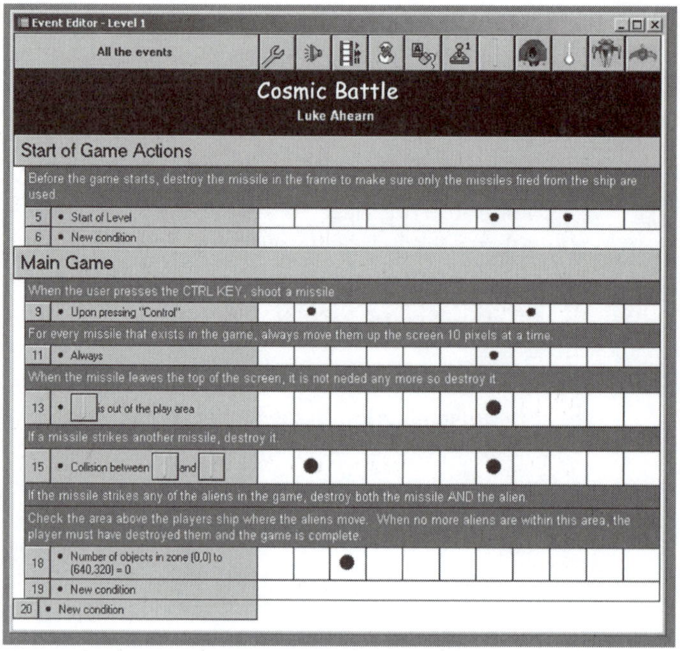

FIGURE 6.16   The *Cosmic Battle* Event Grid.

a spreadsheet before you have entered any information. In *Cosmic Battle*, however, you will see many events already entered.

Look at the Event Editor and you will see a row of icons across the top that represents possible actions. Beyond those, to the right, are all the objects we placed in our game from the Level Editor.

You will also notice that there is a vertical column of gray "event lines." Look below the heading "Start of Game Actions," and you will notice that next to each event line, there is a grid of boxes. Each box lines up with an object icon above it. For example, the first event consists of "start of level," "destroy," and the "missile object." (We will discuss how to insert and edit events and actions in the next chapter.)

You can see the horizontal line at the top of the Event Grid in Figure 6.17. It looks like this in *Cosmic Battle*.

FIGURE 6.17   The top line of the Event Grid in *Cosmic Battle*.

"All the events" is the heading for the vertical column, which is where you insert all the events for the game. We will describe this after talking you through the icons in the horizontal bar at the top.

The icons at the right of the bar refer to all of the level's objects. Shown here are all of the objects (except backdrop) that have been placed on the play area. You can see the enemy objects here, as well as the player's ship and the missile. It will also show any object that you use for bullets, or that you create from within the Event Editor, even if they are not already on the play area.

HINT!

How to shoot an object is described in the next chapter.

The first six icons denote Game Objects, and are always on the Event Grid by default. They can be seen in Figure 6.18.

Special Conditions. Performs special functions when an event occurs.
Sound. Plays or stops sound or music, even a CD track.
Storyboard. Allows you to start, stop, and change levels, and control the flow of the different levels of your game.
Create New Object. Allows you to place or create a new object on the screen at certain times or due to certain events.
Mouse and Keyboard. Lets you control how the player interacts with the mouse and keyboard—interactivity!
Player One. Allows you to change lives and scores.

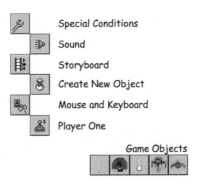

FIGURE 6.18   The six icons on the Event Grid.

Before we go any further, use the vertical scroll buttons on the right side of the screen to move down through the events until you can see events 18 and 19 just appearing on the bottom of the screen. You should now have a screen that looks like Figure 6.19.

You can now see three event lines within the group "Missile Destroys Ship." You can see, starting from left to right, that there are two events that involve the two space ship entities and the missile object.

The logic in line 15 is stated clearly with text and pictures:

Collision between missile and enemy

Now move your cursor over the dots in the grid to the right and you will complete the logic.

Play sound sample.
Add 10 to the score.
Destroy the ship object.
Destroy the missile object.

Notice how the pattern for these two events is identical, except for the ship that is destroyed. Since the two events each refer to the two different

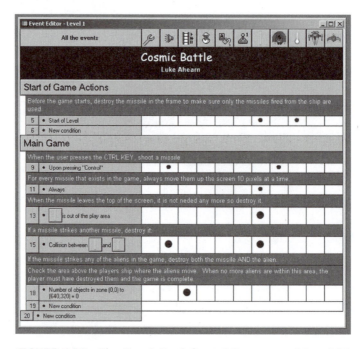

FIGURE 6.19 The *Cosmic Battle* Event Editor, events 18 and 19.

ships when a missile strikes them, logically each different ship is destroyed in each event.

Now look through the rest of the events and move your cursor over the check marks so that you can see which actions are associated with which objects. As you see this relationship unfold, you will see the simplicity of game creation with TGF.

CREATING EVENT LINES

Let's quickly create an "event line." Creating event lines and adding actions is very much like working with a standard spreadsheet and is very easy. All the options are pulled down from menus, and all the information is, too.

1. To create a new event line, move the cursor directly over the text "New condition" on an empty event line. "New condition" means that this line is completely empty. Notice that it has no grid next to it.
2. Now, click the text with the right mouse button. You will now have a dialog box that looks like the one in Figure 6.20.
3. If you move your mouse pointer over each icon in the New Condition window, you will be shown what each one is via the handy hint text balloon.
4. Now, right-click the *Storyboard* controls icon. You will pull down a menu.
5. Click the "Start of level" option with the left mouse button in this menu.

You will now be taken back to the Event Grid, and the new event will read "Start of level." You've created your first event.

Now all you need to do is put in an action associated with that event. Notice the line is devoid of actions.

1. Go across the empty check boxes on line number 10 until you get to the box underneath the icon of the missile.
2. Click the empty box with the right mouse button. You will then see a menu of all the things you can do to the missile object—movement, animation, direction, position, and so forth. We will look at all these options in the next chapter.
3. Now, move down the pop-up menu and, using the left mouse button, click the "Destroy" option. You will then be taken back to the Event Grid and the new event line with the logic that states:

"At the start of the level, destroy the missile object."

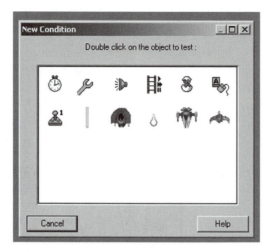

FIGURE 6.20   New Condition window that
pops up when a new condition is added.

ACTIVITIES

Open the battle.gam file we looked at in the chapter and save a copy of it.
Name it whatever you like, just don't overwrite another file. Open the Level
Editor and experiment with the placement of objects on the playing field.
Have fun loading the libraries of art that come with The Games Factory and
placing them on the playing field. You will see that you have a great deal of
art and assets from which to choose when making your own games.

SUMMARY

In this chapter, we loaded and worked with *Cosmic Battle*. Using the Storyboard, Level, and Event Editors, we were able to show how a sample game
can be created. If you are comfortable with the concepts presented in this
chapter, we can move on to the next chapter where you create a game from
the ground up.

Making a Game with The Games Factory

IN THIS CHAPTER

- Creating a New Game
- Starting with the Backdrop
- Placing Objects on the Screen
- Creating Animation
- Adding Sound Effects

Run around the block, wake up, and prepare your mind—you are ready for the serious stuff. In this chapter, we will go deep into TGF and really get our game tweaked out. We will attempt . . . drum roll, please . . . to make Cosmic Battle from the ground up.

By the end of this chapter, you will be able to lay out multiple levels, orchestrate game effects, play music off a CD from within your game, and more.

CREATING COSMIC BATTLE

Okay, now that you've had the guided tour around TGF, let's look at how *Cosmic Battle* was assembled. I will move faster when it comes to areas we covered in the last chapter. For example, I will tell you to create a new event line without telling you exactly how to do it each time, as in the last chapter.

LET'S CREATE A NEW FILE

1. Go to the File heading on the menu bar at the top of the screen.
2. Select the "New" option.
3. The Games Factory will ask you if you want to save the changes that you have made to *Cosmic Battle* if it is open.
4. Select No.
5. You will be asked to select a playfield size. Click the 640 by 480 size.
6. Click OK. This screen size will run faster because it is small, but it is still big enough to be playable.
7. You will now be taken to the Storyboard Editor, with an empty level 1 display.
8. To enter a name for the level, click the "Untitled" text within the level 1 display.
9. Enter the name you would like.
10. Press Return.

ON THE CD

Although the point of this chapter is to have you build *Cosmic Battle* from the ground up, you can go to the CD-ROM and open the file battle.gam to look at the finished version of *Cosmic Battle*.

CONTINUING ON

1. Click inside the empty thumbnail with the right mouse button. From the menu, click the "Edit this level" option.
2. Next, select the "Level Editor" option. You will then be taken to an empty Level Editor screen on which to place your objects.
3. To place new objects on the screen, go to the Level Objects text box on the toolbar at the top of the screen, and click the pull-down button at the side of the text (see Figure 7.1).
4. Now look through all the different object libraries until you get to one called (Tutorial) COSMIC BATTLE. Click this library.

You will now have all the objects from this library displayed in the Object window down the left-hand side of the screen. You will notice that there are large icons within this window. These denote the type of object below it, as shown in Figures 7.2 through 7.4.

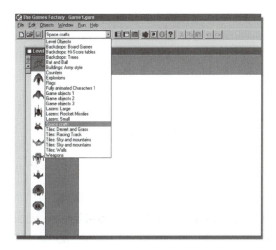

FIGURE 7.1   The pull-down Level Objects button.

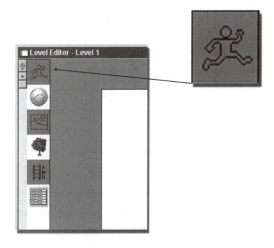

FIGURE 7.2   The Active Objects icon denotes active objects.

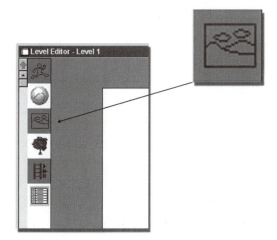

FIGURE 7.3   The Backdrop icon denotes backdrop objects.

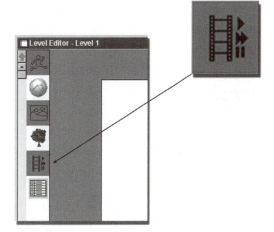

FIGURE 7.4   The Storyboard icon denotes storyboard objects.

Try moving your mouse pointer over the different objects in the window. A handy hint text box will tell you what each one is called.

Before we place the active objects of our game on the play area, we are going to put a backdrop into place, align it perfectly with the edges of the screen, and then lock it into place so it cannot be selected or moved while we are putting all the other objects on the play area.

PLACING THE BACKDROP AND LOCKING IT IN PLACE

1. To place the backdrop on the screen, go to the Object window, and click the Backdrop icon, called Cosmic Battle Backdrop, using the *left* mouse button.
2. Now, move the mouse pointer over the play area—anywhere will do—and then press the left mouse button again. This places the backdrop object on the play area. Your screen should look like Figure 7.5.

FIGURE 7.5   The play field.

HINT!

When the backdrop object and the size of the play area are identical, The Games Factory will automatically align the backdrop object to fit.

We are now going to stop the backdrop object from being selected every time you click it with the mouse. This will make it far easier when you start putting other objects on the play area.

FIGURE 7.6 The Level Editor
Preferences window.

3. Go to the toolbar at the top of the screen, and click the Preferences icon with the left mouse button. You will see the Level Editor Preferences window, as shown in Figure 7.6.
4. In this dialog box, look in the Lock objects area for the "Backdrop" option. There will be an empty check box. Click in the check box with the left mouse button. It will now be filled with a small X, which means that the backdrop is locked in place. Click OK.

HINT!

If you lock the background or any other object in place, don't forget that you did so! There is no indication that the background is locked in place, other than the fact that you cannot move it—it simply doesn't respond to your cursor. This may be confusing if you forget you locked it.

5. Now try clicking the backdrop object—you cannot! As you saw from the different options in the Preferences dialog box, you can also lock many different types of objects into place. To unlock the backdrop object, click the Preferences icon, and then click the Backdrop object radio button again.

PLACING OBJECTS ON THE SCREEN

Now that we have a nice backdrop for our game, we are going to place the active objects on the play area: the enemies, the missile, some obstacles, and the player's spaceship. The trick to getting all the objects lined up so neatly on the screen is to use the *grid tool*.

1. Go to the Preferences icon again, at the top of the screen. Click the icon using the left mouse button. Now, in the Preferences dialog box, select the second tab called Grid. You can see the Grid preferences in Figure 7.7.

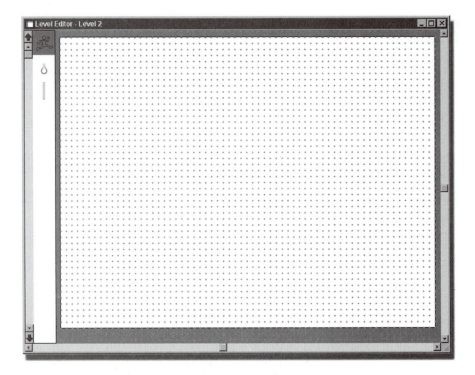

FIGURE 7.7   The grid is used to precisely align objects in the game.

On the Grid tab, you will see several options:

- **Origin**. This dictates where the grid starts. Leave it at zero.
- **Square size**. This dictates how far apart the "line-up points" of the grid are. The larger the number, the farther apart the points, and the less fine control you have over where an object is placed.
- **Width and height boxes**. Let you change the size of the grid.
- **Snap-to and Show grid**. Two radio buttons that allow you to "snap" objects to the grid.

2. Click the numbers in the Width and Height boxes and change them to 10.

3. Check the Snap-to radio button. This function allows any object that you place on the screen to "snap to the grid," or attach to the grid points. If you would like to see the grid, check the Show grid button. You do not have to have it visible to use it.

4. Now click OK at the bottom of the dialog box to take you back to the Level Editor screen.

SCREEN PLACEMENT OF OBJECTS

We are ready to start placing the objects on the screen. Now that we enabled the grid, you will see the objects jump a little as you drag them across the background. This is the grid in effect. If you were to go back to the Preferences dialog box and make the grid squares larger, you would see the objects jumping more.

1. Go to the Object window and select an object—use the left mouse button.

2. Move the object to where you want it on the screen.

3. Next, click the left mouse button and you will place a single copy of the object down. If you were to click the right mouse button, you could place multiple copies of the object down without having to return to the object shelf every time you want to place an object. This is handy for placing an army of drones or building a maze dungeon with many obstacles.

ACTIVITY
· · · · · · · ·

Let's use the right mouse button to lay out a wave of cosmic space ships!

1. Go to the Object window, and click the yellow ship with the left mouse button.

2. Now, move the mouse pointer over the play area.

3. Let's go to the top left of the screen and start placing our ships there. Select the place where you want to place the first ship, but don't press any buttons yet. Don't place it too close to the edge of the screen, or it will disappear off the screen when you play the game because the ships move.

4. Place the ships in a row in the center of the play area, as shown in Figure 7.8.

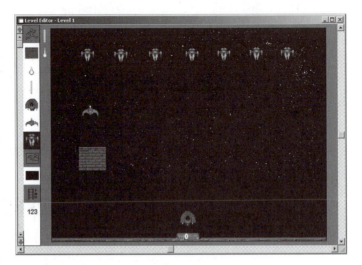

FIGURE 7.8 The ship on the playfield.

HINT!
. . . .

You can still scroll around the display area using the scroll bars even when you are "carrying" an object.

You can use the right mouse button to place ships quickly. You should end up with a line of ships evenly spaced across the top of the screen. Placing your last ship on the screen using the left mouse button will stop you from placing any more clones and will free up the cursor.

PLACING OBJECTS FOR YOUR OPPONENT
. . . .

Since this is a cosmic battle, lets put some ships on the screen with which to battle.

1. Go to the objects, select the Player's Ship, and place that on the bottom of the play area. Place it just slightly above the bottom of the screen.
2. Next, go to the Object window, click a Cosmic Battle Obstacle, and place a row of about four of these immediately above the Player's Ship. Try not to have them too close to the ship—give it some room.
3. Now, place the bullet, "Missile," anywhere on the screen.

HINT!

When we use the Event Editor, we are going to remove any missiles from the display when the level first starts. We are only placing it on the screen so that it will appear in the Event Editor and so we can assign behaviors to it.

4. Scroll through the Object window until you find the Score object. Place that on the bottom of the screen, out of the way of everything else, as shown in Figure 7.9.

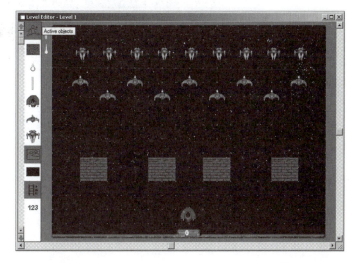

FIGURE 7.9   The objects all laid out in the Level Editor for the *Cosmic Battle* game.

ASSIGNING MOVEMENTS TO OBJECTS

Assigning movement and animation to objects is done in the Level Editor. This is rather easy to do. Right-click an object in the layout area, and you will see the pop-up menu shown in Figure 7.10.

The distinction between movement and animation in TGF is important. *Animation* is the ability to have an active object function (like a short movie), playing frames over and over like an animated cursor in Windows. This makes the active object appear to be walking, running in place, or moving in some way. *Movement* dictates where the active object goes in the game and how it is controlled.

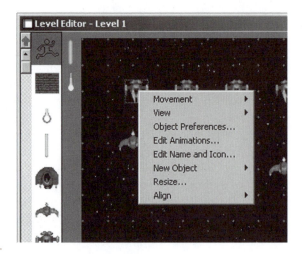

FIGURE 7.10   The pop-up menu associated with an object in the Level Editor.

Now let's look at two of the options in this menu: Movement and Edit Animations.

- **Movement** has an arrow indicating that more choices are available—Change or Edit, in this case.
- **Edit Animations** will open the Animation Editor if selected.

An active object can have more than one animation assigned to it. We will look at that next.

Examples of *animation* include these.

- **Walking**. Legs are moving back and forth, arms swinging.
- **Running**. Like walking, only faster.
- **Dying**. Body falls to the ground.

An example of *movement* is the active object following a path or being controlled by the player. The active object can play the walking animation while being moved by the player, and it looks like it is using its legs to move.

To see this illustrated, go to the Level Editor and right-click the yellow ship. The menu shown in Figure 7.10 appears. Select Choose a Movement, and you will see the Choose a Movement menu appear, as shown in Figure 7.11.

As you can see, you can make the object computer or player controlled. We have our ships computer controlled. Since we have a *Space In-*

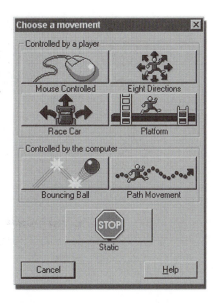

Figure 7.11   The Choose a
Movement menu.

vaders-type game, the best way to emulate that back-and-forth track-type
movement is to use the "Path" option.

The "Path" option allows you to select a track on which the object
moves, whether it loops or plays once, and the speed of the movement.
Most importantly, it allows you to test your movement.

Cancel this after playing with it by right-clicking the spaceship and selecting Edit Animation from the pop-up menu. This opens the Animation
Editor, as shown in Figure 7.12.

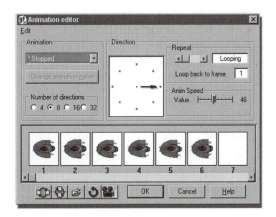

FIGURE 7.12   The Animation Editor.

THE ANIMATION EDITOR

In the Animation Editor, you will see three main areas: the Animation window, the Direction window, and the Animation Frames window. The Animation window has a pull-down text box that stores animation tracks for many events for each active object. This is used later in the Event Editor, where you can make a character (currently using the default walking animation) play the "dying" animation track when he gets hit.

You can pull this list down and select another animation. There will be an asterisk next to the selections that contain an animation. In this case, there are two: "Stopped" and "Getting Hit." "Stopped" is the one that shows the Player Ship swaying, and "Getting Hit" distorts and changes color.

HINT!

When you add your own active objects, you will be brought to the screen. Even if the object is not animated, you will still have to import the images here. Clicking the Create New Object icon on the toolbar and selecting the active object does this. Next, you double-click in the first frame, and then click the Open Folder icon in the Picture Editor.

CHECKING YOUR WORK

Look at what you've done so far.

1. Click the Play button on the toolbar at the top of the screen (see Figure 7.13).
2. Remember to click it again to pause the game.
3. Use the Rewind button to reset the game.

You should have a field of ships moving around the screen. You should also be able to move the spaceship from left to right by using the cursor keys.

Now that we have the basic objects on the screen, we need to add some actions, sound, and so forth. To do this, you need to go to the Event Editor. However, before we do, we'll save the work that we have done.

RESTART   PLAY

RESTART   PAUSE

FIGURE 7.13   The Play button on the toolbar.

THE PROPER WAY TO SAVE A FILE IN TGF

If you created anything unique in the previous exercises that you want to keep, stop and save your work now!

1. Go to the "File" option in the menu bar at the top of the screen.
2. Click it using the left mouse button.
3. Click the "Save as..." option.
4. You will now see a file selector. Select the disk drive to which you want to save.
5. Type in a name for the file. If you are using Windows 3.1, this can be up to eight letters long, and *must always have .gam after it*, denoting that this is a game file. Windows 95/98 allows you filenames with up to 256 characters.
6. Once you have safely saved your work, close your file.

MAKING COSMIC *BATTLE EVENTS* AND ACTIONS

For this section, open the file battle.gam and right-click the thumbnail of the level in the Storyboard Editor. Click the "Edit this level" option (see Figure 7.14) to open up the Event Editor.

The Event Editor is where your gaming really comes to life. You have seen how easy it is to place your objects on the screen, but now you want to fire missiles, destroy aliens, add sound, and change the score.

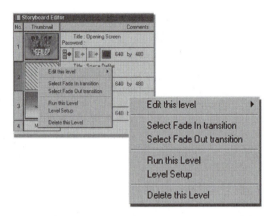

FIGURE 7.14   The pop-up menu to get to the
Event Editor.

We are going to take you step by step through creating a complete set of events that brings *Cosmic Battle* to life. Much of what you will learn in this chapter is basic to all game creation using TGF and other applications.

To begin, before we even create events, we are going to show you how to create *comment lines*, which provide you with notes to refer to in the Event Editor. Although *Cosmic Battle* is a very simple game and presents no navigating problems for experienced users, writing comments in the Event Editor is a very good habit to develop. When you start writing longer, complicated games and applications, you will need to refer to these comments.

We are also going to show you how to define groups of events, which make your event editing far easier to follow and allow you to simplify your game writing.

CREATING A GROUP OF EVENTS

The first thing we'll do is create a group of events called Start of Game Actions.

1. Right-click the number 1 on the New condition line.
2. Next, select the "Insert" option from the menu.
3. Select the "A group of events" option from that menu.
4. You will now have a dialog box asking you to enter the name of the group.
5. Type in the text "Start of Game Actions."

6. When you have done this, make sure that the "Active when frame starts" radio button is selected. It will be selected by default, but check it anyway.
7. When you have the name entered, either press Return or click OK.
8. You should now have a group called Start of Game Actions. Event line number 2 will be indented slightly, denoting it as being within that group.

Next, we are going to create a comment line for event line 2.

CREATING A COMMENT LINE

1. Right-click the number 2 of event line 2.
2. Select the "Insert" option, and then the "A comment" option.
3. You now have a dialog box in which to select the font, color, and background color of your text. We are going to use the standard font but write in white.
4. Click the "Set font color" option, and then click the white square. Click OK.
5. Click the "Set back color" option, select dark green, and then click OK.
6. Click in the top left of the empty text box. Now you can type in the words that you want to appear in the comment.
7. Enter the text "Before the game starts, destroy the missile in the frame to make sure only the missiles fired from the ship are used in the game." Click OK.
8. You should have a comment with a green background and white letters. If you made a mistake, you can edit your comment line by *right-clicking* the text of the comment and then selecting the "Edit Comment" option.

CREATING AN EVENT LINE

Time to get down to the nitty-gritty of your games creation! We are going to insert an actual event, Start of level, which means that when it is the start of the level, all the actions associated with this event line will be performed.

This event is going to be within the group "Start of Game Actions."

1. Click on the text "New condition" of event line number 3 with the *right* mouse button.

2. You will see a dialog box titled New Condition, with the subheading "Double-click the object to test."
3. Move your mouse pointer over the Storyboard Controls icon (the handy hint text will tell you which one it is as you move your mouse pointer over the objects).
4. Either *double left-click* or *single right-click* the object. This will produce a menu from the object (see Figure 7.15).
5. Select the "Start of level" option with the left mouse button. You will have an event line number 3 that reads "Start of level."
6. You can now insert an action, which we will cover in the next section.
7. **Save your game!** If you are working on your own game from the ground up, before you go any further, save the game.

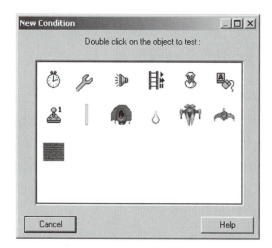

FIGURE 7.15   The New Condition dialog box.

ADDING ACTIONS TO EVENT LINES

Next, we are going to insert an action—destroying the missile—into event line number 3, to destroy the missile. We are continuing from the previous section.

DESTROYING OBJECTS

1. Right-click in the empty box below the Missile icon, on line number 3. This produces a large menu of all the possible actions that you could do to the missile.

2. Select the "Destroy" option with the left mouse button. You will have a complete event line that will destroy the missiles at the very start of the level, within the group Start of Game Actions.
3. Now it's time to start adding the rest of the events. Create a Group called "Main Game."
4. Next, insert the following comment:

"When the user presses the Ctrl key, shoot a missile."

TESTING THE KEYBOARD FOR A SPECIFIC KEY DEPRESSION

During the game, you will want certain keystrokes to do certain things; in this case, the Ctrl key will fire a missile—interactivity, baby!

1. Right-click the "New Condition" text.
2. Now, use the right mouse button to select the Mouse Pointer and Keyboard icon.
3. Select the "Keyboard" option from this menu.
4. Select the "Upon Pressing a Key" option.
5. You will now be asked to press the key with which you want to associate your actions. Press the Ctrl key (next to the arrow keys on most keyboards, as in Figure 7.16).

Figure 7.16   The Control, or Ctrl, key.

6. You will now be taken back to the Event Editor screen, with an event line that reads "Upon pressing Ctrl."

SHOOTING AN OBJECT

Now that you've made your event line to test when the Ctrl key has been pressed, you need to actually shoot something when it is pressed.

1. Go to the empty box that lies directly underneath "Player's ship" and on the same line as the event line we just created.
2. Click it with the right mouse button, and select the "Shoot an Object..." option from the pop-up menu (see Figure 7.17).

FIGURE 7.17 The relationship between the event created and the object it affects.

3. You will see a dialog box displaying all the active objects from the current level.
4. We want to use the Missile object as our bullet, so select that, and then click OK.
5. You will now be asked to select a speed and direction for the bullet. By default, the speed is 100, which is very fast. Use the mouse to move the pointer to 50.
6. Next, you want to select the direction in which to fire, which, in this case, should be *up*. To do this, click the "Shoot in selected directions" button.
7. You can now select the direction in which you want to fire the bullet from the "direction clock face." You can select and deselect directions by clicking the black buttons around the clock face (see Figure 7.18).

WATCHOUT!

Make sure you have just *one* arrow pointing straight up. Note that if you have more than one direction showing, The Games Factory will select from those directions at random. We will use this feature later on the aliens.

FIGURE 7.18   The direction clock face.

8. Now click all the OK buttons to take you back to the Event Editor screen. You should have a complete event line, so that when you press the Ctrl key, a missile is fired up the screen.
9. **Save your game before you go any further.**

THE ALIENS SHOOT BACK

What type of aliens would we have if they just sat there? They need to shoot back, and this is where the real battle comes in. To make the aliens shoot back, go to the Level Editor and follow the same steps you used earlier to place a missile into the scene; only this time, choose the "alien goo" object. Place this under the missile object in the Level Editor simply to keep things neat.

Back in the Event Editor, you need to follow the same steps to destroy the goo object at the start of the game and to destroy the goo if any goes off the screen, just like the missile.

Next, go to the Event Editor, where we'll make the *ships* fight back.

1. Create a new event by right-clicking the "New condition" line and then right-clicking the clock face.
2. Select the "Every" option from the pop-up menu.
3. In the window that pops up, set the time to 1 second. This means that the event will take place every second.

WATCHOUT!

The default active window is minutes. If you fail to move over to the seconds (middle) window, and accidentally set the event at "every 1 minute" instead of "every 1 second," it will look like your event is not happening at all in the game, since it will take a minute instead of a second to happen.

4. Now, go to the empty box that lies directly underneath the yellow ship and on the same line as the event line we just created. Right-click it, and select the "Shoot an object..." option from the pop-up menu.
5. You will see a dialog box displaying all the active objects from the current level. We want to use the alien goo object as our bullet, so select that.
6. Click OK.

You will now be asked to select a speed and direction for the bullet. You should make it a bit slower than we made the player's missile, for game play reasons as well as aesthetics.

1. By default, the speed is 100, which is very fast. Use the mouse to move the pointer to 50 or lower.
2. Click the "Shoot in selected directions" button and deselect the arrow pointing up by clicking the little black square it is pointing at and clicking the down, or 6 o'clock, arrow. Remember, selecting more than one direction makes TGF select a direction at random. This can be annoying if the missile is coming from the player's ship, but when it is coming from the aliens, selecting a square immediately on either side of the 6 o'clock direction gives it a nice random feel that adds to the game.
3. Press all the OK buttons to take you back to the Event Editor screen.
4. Press Play to check your work.

ADDING SOUND EFFECTS

Try running the level with no sound event (or turn your speakers down), and then running the level with sound. You will see firsthand how important sound is in a game.

1. Right-click the empty box beneath the Sound icon on the *active event line.*
2. Select the "Play sample" option from the menu produced, which takes you to a file selector.

3. First, you have to select the correct drive. You can click the button under Drives to pull down a list of the drives available.

4. Look down the list of directories (use the scroll bars) until you find one called Samples. Double-click this directory with the *left* mouse button.

5. From this list select "Weapons" by double-clicking it. You will now have a list of all the noises in the weapons directory.

6. Scroll through the list of noises until you get to one called "phaser03.wav." Left-click it.

7. Now, click Play on the right side of the dialog box to preview the noises. You can always select another sample and preview that using the Play button, or even move to another sound directory. Simply double-click the Samples directory, and then choose another sound directory.

8. When you are happy with the sound that will play every time a missile is fired, click OK.

CREATE A NEW COMMENT LINE

Create a new comment line on the next line, containing the following text: "For every missile that exists in the game, always move them up 10 pixels at a time." Although it seems out of place in the sound section, it is needed here, because it is part of the action we are building.

Create an Always event on the line after that. To do this, right-click the New Condition text, and then right-click the special object. From the "Always/Never" option, select "Always."

MOVING AN OBJECT BY CHANGING ITS COORDINATES

Now we will move an object by changing coordinates, or changing its location.

1. Insert an action on the Always event line, beneath the Missile icon.

2. Right-click the empty box. From the menu, select the "Position" option (see Figure 7.19). This means that every time The Games Factory cycles through the Event Editor, it will always subtract 10 from the Y coordinate of the missile.

3. Click the OK buttons to take you back to the Event Editor.

4. Lean back and rub your eyes.

This method of movement is actually somewhat redundant in this game, since we are already firing the missile at the speed of 50. However,

FIGURE 7.19   The relationship of the Always action to the missile object.

this exercise does show you that you can move objects around quite easily by changing their coordinates. This will help you in the future with more complex games.

1. From this menu, select the "Set Y coordinate" option.
2. Click Edit. This will take you to another Expression Editor.
3. Click the "Retrieve data from an object" button.
4. Next, right-click the missile from the objects displayed.
5. When you select the missile, it will produce a menu. Select the "Position" option.
6. From the menu that this produces, select the "Y coordinate" option.
7. You will now have the text Y("MISSILE") in the text box of the Expression Editor. Without changing this text, add –10 to the end of the text, so that you have an expression that reads Y("MISSILE")–10.

TESTING THE POSITION OF AN OBJECT

Keeping track of objects in the game can be important for the game's efficiency. If we don't keep track of missiles, they will fly forever, and the computer will track them forever, even when they are useless to the game, so we destroy them. For now, we will start with a simple exercise in object tracking. Insert a new comment on the next event line: "When the missile leaves the top of the screen, it is not needed any more, so destroy it." Now insert an event on the line below it to test the position of the missile.

1. Right-click the New Condition line, and select the missile from the dialog box.
2. Select the "Position-Test position of Missile" option.
3. You will have a dialog box that allows you to test the position of the missile in several different ways. Move the mouse pointer over the different buttons and look at all the options available.
4. Click the "Is the object outside?" button. Note that from here, you could select more than one button. You can deselect a button by clicking it again.

5. When only the "Is the object outside?" button is depressed, click OK to take you back to the Event Editor.
6. You will now have an event line that reads "(Missile) is out of the play area."
7. Next, insert an action to destroy the missile, on the same event line (see Figure 7.20).
8. Enter this comment: "If a missile strikes another missile, destroy it."
9. Now insert the following event: Collision between (missile) and (missile)

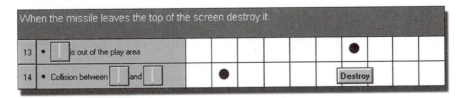

FIGURE 7.20   The relationship between the missile object and the action to destroy it if it goes outside the play area.

10. Right-click the New Condition text, right-click the missile object, and select the "Collisions-Another object" option from the menu.
11. Select the missile from the dialog box with the left mouse button, and then click OK. You will have an event line as described earlier.

    We are doing this in case the player is very fast on the keyboard and fires too many missiles that end up running into each other. If they do, the missiles will destroy each other. This can also be useful if you apply the same action set to any other two objects in a game.

12. Next, insert another action in this group to destroy the missile.

HINT!

You can copy the action from one of the other event lines by clicking and holding on one of the Destroy tick marks, and then dragging it into the empty box beneath the Missile icon, on the Collision between (Missile) and (Missile) event line.

13. **Save your game if you need to!**

DESTROYING A SHIP

In order for your missiles to have any effect when they hit a ship, we have to assign that behavior as well. We will create the necessary events for this now.

1. On the next line, insert the following comment: "If the missile strikes a ship, destroy the missile AND the ship."
2. Next, insert the following event: Collision between (missile) and (yellow ship). Do this by right-clicking the New condition text, then right-clicking the missile icon, and selecting the "Collisions-Another object" option.
3. Now select the yellow ship object.
4. Insert the following event: Collision between (missile) and (yellow ship).
5. Insert the following event: Collision between (missile) and (small ship).
6. You should now have three event lines.
7. Insert a sound action on the first event line, Collision between (missile) and (yellow ship).
8. Pick something appropriate for an explosion. (Right-click the empty box under the Sound icon, select the "Play sample" option, and look in Samples-Tutorials).
9. Copy the sound action into the lines for the yellow ship and small ship. That sound will now play every time a missile collides with any of the ships.

DESTROYING THE MISSILE ON IMPACT

We want the missile to be destroyed when it hits the ship, or it will just keep going. If the missile is destroyed on impact, it adds realism.

1. Insert another Destroy action into the empty box under the missile on each line. (Right-click the box and select the "Destroy" option.)
2. To save time, drag the Destroy action, using the left mouse button, into all the empty boxes beneath the missile, for when the missile collides with an alien.
3. Check your logic. Make sure that it is the *yellow ship* that is destroyed when a missile collides with a yellow ship, and not one of the others! If you make a mistake, you can select a check mark, and then press Delete.

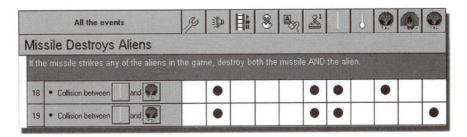

FIGURE 7.21   The two ship collision events.

4. Do the same for the other entities. The events should look like the screen shot in Figure 7.21.
5. **Save your game!**

KEEPING SCORE

Now we want to add to the score every time one of the missiles destroys one of the ships. We are still working with the same three event lines from the previous section.

1. Right-click the empty box underneath the Player 1 object, and select the "Score" option.
2. Select the "Add to Score" option (see Figure 7.22 for the Add to Score menu).

    You can choose how much you are going to add to the score when a yellow ship is destroyed. Since it is big and nasty, you may want it to be worth 100 points.

3. Click OK.

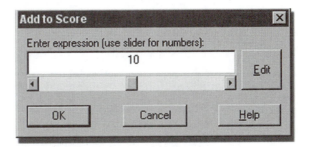

FIGURE 7.22   The Add to Score menu.

4. Do the same for the other entities.

You can also make items deduct points when destroyed. You can make an item worth negative points by typing in a minus sign before the number, thus creating an item the player does not want to hit. To make levels increasingly difficult, you can introduce friendly, or civilian, crafts that you are not supposed to hit.

HINT!

As you develop a game you will decide, for example, how many points a difficult target is worth. This type of decision in your game design is called *game balance*.

IT AIN'T OVER TILL IT'S OVER

Finally, you need to tell TGF when it is over—the game, that is.

The way we will do that is to have the computer look at the playing area, and if all the aliens are dead and gone, the game will end.

1. Insert a comment line, if you wish, that says the following: "Check the area above the player's ship, where the aliens are. If there are no more aliens, the game is complete."

2. Now we are going to insert an event to end the game when all the aliens have been destroyed. To do this, we are going to test for any objects in a zone on the play area.

   a. Right-click on the New Condition text line.

   b. Right-click the New Objects icon.

   c. Select the "Compare to number of objects in a zone" option. You will be taken to a Zone setup screen.

   d. Click in the first box, Horizontal. Enter a 0 in the box. Go to the next box on that line, click it and type 640.

   e. Next, click the first box on the next line down, Vertical. Enter a 0 in the box.

   f. Now enter 320 in the last box. You should have the four boxes filled as follows: 0 to 640, then underneath, 0 to 320. If you have done this successfully, click OK.

   g. Next, a dialog box appears in which you can enter a number that you are comparing to the number of objects in the zone that you just defined.

At the top of the dialog box are several radio buttons, which is where you decide how you are going to compare the number. By default, it is set at Equal. This is the comparison that we want to use, because when the number of objects is equal to zero, we want to end the game. Make sure the Equal radio button is selected.

    h. Now you can enter the number you want to compare. In this case, it is 0, so make sure the text box at the bottom of the dialog box has a 0 in it. You can change it by using the slider, or by clicking the text box and entering the numbers manually.

    i. When you have the comparison set to Equals 0, click OK.

       Your event line will read: "Number of objects in zone (0,0) to (640,320) = 0."

3. Next, insert an action to finish the game. Go to the empty box underneath the Storyboard Controls icon.

    a. Right-click the box.

    b. From the menu produced, select the "End the game" option.

    That's it! *Cosmic Battle* is ready to play!

4. Oh yeah—*save your game!*

In the next chapter, we will take our development with TGF up a notch or two by introducing a new game type.

ACTIVITIES

For this chapter, your activity will be to make your own game—well, make your own version of *Cosmic Battle*. You can do this by simply selecting the assets as you were taught and swapping them for other assets in the libraries. As you do this, you will become more and more comfortable navigating and using The Games Factory by yourself. For example:

1. Click inside the empty thumbnail on the Storyboard Editor with the right mouse button as you did in the beginning of this chapter. From the menu produced, click the "Edit this level" option.

2. Select the Level Editor option. You will then be taken to an empty Level Editor screen, ready for you to place your objects on.

3. To place new objects on the screen, go to the Level Objects text box on the toolbar at the top of the screen.

4. Click the pull-down button at the side of the text (see Figure 7.1 at the beginning of the chapter).

SUMMARY

You made a game with The Games Factory in this chapter. In the process, you learned the foundation for building even more complex and interesting games. In the coming chapter we will do just that, make a more complex game using the Games Factory.

Making Another Game with The Games Factory

IN THIS CHAPTER
• • • • • • • • • • • • •

- Creating a Different Game Using New TGF Features
- Masking Objects
- Adding Music to Your Game
- Adding "Lives" and "Timers"

Okay, are you ready to make a game that will sell a million units and blow right off the sales charts? Well, hold on tight because we are going to make *Dood Hunter* (see Figure 8.1)—a surefire hit! Think about it—*Deer Hunter*, only with Doods.

Well, the design needs work, but we will develop *Dood Hunter* for fun. And behind all this fun, you will be learning the next step of working with TGF. We will be using several more features of TGF and doing a lot more actual development, including tweaking the assets and the game flow. As you will see, *Dood Hunter* is from a different viewpoint than *Cosmic Battle*. Instead of shooting up, we will be shooting at the targets. This will introduce a few new techniques to your growing TGF knowledge base.

Figure 8.1   *Dood Hunter—a surefire hit.*

In this chapter, we will learn new functions of TGF and a few new techniques to keep productions made with TGF organized and running smoothly.

Let's look at *Dood Hunter*.

LOADING *DOOD HUNTER*

You will find the completed version of *Dood Hunter* if you go to the File menu, select Open, and then look for the gametuts directory in which you installed TGF. You are looking for the file Doodhunt. Once you open it, we can begin.

DOOD HUNTER—THE STORYBOARD EDITOR

The first thing you will see in the Doodhunt file is the familiar Storyboard Editor. When you have loaded *Dood Hunter*, you will have a Storyboard Editor screen that looks very similar to the one for *Cosmic Battle*, with all the same options (see Figure 8.2).

While we are here, let's look at a few more things you can do from the Storyboard Editor screen that we didn't look at last time. Click the Preferences icon and look at the dialog box, as shown in Figure 8.3.

In the box, you see one slider bar and two check boxes. The boxes allow you to remove the comments and the header bar, as shown in Figure 8.4.

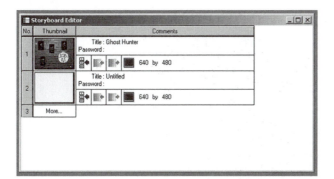

FIGURE 8.2   The familiar Storyboard Editor, as used by *Dood Hunter*.

FIGURE 8.3.   The Preferences icon and the Properties dialog box that pops up from the Storyboard Editor.

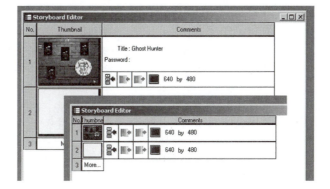

FIGURE 8.4   The Storyboard Editor with the various options enacted from the Properties dialog box.

The slider bar allows you to change the density of the display, which means that the thumbnail picture can be larger or smaller, as shown in Figure 8.4.

HINT!

You have to click OK and exit the dialog box to see the difference it has made to the display.

Setting the density lower can be useful as you become more proficient with TGF and don't need all the visual help. Making the thumbnails smaller makes them harder to see, but if you have been working on a game, you will be intimately familiar with the level names, layout, and general appearance. As your games become more complex and contain more levels, you'll prefer the smaller thumbnails.

You will notice while we are here in the Storyboard Editor that I set the screen at 800x600. Since the average computer today is displaying at larger resolutions, I decided to make the game a bit bigger.

Now let's go to the Level Editor. Right-click the thumbnail of the level, bring up the "Edit this level" option, and select the Level Editor.

DOOD HUNTER—THE LEVEL EDITOR

Remember that you can look at all the objects in the editor by simply placing your cursor over them and reading the handy hint balloons. If you do this, you will see how *Dood Hunter* was created and what objects are contained in the game (see Figure 8.5).

Notice that in the Level Editor, you can see all the Doods, but later on, when you run the level, you will see that they drop down and hide (for good reason) soon after the game starts. When the game is running, all the Doods are hidden from view. They emerge at random to scare you and then hide again. The only shot you have will be when they are out of hiding. You use the mouse to put the crosshairs of your Dood Vaporizer over them and then, pressing the left mouse button, you fire at them.

To make the Doods look like they are actually hiding behind something and then emerging, we have to use a chopped-up copy of the back-

FIGURE 8.5   The *Dood Hunter* Level Editor.

drop. As you have seen before, active objects are placed on top of back-drop objects and appear in front of the backdrop objects. To hide the Doods properly, we are going to make an active object out of part of the backdrop and use it as a Mask object in front of the Doods.

HINT!

You will remember the term *mask* from Part One. A mask not only hides the Doods from view and makes them look like they are hiding and popping up, it also prevents them from being shot while they are hiding, thus increasing the challenge of the game. The mask fits exactly over the background, and it is not obvious when the game runs that there is another ob-ject on the screen because of the way the two pieces fit to-gether (that is, unless we do a sloppy job and place the Doods or the mask improperly).

DOOD HUNTER—THE EVENT EDITOR

To enter the Event Editor, click the Event Editor icon on the toolbar at the top of the screen, or right-click the thumbnail if you have gone back to the Storyboard Editor. You will now be able to look through all of the events used to make the game actions for *Dood Hunter* and read the comments. You will see that now we have more events and a few new icons to work with. Figure 8.6 shows the *Dood Hunter* Event Editor.

You will also notice that groups are used to a much greater degree in this game. One reason is that the game is larger and so groups are neces-sary to help with the organization of the game. In addition, groups are also used because you can deactivate and activate them during the game, which makes the game easier to control.

If you scroll through the events and move your mouse pointer over the check marks in the boxes to see the actions that are associated with the events, you will get a feel for the logic, or flow, of the game. Some of the first events you will see are the group deactivation events I mentioned. Deactivation events help speed up the game during play by preventing unneeded events from running. This will be useful in boosting perfor-mance when you start making larger and more complex games.

For example, you will notice a group of Level Won events, as shown in Figure 8.7. This group is inactive until it is needed, when the player wins the game. Then it is activated and other groups are deactivated.

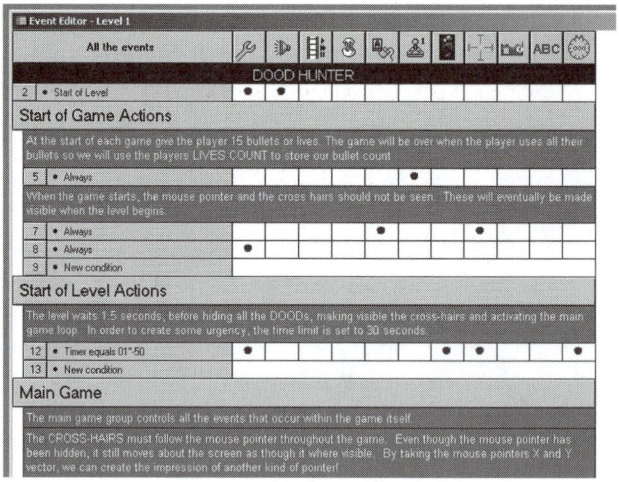

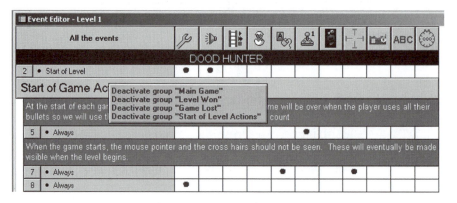

FIGURE 8.6 The *Dood Hunter* Event Editor.

FIGURE 8.7 The events for activating and deactivating groups.

You can also collapse a group of events by double-clicking the header. Do this to all the groups and you can see how this makes it far easier to move around the Event Grid. Collapsing events also makes it easier to see the major steps of the game. *Dood Hunter* has five major groups of events (see Figure 8.8). As you double-click each group and open it, you'll see the events that make up that portion of the game.

Now that we have had a look around in the Event Editor, let's play the game a little before we start to recreate it, so you have a frame of reference for the events we are setting up.

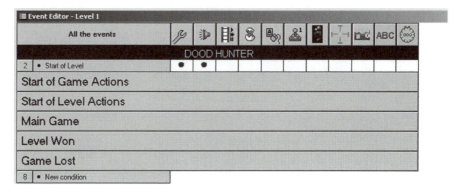

FIGURE 8.8   The Event Editor, with all events collapsed into group headings.

Use the Run Game button on the toolbar at the top of the screen to run *Dood Hunter*.

HINT!

When you are ready to exit the game, press Alt and F4 together.

ASSEMBLING *DOOD HUNTER* YOURSELF

We will now walk through the steps of assembling *Dood Hunter*. When you are finished playing *Dood Hunter*, load a new file. You should by default be in the Storyboard Editor. Set the play area to 640x480, and then click OK.

IN THE *DOOD HUNTER* LEVEL EDITOR

To get into the Level Editor from the Storyboard Editor, click the empty thumbnail with the right mouse button, and select the "Edit this level" and "Level Editor" options.

First, we need to go and get all the assets and objects we will be using for this project. Go to the Level Objects pull-down menu on the toolbar. Click the button at the side of this menu to pull down a list of all the object libraries, and select the library called (Tutorial) DOOD HUNTER (see Figure 8.9). You can see all the objects used to create *Dood Hunter* in the Object window down the left-hand side of the screen.

FIGURE 8.9   The library of items used in *Dood Hunter*.

PLACING THE BACKDROP OBJECT

Place the backdrop object onto the screen by selecting it and then placing it anywhere in the play area. You will remember from the previous chapters that because it is exactly the same size as the play area, it will align itself automatically.

PLACING THE DOODS

Next, click the active object for the Dood, named Dood, and, using the right mouse button, place copies of it in the window part of the house, on the door, and over the fence. Line up the bottom of the Dood so it fits nicely into the areas. You will also remember that using the right mouse button allows you to lay down more than one copy of the Dood, and using the left mouse button lays down a single copy.

THE MASK OBJECT

Now you can place the mask object in front of the Doods. Be careful to line it up perfectly with the backdrop. It should cover up the bottom part of the Doods a little. The mask is to stop you from being able to shoot the Doods when they are hiding. Since they are behind an active object, the mask, they are protected (see Figure 8.10).

FIGURE 8.10 The mask (notice the blocks of color used for transparency).

HINT!

The mask is nothing more than the backdrop image copied, with the large areas being filled in with a color that is very different from the rest of the image, to be used as the transparency color. If you are creating your own mask object, be careful to use no anti-aliasing (see previous chapters), since this causes a colored line around the masked portions of the image. The reason for this is also explained in the previous chapters on image manipulation.

PLACING THE CROSSHAIRS OBJECT

Now we are going to place the object that we will be using as the crosshairs of our gun onto the play area. Later, these crosshairs will replace the mouse cursor in the game.

Go to the Object window and select the Crosshairs object. Place it anywhere on the screen. It does not matter where you place it, since we are going to hide it at the very beginning of the level. We will deal with making it replace the mouse cursor later in the Event Editor.

PLACING THE COUNTDOWN OBJECT

Select the countdown object and put this on the play area in a place where you will be able to see it readily, but not so it interferes with the Doods, such as one of the corners.

PLACING THE TEXT OBJECT

Now place the "DOOD! Ya' got me!" text object on the far left of the Dood play area, at about the same height as the top of the Doods.

PLACING THE AMMO OBJECT

Place the live ammo on the bottom left of the play area. This is the display for the number of bullets that you have left.

PLACING THE SCORE OBJECT

Place the score object on the play area near the countdown object. This displays your score during the game. You should now have a screen that looks like Figure 8.11.

CHANGING THE VIEW ORDER OF OBJECTS

While we are in the Level Editor, let's look at a small but useful feature of TGF—changing the view order of objects.

Let's say that you accidentally placed the mask object on the screen before the Doods, and then placed the Doods on top of the mask. You then noticed that the mask does not cover the Doods. If you had done this, however, you would not need to delete everything and start over. You could simply right-click the mask and change the order of the layers, just like you can in Photoshop, Paint Shop Pro, and other paint programs.

FIGURE 8.11 The *Dood Hunter* Level Editor, with objects laid out.

What this means is simply that you can make the mask move forward and cover the Doods.

To change the order of the layer of either the Doods or the mask:

1. Right-click the mask object. This produces a menu with several options, as shown in Figure 8.12.
2. Select the "View" option from this menu.
3. Now select the "To front" option. This will place the mask object "in front" of all the other objects on the screen.

FIGURE 8.12   The pop-up menu from the mask object.

This is a simple and very useful tool to be aware of. You may have noticed that your other options were to bring forward one or go back one. You can see how this will save you time if you have many items on the screen, or if you decide to stick another active object in and have to get it behind the mask. You can lay it in and then change its order.

CHANGING THE GAME SETUP

We'll look at the Game Setup menu before we go any farther (Figure 8.13). We are going to change the game setup because some of the objects we are using need to have their initial values changed. We also want to hide the mouse pointer and the menu bar that is normally displayed when you do a full run of your game using the Run Game button.

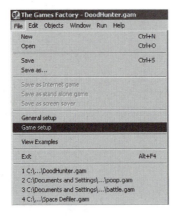

FIGURE 8.13 The Game
Setup menu.

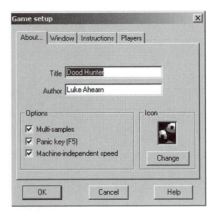

FIGURE 8.14 The About tab of the
Game Setup dialog box.

1. Select the File menu heading at the top of the screen.
2. Select the "Game setup" option from this menu. Be careful not to select General Setup by accident.
3. On the first "layer" of the dialog box, you can enter a name for your game in the Title text box, then your name underneath in the Author text box, as shown in Figure 8.14.
4. Now go to the Window layer by clicking its tab at the top of the dialog box, as shown in Figure 8.15.
5. Next, make sure that all of the tick boxes are unselected (that is, that they are all empty). This keeps the menu bar and heading from being displayed when you run your game.
6. Select the Players tab (see Figure 8.16). In the Lives box at the bottom right, change the Initial setting to 15. You can enter the numbers directly by clicking the text box, using the Delete key to clear the box, and then entering 15.
7. Change the Maximum value to 15.
8. Click OK.

HINT!

We didn't look at several options in the Game Setup dialog box, but we will get back to these later.

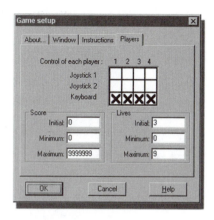

FIGURE 8.15   The Window tab of
the Game Setup dialog box.

FIGURE 8.16   The Players tab of
the Game Setup dialog box.

THE *DOOD HUNTER* EVENT EDITOR

Once you have made those changes to the Game Setup dialog box and
you have all the game objects placed the way you want them on the play
area in the Level Editor, go to the Event Editor. To do this, select its icon
from the toolbar at the top of the screen (see Figure 8.17).

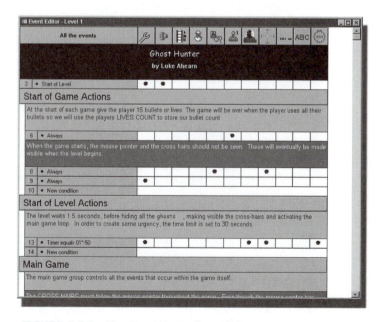

FIGURE 8.17   The *Dood Hunter* Event Editor.

We are now going to start inserting events. We'll begin with a "Start of level" event, and then add some actions.

1. Right-click the "New condition" text of event line 1.
2. Right-click the Storyboard icon, and then select the "Start of level" option from its menu.

PLAYING MUSIC

The first thing we are going to do at the start of the level is play some music, so we will insert an action to play some music on this event line. We are also going to add four actions to deactivate other groups of actions, as we talked about earlier. Since we have not yet created these groups, TGF will not let us deactivate them yet.

1. Right-click the empty box directly beneath the Sound icon. Select the "Play and loop music" option. You will then be able to select a file. If you have done a normal installation of The Games Factory, the sound files will be on your hard drive in the default installation folder.
2. Go to the directory called Midi, and then look for the file named Melanitr.mid. Select this file, and then click OK.
3. You will now be asked to enter the number of times you want the music to loop. Enter 99 times.
4. Click OK.
5. A check mark is displayed under the Sound icon. If you move your mouse pointer over it, the event will read "Play music Melanitr.mid 99 times" (see Figure 8.18).

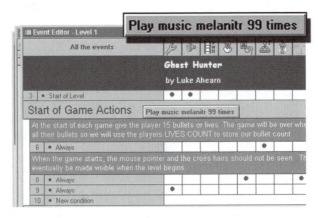

FIGURE 8.18 The pop-up handy hint balloon for the Start of Level event, Play music Melanitr.mid 99 times.

INSERTING THE START OF GAME ACTIONS GROUP

Now we are going to create a group called Start of Game Actions.

1. Right-click event line 2.
2. Select Insert from the pop-up menu, and then select "A group of events."
3. Enter "Start of Game Actions" in the text box, and then click OK.

INSERTING A COMMENT

We are now ready to place events within this group. Make sure that each event line on which you insert a new condition is indented slightly from the left. This shows that the specific event line is within the group directly above it.

1. Insert this comment on line 3: "At the start of each game, give the player 15 bullets, or lives. The game will be over when the player uses all his or her bullets, so we will use the player's LIVES COUNT to store our bullet count."
2. To insert a comment, right-click the number of the event line. Select the "Insert" option, and then select the "A comment" option.

Of course, to make the comments stand out, you can change the text and background color. Color is also useful for grouping the events visually. As your games get increasingly longer and more complex, color-coding the comments will help you keep track of your game.

INSERTING AN ALWAYS EVENT

Insert an always event on line 4.

1. Right-click the "New condition" text line.
2. Right-click the Special Object icon in the window.
3. From the "Always/Never" option that pops up, select the "Always" option.

SETTING LIVES

1. Right-click the box under the Player 1 object, on line 4.
2. Select the "Number of lives" option, and then select the "Set number of lives" option.

3. You can enter the number in the text box or use the slider.

4. When it is set to 15, click OK.

INSERTING A COMMENT

Insert the following comment on line 5: "When the game starts, the mouse pointer and crosshairs will not be seen, but the crosshairs will be made visible when the game starts."

INSERTING AN ALWAYS EVENT

Insert an always event on line 6. (Right-click "New Condition," right-click the special object, and select the "Always" option.)

HIDING THE MOUSE POINTER

We will hide the Windows mouse pointer so we can replace it with the custom crosshairs object. On the same line as the always event we just created, insert the Hide Windows mouse pointer action.

To do this, right-click the empty box beneath the Mouse pointer and Keyboard icon, and then select the "Hide Windows mouse pointer" option.

MAKING THE CROSSHAIRS OBJECT INVISIBLE

Insert another action on line 6 to make the crosshairs invisible. To do this, right-click the box under the crosshairs object, select the "Visibility" option, and then select the "Make object invisible" option.

We are hiding the crosshairs at the start of the game to add to the game play. Maybe you noticed that when you run the game, the Doods taunt you for a second before hiding—you can't shoot them at this time. This adds a bit of production value as a sort of introduction to the action of the game.

INSERTING AN ALWAYS EVENT

Insert an always event on line 7. We are going to activate and deactivate some of the groups here, but as explained earlier, you cannot do this until you have created those groups.

HINT!

Save your game.

INSERTING "START OF LEVEL ACTIONS" GROUP OF EVENTS

Insert a group of events called "Start of Level Actions" on line 8. You must create this group on a line that is not indented so it will function properly in the game.

When you have done this, line 8 should be empty and still be within the "Start of Game Actions" group, as shown in Figure 8.19.

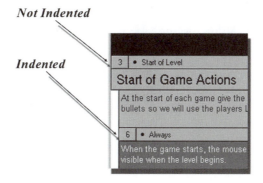

FIGURE 8.19   The "Start of Level Actions" group on line 9, not indented.

INSERTING A COMMENT

To increase excitement, we will create a sense of urgency and set the time limit to 30 seconds. Right-click the number in the border, and select the "Insert a comment" option.

Enter the following comment on line 10: "The level waits 1.5 seconds before hiding all the Doods, making the crosshairs visible, and activating the main game loop." Click OK.

READING THE TIMER

Now insert an event on line 11 "Timer is greater than 1".

1. Right-click the "New condition" text and right-click the timer object.
2. Select the "Is the timer greater than a certain value?" option.
3. Now you can enter the time. By default, the value is 1 second, so you need to change only the 1/100 box. Click in it, enter the number 50, and then click OK.

CHANGING AN ANIMATION SEQUENCE

Insert a Change animation to hiding action under the Doods icon on line 11.

1. Right-click the box, select the "Animation" option, select the "Change" option, and then select the "Animation sequence" option.
2. From the dialog box that appears, select the "Hiding" option. Click OK.

MAKING THE CROSSHAIRS REAPPEAR

Insert reappear action on line 11, under the crosshairs icon.

1. Right-click the box and, from the menu, select the "Visibility" option, and then select the "Make object reappear" option.
2. Next, insert an action to set the counter to 30.
3. Right-click the empty box under the countdown object on line 11, and then select the "Set counter" option.
4. You will see a dialog box where you can either enter the numbers directly in the text box, or use the buttons on the slider to change the number. Make sure that the value entered is 30, and then click OK.

INSERTING THE MAIN GAME GROUP

Insert a group called Main Game.

HINT!

You must do this on line 13, which is outside of the Start of Level Actions group. If you used line 12, which is indented, then you would put a group within a group, which The Games Factory will not allow.

To insert a group, right-click the number of line 13, select the "Insert a group of events" option, enter "Main Game," and click OK.

INSERTING COMMENTS

Insert this comment on line 14: "The Main Game group controls all the events that occur within the game itself."

Right-click the number, select the "Insert a comment" option, enter the text, and then click OK.

Insert another comment, preferably in a different color: "The crosshairs will follow the hidden mouse pointer throughout the game."

HINT!

Even though the Windows mouse pointer has been hidden, it is still there, moving about and functioning as though it were visible. If your game window is smaller than your screen size, then you will see the cursor reappear if you move it off the game and onto the Windows desktop.

By taking the mouse pointer's X and Y coordinates, we can make the crosshairs follow the movement of the mouse pointer.

INSERTING AN ALWAYS EVENT

Insert an always event on the next event line (line 16).

MAKING AN OBJECT FOLLOW THE MOUSE POINTER

Now we will make the crosshairs follow the invisible cursor. Insert an action on line 16 to set the coordinates of the crosshairs to the same as those of the mouse.

1. Right-click the empty box under the crosshairs object on line 16.
2. Select the "Position" option.
3. Select the "Set X coordinate..." option.
4. Click Edit.

5. Click the "Retrieve data from an object" button.
6. Now, right-click the mouse pointer and keyboard object.
7. Select the "Current X position of the mouse" option.

You should have an action under the crosshairs object that reads "Set position to X mouse." To set the Y coordinate to be the same as the mouse, do the following.

1. Right-click the filled box under the crosshairs object on line 16.
2. Select the "Position" option.
3. Select the "Set Y coordinate..." option.
4. Click Edit.
5. Click the "Retrieve data from an object" button.
6. Now, right-click the mouse pointer and keyboard object.
7. Select the "Current Y position of the mouse" option, and then click OK. This sets the crosshairs object to follow the movement of the mouse pointer exactly.
8. **Save your game!**

INSERTING A COMMENT

Insert this comment on line 17: "Every second, deduct 1 from the counter that holds the time limit."

TESTING THE TIMER

Now insert an every 1"-00 event.

1. Right-click the "New condition" text of line number 18, and then right-click the timer object.
2. Select the "Every" option.
3. Make sure the time entered is 1 second, and then click OK.

CHANGING THE VALUE OF THE COUNTER

Insert the subtract 1 from counter action.

1. Right-click the box under the countdown object.
2. Select the "Subtract from counter" option.
3. Now enter the number 1 in the text box of the Expression Editor that appears, and then click OK.

INSERTING A COMMENT

Insert the following comment on line 19: "Every 2 seconds, select one of the many Dood objects from the game, and if that Dood is currently hiding, run its Appear from Hiding animation."

Right-click on the number, and select the "Insert a comment" option.

TESTING THE TIMER EVERY TWO SECONDS

Insert an event every 2 seconds.

1. Right-click the "New condition" text of line 20.
2. Right-click the timer object, and then select the "Every" option. Make sure the time entered is 2 seconds, and then click OK.

ADDING A CONDITION TO A TIMER EVENT

Now add a condition to the preceding event.

1. Right-click the text "Every 2"-00," and select the "Insert" option.
2. Now, right-click the Dood object, select the "Pick or count" option, and then select the "Pick 'Dood' at random" option.

ADDING A FURTHER CONDITION

1. Right-click on any of the texts of line 20, and select the "Insert" option.
2. Right-click the Dood, and then select the "Animation" option.
3. Select the "Which animation of 'Dood' is playing?" option.
4. Select the hiding animation from the list in the dialog box. Click OK.

You will have three conditions on one event line.

HINT!

You should move the every 2"-00 event to the top of this event line, so that TGF goes through the rest of the conditions only once every 2 seconds. This speeds up your game play slightly, especially if you have many event lines like this. For example, if you placed the "Pick one of 'Dood'" condition at the top, then TGF would go through the actions of picking a Dood before looking at the other conditions.

CHANGING AN ANIMATION SEQUENCE

1. Right-click the box under the Dood object on line 20.
2. Select the "Animation" option, select the "Change" option, and then select the "Animation sequence…" option.
3. From the dialog box, select the "Appear from hiding" animation, and then click OK.

INSERTING A COMMENT

Insert this comment on line 21: "Four times a second, select one of the Dood objects from the game, and if that Dood is currently hiding, run its Appear from Hiding animation."

TESTING THE TIMER

Insert an every 00"-25 event on line 22.

Right-click the "New condition" text, right-click the timer object, and select the "Every" option from its menu. Make sure that the time entered is 25 hundredths of a second, and then click OK.

PICKING A DOOD AT RANDOM

Insert a condition on line 22, "Pick one of (Dood)."

1. Right-click the text "Every 00"25" of line 22, and select the "Insert" option.
2. Right-click the Dood object, select the "Pick or count" option from its menu, and then select the "Pick 'Dood' at random" option.

TESTING WHICH ANIMATION IS PLAYING

1. Right-click either of the condition texts on line 22, select the "Insert" option, right-click the Dood object from its menu, and select the "Animation" option.
2. Next, select the "Which animation of 'Dood' is playing?" option. From the dialog box produced, select the "Stopped" animation, and then click OK.

CHANGING THE ANIMATION SEQUENCE

You can insert an action into line 22 to hide the "Dood" that has been picked.

1. Right-click the empty box on line 22, underneath the "Dood" object. From its menu, select the "Animation" option, select the "Change" option, and then select the "Animation sequence" option.
2. From the dialog box, select the hiding animation, and then click OK.

INSERTING A COMMENT

Insert this comment on line 23: "If the player manages to click the mouse pointer (appearing as crosshairs) on a Dood, destroy the Dood and add 10 points to the score."

TESTING THE MOUSE TO SEE IF IT HAS CLICKED A DOOD

1. Right-click the "New condition" text of line 24, and then right-click the mouse pointer and keyboard object.
2. Select the "The mouse" option, and then select the "User clicks on an object" option.
3. You will be taken to a dialog box. Make sure that there are tick marks in the Left button and Single click radio buttons, and then click OK.
4. Select the Dood object, and then click OK.

INSERTING SOUND

Now we will insert two sound actions on line 24.

1. Right-click the empty box under the sound object, and select the "Play sample" option.
2. A file selector appears. If you have done a normal installation, the sound files are on your computer in the default directory. Look for the directory called Samples.
3. Within the Samples directory, look for the subdirectory Weapons. From here we will select the noise for the gun being fired. Try the gun3.wav file. You can preview the sound by clicking the Play button. Then, click Open.

4. Insert a second noise, the yelp of the Dood, from the Dood Hunter tutorial folder.

HINT!

To insert a further action in the same check box, left-click in the box to which you want to add an action.

5. Click under the sound object again, and then right-click the "New action" option. Select the "Play sample" option.

6. Look again in the Samples directory, but this time, look in the Dood Hunter subdirectory for the file Ricchet2.wav. Try playing it a few times. If you are happy with your selection, click the OK buttons until you are returned to the Event Editor.

CHANGING THE SCORE

You are now going to change the score at the same time as you destroy a Dood. That way, every time the user clicks a Dood, not only will a gun sample and a Ricchet2.wav sample play, but you will also add to the score and destroy the Dood.

1. Right-click the empty check box underneath the Player 1 object. From the menu produced, select the "Score" option, and then select the "Add to score" option.

2. Here you can enter the score via the keyboard, by clicking within the text box or clicking the slider. You can add any score you like, but we are going to add 10 to the score. Click OK.

DESTROYING A DOOD

1. Right-click in the empty check box underneath the Dood object. From the menu produced, select the "Destroy" option.

2. Next, add an action to deduct a life from Player 1. In the context of this game, it means that Player 1 has used a bullet each time he or she fires the gun. When there are no more bullets, the game is over, since there is nothing else to do. This is an example of using set tools in a different way than they are labeled to make a better or more in-

teresting game. Just because the word *life* is used, doesn't mean you have to literally make the action apply to a life.

3. Click the box underneath the Player 1 object, where you just inserted the action to add to the score.

4. Right-click the "New action" option, select the "Number of lives" option, and then select the "Subtract from number of lives" option. Now, enter the number 1 in the text box, or use the slider bar to change the value.

5. Click the OK buttons to return to the Event Editor.

INSERTING A COMMENT

Insert this comment on line 25: "When the player presses the left button and misses, deduct 1 life and play the sample gun04.wav. The sound condition makes sure that these actions are not repeated very rapidly."

TESTING THE MOUSE TO SEE IF THE LEFT BUTTON HAS BEEN CLICKED

Insert an event on line 26 to check whether the user has clicked the left mouse button. We are then going to add a condition to this, so the actions associated with this line will only take place if a sound is not playing (in other words, if the player has not hit a Dood).

1. Right-click the "New condition" text of line 26, select the mouse pointer and keyboard object, select the "The mouse" option, and then select the "User clicks" option.

2. Make sure that the Left button and Single click radio buttons are selected, and then click OK.

TESTING TO SEE THAT NO SAMPLES ARE ALREADY BEING PLAYED

Now we'll make sure that the user has not already just killed a Dood.

Insert a condition on line 26 to check that no samples are being played. Right-click the text of line 26 and select the "Insert" option. Then, click the sound object. Choose the "Samples" option, and then select the "Is a sample not playing?" option.

PLAYING A SAMPLE AND DEDUCTING A LIFE

Now you can insert actions into line 26 to play a sample and to deduct 1 from Player 1's lives; in other words, one bullet.

1. Right-click the empty box under the sound object and select the "Play sample" option.
2. Look in the Samples directory, and then in the Weapons subdirectory. From here, select the sample gun04.wav.
3. Click the empty box under the Player 1 object, select the "Lives" option, and then select the "Subtract from number of lives" option. Set the Expression Editor value to 1, and then click OK.

INSERTING A COMMENT

Insert this comment on line 27: "If all the Doods in the game have been destroyed, the player has completed the level. Reveal the 'It's a shame!' message and activate the Level Won group."

TESTING TO SEE IF ALL THE DOODS HAVE BEEN SHOT

Insert the last Dood has been destroyed event on line 28.

1. Right-click the "New condition" text, and then right-click the Doods object.
2. Select the "Pick or count" option, and then select the "Have all Doods been destroyed?" option.

PLAYING VICTORY MUSIC AND DISPLAYING THE VICTORY TEXT

We cannot activate or deactivate a group until it has been created, so we will insert the action to activate the Level Won group after it has been created. For now, you can insert several actions on line 28. First, insert an action to play some music.

1. Right-click under the sound object, select the "Play music" option, and then look in the midi directory and select the soldier2.mid file. Now, insert an action to display the text "It's a shame!"
2. Right-click under the Good Shooting object, and then select the "Display text..." option. You will now see a position selector. Enter 0 in the X coordinate box, and 64 into the Y coordinate box. Click OK.

INSERTING A COMMENT

Insert the following comment on line 29: "There are two ways in which the player can lose the game. The bullets can run out or the time limit can expire. In each case, the Game Lost group will be activated."

Insert an event on line 30, right-click the "New condition" text, select the Player 1 object, and then select the "Compare to player's number of lives" option. Now make sure that the value is 0, and that the Equals radio button is selected. Click OK.

INSERTING SOUND

Insert a sound action on line 29. Play a piece of music that you feel is appropriate to losing the game.

COMPARING THE VALUE OF THE COUNTDOWN OBJECT TO A NUMBER

Insert an event on line 31. Click the line's text, and then select the countdown object. Next, select the "Compare the counter to a value" option. Make sure the value it is being compared to is 0, and then make sure that the Equals radio button is selected.

COPYING AN ACTION

Click and drag the music action from line 30 down into line 31. This copies that sound action onto line 31.

INSERTING A GROUP

On line 33, insert a Level Won group. Note that this must go on this line so that it falls outside of the Main Game group. If you were to place it on line 32, The Games Factory would be unable to run your game.

INSERTING A COMMENT

On line 34, insert the following comment: "When the congratulations music has finished, restart the level, which keeps the score and allows the player to play again with all the Doods back as they were at the start of the level."

TESTING TO SEE IF NO MUSIC IS PLAYING

Insert an event on line 35. Right-click the line, select the sound object, select the "Music" option, and then select the "Is music not playing?" option.

RESTARTING THE CURRENT LEVEL

Insert an action on line 35. Right-click under the storyboard object, and then select the "Restart the current level" option.

INSERTING A GROUP

Now, insert a Game Lost group on line 37.

INSERTING A COMMENT

Insert the following comment on line 38: "When the game lost sound has ended, restart the game to clear the score and begin the entire game from the very start."

COPYING AN EVENT

Copy an event onto line 39. Click and hold on the "No sample is playing" text of line 35 and drag it into line 39. This will copy that event.

RESTARTING THE GAME

Insert an action on line 39 to restart the game. Right-click the box under the storyboard object, and then select the "Restart game" option.

INSERTING ALL THE ACTIONS TO ACTIVATE OR DEACTIVATE THE GROUPS

That's almost it. All we need to do is go back and insert all the actions to activate or deactivate the groups, now that we have created them all.

1. Go to line 1, right-click the box under the special object, select the "Group of events" option, and then select the "Deactivate" option. You will then be taken to a dialog box where you can select the groups that you want to deactivate (see Figure 8.20). First, pick the Start of Level Actions group, and then click OK.
2. Now you need to insert the rest of the actions into the same check mark. To do this, click the check mark. A dialog box appears that

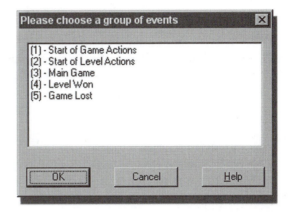

FIGURE 8.20   The dialog box where you activate and deactivate groups.

lists all the actions from within that check mark. You also have a "New action" option. Right-click this option. You will see the same menu produced as when you first right-clicked under the special object. Select the "Group of events" option, and then the "Deactivate" option. Now select the Main Game group.

You will be able to deactivate the Level Won and Game Lost groups using the preceding method.

3. Go to line 7 and insert the following actions: deactivate group—Start of game actions, and activate group—Start of level actions.

4. Right-click under the Special object, select Group of events, select Deactivate, Start of game actions, and then click OK.

5. Click the check mark, right-click New actions, select Group of events, select Activate, select Start of level actions, and then click OK.

6. Go to line 11 and insert the following actions: deactivate group—Start of level actions, and activate group—Main Game.

7. Go to line 28 and insert the following actions: deactivate group—Main Game, and activate group—Level Won.

8. Go to line 30 and insert the following actions: deactivate group—Main Game, and activate group—Game Lost.

9. Now copy these actions into line 31 by clicking and holding on the check mark, and then dragging it into line 31.

CONGRATULATIONS

That's it. *Dood Hunter* is ready to take the market by storm. You have just completed a more advanced game in TGF and learned some functions and techniques to help you with your organization while making a game with TGF and to help TGF run more efficiently.

Next, we will take yet another big step in game development and create a game that adds to our growing bag of tools. Once again, we will change the perspective you have of the game world and attempt a different type of game to further explore the abilities of TGF.

ACTIVITIES

A good activity for this chapter is to simply go into the Event Editor and change the score, as we did earlier in this chapter. In the game, when you destroy a Dood the score changes, and in the Event Editor, you can experiment with the values of the score. This will give you an idea of what goes into game balance. Try going back and changing other values for the game balance effect, as well as changing the text message that displays at the end of the game. This is easy to do and can affect what the player feels at the completion of the game. For example, if you put a rather mean message, such as "That was some really bad shooting!" as opposed to "Good shooting, try again!" you will leave the player with drastically different feelings about you and your game. You can even do an experiment on a friend using different messages and see how long he or she plays your game.

SUMMARY

In Chapter 8, you learned to make a more complex game with The Games Factory. Not only did we look at the action from a different point of view, but you learned many more functions of TGF. In the coming chapter, you will go even further with TGF and make yet another type of game.

Making a More Advanced Game with The Games Factory

IN THIS CHAPTER
- Creating a Different Type of Game, *Bat Flight*
- Adding Obstacles

Okay. Ready to make another game? This time we will do a game that is a bit more advanced. We will explore a few more functions of The Games Factory. We will look at side scrolling on a screen larger than the play area and use groups to speed up game development and make the Event Editor easier to look at.

We will be developing *Bat Flight*.

BAT FLIGHT
• • • • • • • • •

By now, you should have a good feel for the different editor screens and their purposes. As you know, most game action is created in the Event Editor, and the levels themselves are assembled in the Level Editor. The Storyboard Editor allows you to control the flow of your game as a

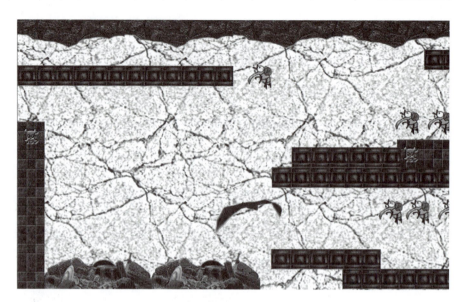

FIGURE 9.1 A screen shot of *Bat Flight*.

production—level order, transitions, and progress of the game. Now we will look deeper into some fairly complex game creation techniques, but don't be intimidated. We will go through these step by step.

Bat Flight (Figure 9.1) is a simple game of racing against the clock. The bat is trying to fly out of its cave and has to dodge the walls and its own firetraps. Although fairly simple in terms of game play, *Bat Flight* uses some fairly advanced techniques to achieve the end result. Let's load up the game and have a look around.

Go to the File menu heading at the top of the screen, and select the "Open" option.

Now, look for the directory Sample games, and then look in the subdirectory Bat for the file Bat.gam.

STORYBOARD EDITOR—*BAT FLIGHT* PART 1

Let's look at the *Bat Flight* Storyboard Editor to see the various preferences that have been changed (see Figure 9.2).

First, go to the File menu in the toolbar and select the "Game setup" option. The first layer of this dialog box shows the author and title of the game. You can see that the Panic key has been enabled (see Figure 9.3).

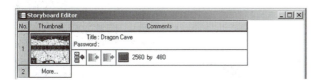

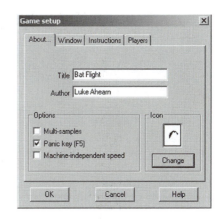

FIGURE 9.2   The *Bat Flight* Storyboard Editor.

FIGURE 9.3   The Game Setup menu for *Bat Flight*, with the Panic button activated.

The Panic key is there in case you panic during the game (like when your boss walks in when you are playing). If you press the key (F5) during the game, The Games Factory will take you back to the Windows screen, leaving the game to run in the background. The Panic key turns off the sound and minimizes the display. When you click the button in the Windows bar to restore the game, the sound effects will work, but the looped music will not play again until the level is restarted.

Click the Windows tab and look on the next layer. There are some significant changes here from the default settings. These have a dramatic effect on the final look of the game when it is run, and it is important to understand these changes (see Figure 9.4).

The first line is "Maximized on boot up," which maximizes the window used to display the game when it is first loaded, not the game itself. That is, as in any Windows application, The Games Factory uses a window to display your game. Having this option turned on stretches the window out to fill the screen to the very edge (see Figure 9.5).

HINT!

You will not be able to change the dimensions of the window using the mouse pointer "maximized on boot up" is enabled.

The "Resize display to fill current window size" option fills whatever window size you are using with the game display.

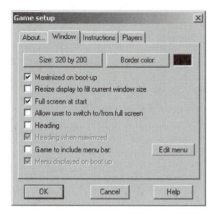

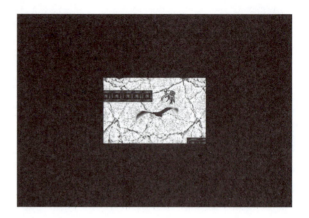

FIGURE 9.4   The changes made on the Windows tab of the Game Setup menu.

FIGURE 9.5   The maximized game window (note that the game is not maximized).

HINT!

If you disable the "Maximized on boot up" option, you will be able to shrink or stretch the window used to display your game, using the mouse pointer to "grab" the edges of the window. When the window is large, this option can dramatically slow the game action due to the complicated nature of the calculations necessary to resize the display.

The "Full screen at start" option is for use on the 16-bit version only. It was designed specifically for use with the 320x200 graphics mode that the 16-bit version supports.

HINT!

Changing the "Full screen at start" option will have no effect when used with any window sizes other than the 320x200. It allows very fast game play of a low resolution that still fills the screen. Notice that at the top of this layer, the size of the window has been changed to 320x200, which means that only an area of 320x200 pixels will be shown on the screen. By enabling the "Full screen at start" option, you expand this small chunk of the play area to fill the screen.

When you go back to the Storyboard Editor, look at the size of the play area; it is, in fact, larger than the size of the screen (see Figure 9.6). The

FIGURE 9.6   The play field size is set larger than the screen size.

Windows preference being set to 320x200 means that only a window 320x200 will be shown from this play area, and "Full screen at start" means that it is expanded to fill the screen. This very important feature of The Games Factory can be used to change the way your games are displayed.

To achieve the same effect as the "Full screen at start" option has on the 16-bit version, 32-bit users should enable the "Maximized on boot up" and "Resize display to fill current window size" options. This will make the window being used to display the game fill the screen to the edge. The display is then resized to fit this larger window.

HINT!

If you maximized the window without resizing the display, the screen will show a chunk of the play area 320x200, surrounded by a huge black border. Notice that the "Heading" and "Game to include" menu bar options on the Windows tab have been disabled. This means that when your game is run, there will be no menu heading at the top of the screen and no heading telling what the game is (see Figure 9.7).

HINT!

Only the actual play area window will be displayed, so the only way to escape from a game when these options are turned off is to use the Alt + F4 keys. The mouse pointer is hidden via the Event Editor and is inaccessible. There are no menus to click even if the pointer was there.

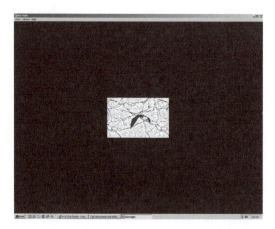

Figure 9.7 The different Header bar options,
enabled and disabled.

No other changes have been made to the default settings in the Game Setup menu, so you can "OK" your way out of this dialog box or cancel if you are not sure if you made any changes.

Now we will explore the levels of *Bat Flight*. First, notice the play area size: it is 2560x480, a long horizontal strip. We made the game world much longer than it is wide because one of the things we are going to do in *Bat Flight* is to scroll the screen through the bat's lair. We need a long screen so that the whole level isn't visible all at once.

Now let's look in the Level Editor. I am sure you remember how to open the Level Editor by now.

LEVEL EDITOR—*BAT FLIGHT*, PART 1

As you have done in previous tutorial games, run your mouse pointer over the different objects on the screen to see what they are and how they relate to each other. Not all of the objects that we are going to use are on this screen yet—they are being saved for later tutorials.

Move your mouse pointer over the cave wall backdrop object, and right-click it. Select the "Obstacle" menu option and note that the "No" option is selected. This means that active objects cannot collide with it. This is the "wall" of the cave in the background. Our Bat is going to move **through** the cave with this wall in the background. See Figure 9.8 for the **backdrop** pop-up menu.

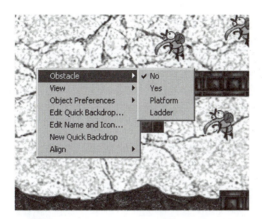

FIGURE 9.8   The pop-up menu for the cave wall, indicating that it is not an obstacle.

FIGURE 9.9   The "Movement" options for the Bat.

Look at the pop-up menus for the other objects, and notice that the Obstacle menus all have the "Yes" option checked. This means that active objects can collide with them, as you can see when you run the game.

Now go and find the Bat object. It is on the far left of the play area, which is where the game starts.

Right-click the Bat object to show the menu options.

Look at the "Movement" and "Edit" movement options. Note that Eight-direction movement is being used. The maximum speed is set quite low, making the object slow, and the deceleration is set quite high, making the object slow down quickly. To make the Bat reasonably responsive, the acceleration is set high (see Figure 9.9).

While you are here, you can look around at the other objects. Make sure you don't change anything, or make a backup copy if you want to experiment. If you look at all the different menu options of all the different objects on this screen, you will recognize many functions from the previous chapters.

Now look at all the objects in the Object window. There are many different active objects in this game level, mostly the cave walls.

HINT!

There are two different walls, but they look exactly the same. One is indestructible; the other you will be able to shoot out of the way during the game.

You can make two different objects look exactly the same. Place the first object on the play area, and then from its menu, select the "New object" option (see Figure 9.10), which makes the second object an active object. Then select the "Edit name and icon" option to change its name. Apart from that, the two objects are identical. The differences in the way they behave are all done in the Event Editor.

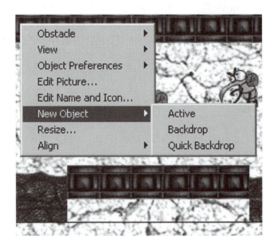

FIGURE 9.10   The pop-up menu in the Level Editor to make a new object from an existing one.

As you scroll through all the other objects in the Object window, you will see that the background has been made out of many objects placed individually on the screen. Using TGF's libraries, you will be able to do the same thing to create similar backgrounds or platforms.

At the very bottom of the object library is the counter object, which is used to display the time remaining, and a lives object, which in this case is used to count the number of fireballs the player (bat) has left.

When you are finished looking around the Level Editor, move on to the Event Editor by clicking its icon on the toolbar.

EVENT EDITOR—*BAT FLIGHT*, PART 1

One of the first things you will notice is that there are lots of objects displayed across the top of the event grid; so many, in fact, that you may have to scroll through them using the scroll bar at the base of the screen. You will also notice two funny face icons—Group.Bad and Group.Neutral. Ignore these for now. We will talk about them at the end of the chapter.

HINT!

 If you have a small monitor or are displaying at a low resolution, you can make all the events fit on the screen. You can do this by clicking the preferences icon on the toolbar, selecting the display layer of the dialog box, and then moving the number of events on the screen slider to High.

Try experimenting with this slider until you are happy with the result. This is similar to the Storyboard Display properties that we looked at earlier.

Read through all the comments in the event grid. These will clearly explain what has been done at each stage of the game. Remember that you can collapse groups, sort events, and manipulate the display for your convenience to see all the events.

An interesting side note: As I mentioned at the beginning of this book, the drag-and-drop tools available to us now, like TGF, have made our lives easier—so much so that we may take things like this first actual event line for granted. In this event, we click one button and make a few menu selections to tell TGF to allow the screen to scroll. What used to take hours of programming is done in just one line with TGF. The event line makes the rest of the screen scroll around, using the Bat object as the center when it is moved. The Bat will always be in the center of the screen—it's the play area that moves instead.

KEEPING THE BAT ALWAYS IN THE CENTER

To make this event, create an always event.

1. Right-click the square under the Storyboard Actions icon.
2. Click the Center horizontal position in the playfield button.
3. Click the Center vertical position in the playfield button.
4. Click the Retrieve data from an object button from these menus, and then select the Bat object to use the X and Y coordinates of the Bat object for the scrolling actions. See Figure 9.11 for the menu progression of this function.

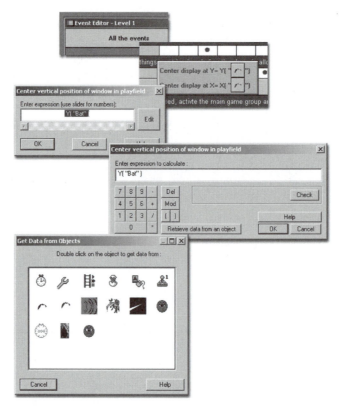

FIGURE 9.11   The menu progression for making the screen scroll with the Bat object.

DECREASING THE COUNTER

In *Bat Flight*, we make the counter decrease in value by 1 for every second that passes. This is the clock you are racing against. To create this event we added the event line "Every 1" 00," then selected the "Subtract from Counter" option, and set the value to 1.

MOVING FIRETRAPS

To move the firetrap objects, you start by making their Y values the same as the Y value of the Bat. This means that the firetraps are always "in the way" or in the same location as the Bat going up and down, but not side to side. The player has to shoot the firetraps in order to get past them.

This was done in a similar manner to the scrolling function presented earlier. If you right-click the square below the firetrap and select the "Position" option from the pop-up menu, you can then select the "Set Y coordinate" option. Then, all you have to do is click the "Retrieve data from an object" button and select the Bat object from the pop-up window.

During the game, the firetrap objects will get, or retrieve, their Y coordinate values from the position of the Bat.

Use the Play button on the top right of the toolbar to see how all of these events and actions fit together, and save your game file if you are creating this from the ground up.

LEVEL EDITOR—*BAT FLIGHT*, PART 2

Let's look at another significant feature of *Bat Flight*—an easy one to pull off, but a very useful one. Look in the Object window for an object called the real collider. This is the object that is actually going to be tested for collisions instead of the Bat object. The reason for this is that the Bat object itself is fairly big—or the square image that contains it is big—but the body of the Bat is actually rather slender.

It is the flapping wings and flames that make the image so big. The players will never get through the cave if the entire area of the Bat image is tested for collisions, so we will make things a bit more fair for them by testing another object.

To explain further, TGF by default detects for a collision using the entire image border. Thus, a collision would be detected if any part of the Bat collided with anything else, including the flames and wings. Since we want only the Bat's body to be what causes a collision, we will use an active object created for this purpose that has an outline matching that of the Bat object. This is helpful to artists, since some of us may want to have an impressive object that shoots lightning bolts off in every direction while being small enough to pass through the caves or tunnels of the game. If the entire image was tested, even the tips of a lightning bolt, with no apparent mass, would cause a collision. See Figure 9.12 for a visual representation of these concepts.

The real collider object is made invisible, and given the same X and Y coordinates as the Bat, via the Event Editor. Let's see how that looks in the Event Editor.

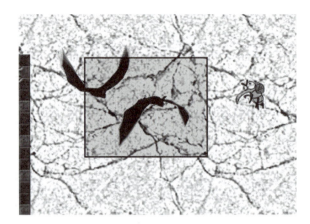

FIGURE 9.12 The large Bat bitmap, the real collider objects, and how they function in the game.

EVENT EDITOR—*BAT FLIGHT*, PART 2

Let's look at the groups Lost Race and Won Race (see Figure 9.13). These groups perform sets of actions when the race is won or lost. They are deactivated here to stop their actions from being performed during the game. When the game is won or lost, one of the two groups is activated and the Main Game group is deactivated.

You can see that this very much simplifies your game creation. Rather than having a condition on all the lines for the Lost Race group that tests to see if the game has been lost, the group is simply deactivated, and then activated when needed. Also on this line is the action that makes the real collider object invisible. The next significant new line is line 23. This is where the real collider object is given exactly the same position as the Bat.

To give the real collider object the exact same position as the Bat object, do the following.

Lost Race																
When the race has been lost, wait 4 seconds then RESTART THE GAME loosing all the score points accumilated thus far.																
48	• No sample is playing															
49	• Every 04"-00		•													
50	• New condition															
Won Race																
52	• New condition															

FIGURE 9.13 The Lost Race and Won Race groups of events in the Event Editor.

1. Set up an always event, right-click the square under the special object, and select the "Position" option from the pop-up menu.
2. Select the real collider object.
3. Select the "Select position" option.
4. The position should be set at 0,0 relative to the Bat object.

LOSING THE GAME BY COLLISION

The game can be lost if the Bat hits the walls of the cave. Line 25 is where you make this happen.

1. Insert an event that detects if a collision has occurred between the real collider object and the background. Remember, do not use the Bat object for this collision test.
2. To set this line up correctly, select the "New condition" text.
3. Right-click the real collider object.
4. From the pop-up menu, select the "Collisions" menu option.
5. Next, select the Backdrop option.

The Main Game group is then deactivated to stop the game, and the Lost Race group is activated.

An explosion sample is also played on this line. The player's control is taken away here, and the Bat object is destroyed.

Because the Main Game group is deactivated here, all the lines hereafter will be ignored when the game is lost, and only the lines in the Lost Race group will be active.

THE RACING FLAVOR

The next line is the one that controls when the game is won. To give the game a true racing flavor, only the X coordinate of the finishing portal object has to be passed in order to win, thus making it a true "finish line."

To create the finish line, do the following.

1. Select the "Position" option of the Bat object.
2. Select the "Compare X position to a value" option.
3. The X position of the finishing portal is retrieved via the "Retrieve data from an object" button. This was compared using the "Greater than" comparison.
4. On this line, the Main Game group is deactivated and the Game Won group is activated. Notice that in order to stop the player from moving any farther, the player's control is ignored.

5. At this stage, the Lost Race group merely waits four seconds and then restarts the game, which resets the score.

6. The Game Won group waits one second and then restarts the level, which does not reset the score. It also adds 2 to the value of the score. The score is not going to be used to display the score, but will be used to subtract from the time at the beginning of the game. Therefore, each time you win, you have less and less time to reach the end.

7. Now run this version of *Bat Flight* and see how the Bat collides with obstacles and how the won/lost game sections work.

LEVEL EDITOR—*BAT FLIGHT*, PART 3

Now we'll add another important function. If you look in the Object window and on the play area, you will see our fireball object. It is used to replenish your stock of Fire Breath, without which you would be unable to get past the various traps and obstacles.

Something that you may have noticed is that there are bad and neutral groups in the game: Group.Bad and Group.Neutral. Find out which objects belong to which groups by right-clicking them on the play area, and then selecting their Object Preferences menus. This will show you to which groups they belong.

EVENT EDITOR—*BAT FLIGHT*, PART 3

This time we look at the event that will destroy all the fireball objects that might be left on the play area before the game begins. In addition, we will add a neat little start to the game for effect. While the music is being played, the Bat moves down and along a path as if it has just launched off its perch and is ready to fly out of the cave.

As soon as the music that was played from line 11 has finished, this line plays another sound sample and then deactivates the Start of Race Actions group, which stops the Bat from being moved any farther. It also launches you into the main game by activating the Main Game group.

LAUNCHING A FIREBALL

The next major event is blasting something with a fireball. First, we must check that we have fireballs in our possession, and to do that we check to see if the number of lives (fireballs) is greater than 0. If it is, when the key is pressed, all the actions on this line will be performed.

1. To create this line, first create the "Upon pressing the key" event.
2. Then, insert the "Number of lives >0" condition.
3. Right-click the "Upon pressing the key" text.
4. Select the "Insert" option. Selecting its "Compare to the player's number of lives" option tests the "player 1 object."
5. Now, associate the action shown in Figure 9.14 to this event line, using the Event Editor as a guide.

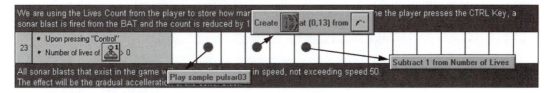

FIGURE 9.14   The events associated with breathing a fireball.

6. Play a sample.
7. Create a fireball just in front of the Bat. Note that the fireball is not fired and is stationary when it is first created. It needs an event line to accelerate it, which is placed elsewhere in the Main Game group. The fireball's movement is controlled in this way so as to create a realistic effect of the fireball slowly accelerating through the air.
8. Subtract one fireball, since one was just fired. In addition to the preceding actions, 1 is subtracted from the player's number of lives (fireballs) to signify that a fireball has been used up.

ACCELERATING A FIREBALL

Next in the Event Editor, the fireballs are accelerated up to a maximum speed of 50.

1. Select the fireball object's Movement menu.
2. Select its "Compare speed of 'fireball' to a value" option.
3. Using the "Less than comparison," compare this with the value 50.
4. Place the action to set its direction in the check box first.
5. Insert the action to increase its speed afterward by left-clicking the box, right-clicking the "New action" text, selecting the "Movement"

option, and then selecting the "Set speed" option. Retrieve its own speed by using the "Retrieve data from an object" button and adding +5 to the end of the expression (see Figure 9.15).

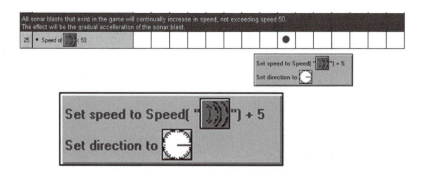

FIGURE 9.15 The steps for accelerating a fireball from a dead stop to 50, but no faster.

The logic of these steps is as follows: the speed of the object is set to the speed of itself, +5.

You can then set an action to destroy the fireballs if they collide with the background. This is associated with a sound sample as well.

To speed up and simplify game development, you can use the Bad and Neutral groups. You can set an event to say, "Anything belonging to Group.Neutral is destroyed when hit by the fireball," as opposed to going through the motions for every object you want destroyed by the fireball.

GAME BALANCE AND INDESTRUCTIBLE WALLS

In this game, we have placed some walls that react when hit with a fireball but are indestructible. Placing these walls may seem cruel to the player since he or she will no doubt waste precious time and fireballs trying to get through them and therefore will lose the game a few times. However, these initial defeats make players want to play the game again, since they know what to do differently the next time around—or they think they do, until they hit your next trick.

This is ultimately a gift to the players, since they will have a more enjoyable experience in the long run. They will gain a feeling of accomplishment after having played your game a few times and eventually winning. This simple aspect of a rather simple game increases game play enormously. With game balance, you literally balance the game play—too hard and you lose the players to frustration; too easy, and they are done in a flash and become bored.

Indestructible walls also add a great deal to the atmosphere. Remember from our discussions on game design that interactivity is a very important aspect of game development. Game worlds that feel flat and dead reduce the playability of the game. Adding little things like this make a big difference in the quality of your game. You can call it increasing production values, adding professional polish, or tweaking. Walls and objects that can be poked or prodded and tested for a result make the players feel that they are exploring a real world and not just driving through tunnels.

DESTRUCTIBLE WALLS

Now we will create walls that are destructible. These are actually animated active objects that allow a hole to be blasted through a weak wall. The object is not completely destroyed, but the animation creates a hole, the fireball is destroyed, and a sound sample is played—and the Bat can pass through the hole.

GAME STEPS

Collecting Fireball Energy. The action that controls the collection of fireballs is done simply by adding 2 to the number of lives and destroying the fireball power rune object when the real collider object collides with the ammo object.

Countdown. If the value of the counter is zero, the game has been lost. The associated actions deactivate the Main Game group and the player's controls, as well as playing a sample and activating the Lost Race group.

Real Collider Hits Backdrop. The game is lost if the real collider object hits any of the backdrop objects. The same actions are performed as shown previously, with the addition of destroying the Bat object.

Real Collider and the Group.Neutral. This step tests to see if the real collider object hits any of the other active objects that belong to Group.Neutral, which includes the walls, both weak and indestructible, and any of the firetrap objects or boulder objects.

Guess what? You just made another game with TGF. By now you should understand how this game was constructed and why it was constructed in this way, using groups.

If there are any points you are finding difficult to understand, it can be very helpful to try and recreate an event line on a spare "New condition" line. You can always delete it afterward. You can also look at most of the actions and events by right-clicking them and selecting the "Edit" option. Note that you cannot edit some of the very simple actions, such as Destroy.

Now you may be itching to get on with game developments of your own. The next few chapters will look in depth at some of the most commonly used tools in game development with TGF.

ACTIVITIES

Here is another exercise that will help you learn the editor as well as game balance. Go back to the section of this chapter "Losing the Game by Collision" and review it. Remember that the game can be lost if the Bat hits the walls of the cave; line 25 is where you make this happen in the Event Editor. You can go back to that line and alter the event that detects if a collision has occurred between the real collider object and the background. Make it so that the Bat cannot die. This will make the game easier, so you will also have to reduce the time limit or add more fireballs to compensate.

SUMMARY

In Chapter 9, you made yet another type of game with The Games Factory (your body of work is growing). In addition, you learned even more functions of TGF. Next, we will look at some of the advanced control of game objects in TGF.

Advanced Control of Active Objects

IN THIS CHAPTER

- Controlling the Actions of Objects on the Screen
- Allowing the Computer to Control Movement
- Using the Joystick to Control Movement
- Some Design Elements

Now that you have a firm background in TGF, you will want to experiment on your own more. You will start digging deeper into the menus. Detailed here are a few of the most important things you will do with active objects in TGF.

In the previous chapters, you were never called on to create assets or animate objects. Over the next few chapters, we will look at ways to create and manage assets. We will start by looking at all the active objects and their movement menus, the text objects, and the backdrop objects—the mainstays of TGF games.

ACTIVE OBJECTS

Active objects are mostly used as the main characters of your games. These are the characters and objects to which we've assigned behavior and controls. We did this by either allowing the player to use the mouse

FIGURE 10.1   The Active Object icon in the
Level Editor screen.

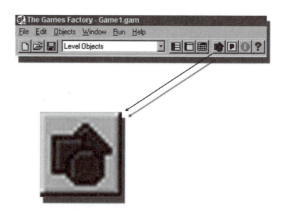

FIGURE 10.2   The New Object icon in the Level
Editor screen.

or keyboard or having the computer control the objects for us. You can
also animate your active objects, making them run, jump, or do whatever
you decide.

An icon on the Object Shelf in the Level Editor screen denotes Active
Objects (see Figure 10.1). Open a tutorial that showed a moving character, like the bat in *Bat Flight*, from the last chapter. Try grabbing the bat
active object and dragging it onto the screen of the Level Editor.

You can create your own active object by clicking the New Object icon
on the toolbar at the top of the Level Editor screen, as shown in Figure
10.2. Once you have done this, you can change the options by clicking the
object with the right mouse button. Don't worry about the images and
object animation just yet. We will talk about that in the next chapter.

MOVEMENT

To change an object's movement from the Level Editor, select the object
using the right mouse button, select the "Movement" option from its
pull-down menu, and then select the "Select movement" option. The
menu in Figure 10.3 will pop up.

The first item on this menu is the player-controlled Movement area.
Obviously, this allows the player to control the object in several ways.

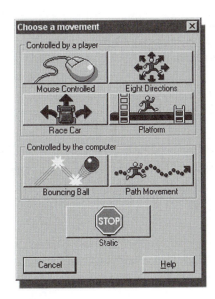

FIGURE 10.3   The Movement pop-up menu.

MOUSE CONTROLLED

The mouse-controlled icon assigns your object to follow exactly the movement of the mouse. Notice that when you call this option (see Figure 10.4), your object will be surrounded by a box, which represents the object's limits of movement, as shown in Figure 10.5.

You can stretch or shrink the area by grabbing the pick points with your mouse and dragging them around. Note that this box takes its

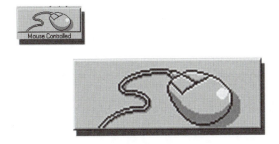

FIGURE 10.4   Mouse-controlled icon.

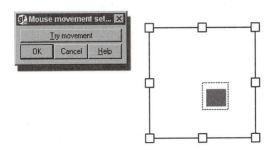

FIGURE 10.5   The mouse movement area control box.

position from the object, not the screen. Therefore, if you move your object to a new position on the Level Editor screen, you may need to edit this box again.

The following parameters are used for several of the movements, so they have been summarized here.

SPEED

Speed sets the maximum speed at which your object will be able to move.

ACCELERATION

Acceleration sets the rate at which your object will reach its maximum speed. If your object is a car, for example, you may want the acceleration quite high. If it is a heavier object, like an elephant, you would want it set lower.

DECELERATION

Deceleration affects the rate at which your object slows down. A high value stops the object quickly when you release the key to move it. A low value will results in a very gradual slowing down, as if the object were really heavy, like an oil tanker.

INITIAL DIRECTION

Initial Direction allows you to decide the first direction in which an object will move. If you select more than one direction, the computer will choose a direction at random.

MOVING AT START

Moving at Start is a toggle switch to indicate whether you want your object to be moving at the start of a game.

TRY MOVEMENT

Try Movement tests your movement on the screen. Use the Esc key, or select the Stop icon to take you back to the Direction Editor.

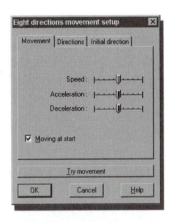

FIGURE 10.6   The Eight Directions icon.

FIGURE 10.7   The Movement Direction dialog box.

EIGHT DIRECTIONS

The Eight Directions icon (shown in Figure 10.6) provides you with the classic eight different directions that are used by a joystick. You can also use the cursor keys to control this movement. There are several basic controls. Speed, acceleration, and deceleration have been described previously. The "Possible directions" option allows you to select or de-select the number of directions in which your object can move. See Figure 10.7 for the Movement Direction dialog box.

To select or de-select a direction, simply click the relevant box. Having an arrow pointing to that box shows possible directions. In Figure 10.7, the only possible direction that the object could move in is to the right.

RACE CAR

Figure 10.8 shows a bird's-eye view of a car's movement, with controls for steering, braking, and accelerating.

Action	**Keyboard**	**Joystick**
Accelerator	Up Arrow	Joystick Up
Brake	Down Arrow	Joystick Down
Turn Left	Left Arrow	Joystick Left
Turn Right	Right Arrow	Joystick Right

In addition to speed, acceleration, and deceleration settings, there are three more options.

FIGURE 10.8 The Race Car icon.

ENABLE REVERSE MOVEMENT

This option gives your object the ability to go backward. With it turned off, you have only forward movement.

DIRECTIONS

"Directions" lets you decide how many different directions it is possible for the vehicle to move in. Selecting 4 gives you left, right, up, and down; selecting 32 gives you the smoothest possible direction changes.

HINT!

You can easily create all the different animation tracks needed for each direction by using the Animation Editor. We discuss this later in the book.

ROTATING SPEED

"Rotating Speed" sets the rate of turn. Having a high value will allow tight corners to be turned; having a low value reduces the cornering ability.

PLATFORM MOVEMENT

This movement (see Figure 10.9) is used mainly to define platform game-type movement (for example, characters who walk along a platform on the screen, viewed from the side, as in *Commander Keen* or *Zeb*). The cur-

FIGURE 10.9   The Platform Movement icon.

sor keys or the joystick controls them. In addition to the usual acceleration, deceleration, and speed, there are a large number of controls pecu-
liar to platform movement.

You can make platforms and ladders that are obstacles out of backdrop objects.

HINT!

You must still test for a collision with a backdrop platform
object; otherwise, your active object will fall through the platform as if it weren't there.

GRAVITY

As it suggests, this option selects the effect of gravity. A high setting
makes an your object fall rapidly, allowing only short jumps.

JUMP STRENGTH

Jump Strength selects the jumping power of your character. Changing
the gravity will also affect this parameter.

JUMP CONTROLS

Jump Controls are used to change the control system for jumps.

NO JUMP

Obviously, this option turns the jumping off.

UP LEFT/RIGHT ARROW

This option makes the object jump when both the up arrow key and either the left or right cursor keys are pressed.

BUTTON 1

Button 1 uses fire button one or the Shift key to control the jump.

BUTTON 2

Button 2 uses the second fire button or the Ctrl key to activate a jump.

COMPUTER-CONTROLLED MOVEMENTS

There are two computer-controlled options: "Bouncing Ball" and "Path Movement."

The first option is "Bouncing Ball" and, as the name indicates, this option is used to allow the computer to move or control the other objects in your games—a simple bouncing ball, an attack wave of aliens, or even a preset path on which a guard walks his patrol.

BOUNCING BALL

This movement option (Figure 10.10) is normally used to produce an object that bounces around the screen. However, changing several parameters and using the Event Editor can make this option control the movement of a host of aliens or other enemies that will chase you around.

FIGURE 10.10   The Bouncing Ball icon.

Speed

Speed is set as for all the other types of movement.

Ball Deceleration

When this option is set to zero, the ball will keep on bouncing around for-ever. Increasing this value gradually slows your object down until it eventually grinds to a halt.

Bounce Randomizer

As the name suggests, this option makes the bounces more random in their direction when this control is set high.

Bounce Security

Bounce security jiggles objects to keep them from getting stuck in cor-ners. However, as a result, the rebound effects are made slightly more random.

We will look at Bouncing Ball in a little more detail later.

PATH MOVEMENT

The "Path Movement" icon (shown in Figure 10.11) sets an object moving on a predetermined path that you define (for example, a patrolling guard who walks a set distance and then turns around or who has a preset walk around a corridor). With this movement, you can script some neat effects since you can control many parameters, such as the looping and speed of different sections of the path as the object moves along.

FIGURE 10.11   The Path Movement icon.

PATH EDITOR

Figure 10.12 shows six different buttons to define movement, plus the speed bar, which changes the speed at which the object moves along its path. A path-type movement is entered using your mouse to define the path (see Figure 10.13).

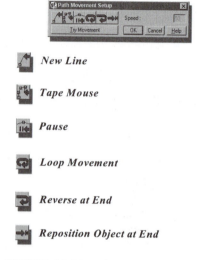

New Line

Tape Mouse

Pause

Loop Movement

Reverse at End

Reposition Object at End

FIGURE 10.12   The Path Editor menu window.

FIGURE 10.13   The Path Editor option buttons.

NEW LINE

This function adds a single line to your movement.

HINT!

If you have already defined a movement, New Line will be added at the end of it by default, unless you insert it by choosing the insertion point with the mouse.

TAPE MOUSE

This function allows you to set a very complex path movement. By holding down the left mouse button and dragging it around the screen, you set the movement you want.

. . . .

Tape Mouse changes the speed of the object, depending on how fast you move the mouse.

PAUSE

Pause stops an object at its current position for a pause that you define in seconds.

LOOP THE MOVEMENT

This function runs whatever movement you have defined over and over.

. . . .

Loop the Movement repositions the object at its original starting position to continue the loop, so try to ensure that your path finishes at the object's start point, or it will jump around the screen.

REVERSE AT END

This function simply reverses an object's movement and sends it back along the original path, backward. This function is good for a guard patrolling the grounds.

REPOSITION OBJECT AT END

This function replaces your object to its original starting position when it has completed the movement.

TRY MOVEMENT

This function allows you to try the movement before finally deciding to use it.

EDITING A PATH

Once you have added a movement to your object, you can edit it very easily from the Level Editor by selecting the object and then choosing the "Edit Movement" option. This reopens the Path Editor. You can select individual points of the movement or whole sections by dragging a box around them. You can then manipulate these selected pieces by either deleting them, or using the "Cut," "Copy," and "Paste" options from the Edit menu (the drop-down menu at the top of the screen). You can simply drag one of the points that you select using the left mouse button.

INSERTING A CONDITION

By using the right mouse button on one of the points, you can insert one of the previously defined conditions at any point along a path (for example, set a pause, tape mouse, or new line).

BOUNCING BALL MOVEMENT

The Bouncing Ball movement is normally used to provide a ball-like movement that will bounce off other obstacles on the screen. However, by setting all the parameters to zero, you will have a movement "blank page," which you can then manipulate entirely from the Event Editor. This is useful for enemy movements.

Movement

When you first select the Ball movement setup option, you will see a three-layered dialog box. You can change the layer being shown by clicking its tab (see Figure 10.14).

Speed

This option sets the maximum speed at which your object can move.

Deceleration

Deceleration sets the rate at which your bouncing object will slow down. Having this option set to zero will bounce your object around endlessly.

FIGURE 10.14 The Bouncing
Ball dialog box—Movement tab.

Moving at start

The "Moving at Start" option will set off the movement in one of the directions you choose, right from the start of the game. Having it set off means that the object will remain stationary until it collides with another object.

Bounces

This option (see Figures 10.15 and 10.16) sets the number of angles in which it is possible for your object to bounce. Having it set to 32 will result in the smoothest, most realistic effect. Having it set to 8 will result in an object that can only move left, right, up, down, and diagonally in between, and would not suit an object that is supposed to bounce like a ball.

FIGURE 10.15 The Bouncing Ball dialog
box—Bounces tab.

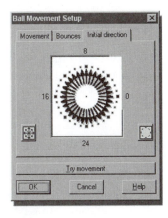

FIGURE 10.16 The Bouncing Ball
dialog box—Initial Direction tab.

Randomizer

The Randomizer gives an object a chance of bouncing off in a different direction from what you would normally expect. The higher the setting, the more unpredictable your bounces will be.

Security

This option jiggles objects to keep them from getting stuck in corners. As a result, the rebound effects become slightly more random.

Initial Direction

Initial Direction allows you to choose one or more directions for your object to move in when the game begins. Having more than one direction selected will result in a random choice being made between the directions that you have selected. You can select and deselect the directions individually by clicking the box at the end of each direction arrow. A selected direction will show an arrow in that box; deselecting a direction will remove the arrow. You can select all the possible directions using the icon on the bottom left, or deselect all directions by using the icon on the bottom right.

Backdrop Objects and Quick Backdrop Objects

All of the following parameters apply to both backdrop and quick backdrop objects, except that quick backdrop objects can be constructed without using the Picture Editor if their appearance is going to be relatively simple. (This option is discussed in the next chapter.)

Backdrop objects are normally used to "set the scene" in games. They provide backdrops for your players to move over, or even with which to interact. You cannot move backdrop objects or change their appearance when the game is playing, as you can with active objects. However, you can change their position on the screen, as well as their size, shape, and color, from the Level Editor.

You can either select one of the many backdrop objects from an object library or create your own backdrop and quick backdrop objects using the icon on the toolbar at the top of the Level Editor screen.

Most of the changes that you make to the actual appearance of the backdrop object are done using the Picture Editor (see next chapter). You use this only when you have selected the "Mosaic" option when using a quick backdrop object.

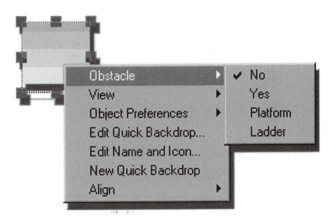

FIGURE 10.17   The Backdrop Object pop-up menu in
the Level Editor.

All the other changes to backdrop objects are done from the main
menu that you pull down when you right-click the actual backdrop object from the Level Editor screen. The pop-up menu from the backdrop
object can be seen in Figure 10.17.

OBSTACLE

You can change the way that other objects on the screen will interact with
a backdrop by turning the menu options on or off here. There are four
options.

NO

This option means the backdrop object will not be an obstacle to active
objects. You will not be able to detect a collision with an active object
when this option is turned on.

YES

This option means it will be possible to detect a collision with an active
object. You must test for a collision with a backdrop object in the Event
Editor and insert a stop action.

PLATFORM

This option means that the backdrop object will act as a platform for active objects controlled by platform-type movement. This is not the same as the "Obstacle" option because you will not be able to detect a collision from an active object that has been assigned a platform-type movement.

LADDER

This option will treat the backdrop object as a ladder when you are using a platform-type movement. For animated objects that have a relevant animation sequence, the animation will automatically be changed when they are climbing a ladder. If not, you could change the animation via the Event Editor. We discuss Active Animation later in the book.

EDIT PICTURE

The "Edit picture" option allows you to change the appearance of the backdrop object using the Picture Editor. We will look at this in the next chapter.

NEW OBJECT

The "New object" option is available for both backdrop objects as well as active objects. It allows you to produce another object that looks exactly the same as the original object, only it exists as either a backdrop, quick backdrop, or an active object. You can then place this object on the Level Editor screen and, although it looks exactly like the original backdrop object, it takes on all the qualities of whichever object type you selected. We used this in the last chapter, if you remember, to create walls that were indestructible and destructible.

NEW QUICK BACKDROP OBJECT

This is only available from the menu of a quick backdrop object. It produces a clone of the original, with a different name, one up in numerical order.

For example, if you created a quick backdrop object and it was the first one that you had produced in that game, TGF would call it Quick Backdrop 1. If you cloned that object using this method, even though it would take on all the same parameters as the original object, it would be called Quick Backdrop 2.

HINT!

 New Quick Backdrop Object differs from using the right mouse button to lay down multiple copies of the same object. Using that method results in producing genuine clones with the same name. If you made a change to one, that change would occur to all of them.

RESIZE

Resize allows you to resize your object by using the pick points on the box that will appear around the object.

ALIGN

This option will correctly align your backdrop object. You can push it up against the left-hand or right-hand edge of the play field or center it horizontally using the "Horizontally" option. You can align it against the top or bottom, or center it vertically, using the "Vertically" option from the menu.

SPECIAL OPTIONS FOR QUICK BACKDROP OBJECTS

The reason that there are two different types of backdrop objects is that for many purposes, it is only necessary to produce a block of color or a gradient of color.

For example, to produce a plain black backdrop, simply select a block color for a quick backdrop and then stretch it to fit the screen, rather than going into the Picture Editor and filling a picture. Simple structures, such as platforms and ladders, are very quick to produce.

You have several options within the Quick Backdrop Editor, as shown in Figure 10.18.

SOLID

The "Solid" option will fill your object with a solid color, selected from the palette.

FIGURE 10.18   The Quick Backdrop
Editor.

MOSAIC

The "Mosaic" option will take you to the Picture Editor. We will discuss
this more in the next chapter.

GRADIENT

The "Gradient" option will produce a smooth gradient from one color to
another. To use this function, click the Gradient button, then click the
From button. Choose your first color from the palette. Then, click the To
button, and select the second color from the palette. You will see a
smooth gradation of color from one to another. You can change the orientation of the gradation using the Vertical and Horizontal buttons.

PATTERN

The "Pattern" option uses cross-hatching to grade the colors from one to
another rather than smoothly fading the color.

TEXT OBJECTS

HINT!

Only the options related specifically to text objects are described
in this section. All the other options available have already been
described for the majority of the other active objects. You can
see the options we describe in the pop-up menu in Figure 10.19.

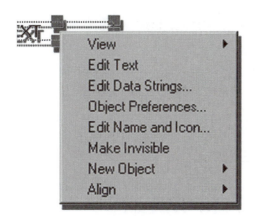

FIGURE 10.19   The Text pop-up menu.

FIGURE 10.20   The Text Options dialog box.

Text objects are used to put text on the screen. You can use them for instructions, comments, end-of-game displays, or just about anything where you need to place text on the screen. There are some texts already in the object libraries, but you will no doubt want to make your own.

To make your own text objects, select the Create New Object icon from the toolbar at the top of the Level Editor screen, and then click the Text icon. The mouse pointer will be replaced with a cursor. You place this cursor at the point where you want the text to start.

You will also have a dialog box, which is where you select fonts, the size and color of text, and the justification style you want to use (see Figure 10.20).

SELECTING A FONT, SIZE, AND COLOR

Clicking the Font icon opens a dialog box from which you can choose the size, style, and font that you want to use for the text in your text object, as shown in Figure 10.21.

To change the parameters, simply click each text box. All the text boxes have scroll bars so that you can view all the options available. The Sample box will give you a preview of the style you have chosen.

THE COLOR SELECTOR

This option is merely a shortcut to changing the color of the text via the Font Editor, and brings up a palette from which to choose the text color.

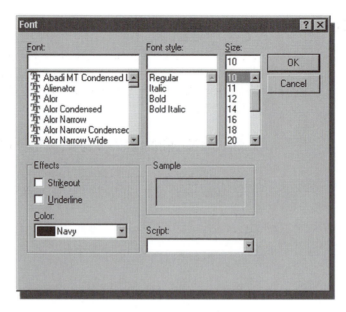

FIGURE 10.21   The text formatting dialog box.

LEFT ALIGNMENT

When you have more than one line of text, this option will align it all so that each line starts evenly from the left-most margin.

CENTER ALIGN

This option will align all the text centrally, so the length of the lines will be mirrored about a central line.

RIGHT ALIGN

This option aligns all your text to butt up against the right margin.

IMPORT

This option allows you to load up .txt files and place them into your text object from disk rather than typing them into the window. This allows the creation of text in a word processor, where things such as spell-checking and organized storage of the text can be done.

EDIT DATA STRINGS...

The "Edit Data Strings..." option allows you to have one text object used to display several different paragraphs of text during the game. When you select this option, you will be presented with a dialog box like the one in Figure 10.22.

FIGURE 10.22   The Text setup dialog box.

You can edit or clear the selected paragraph, or change its order, using the up and down arrows on the right of the dialog box.

You can add more paragraphs using the Add button, which then takes you to a text box where you enter the text for your new paragraph.

On the left of each paragraph is a number. This number is used to identify the paragraph when you display it in the Event Editor.

For example, an action you could insert under the text object on the event grid would be Display paragraph 1, which would display the text in paragraph 1 on the play area during a game.

Once you have placed your text object on the play area, you can right-click it to produce its menu and edit it as you can the other active objects.

ACTIVITIES

A fun exercise for this chapter is editing the path of an object, as discussed in the section "Editing a Path." You can apply this to the game *Cosmic Battle* and assign different paths to the objects. Once you have added a movement to your object, you can edit it very easily from the Level Editor, by selecting the object and then choosing the Edit Movement option. This reopens the Path Editor. You can select individual points of the movement, or entire sections, by dragging a box around them. You can then manipulate these selected pieces by either deleting them or using the Cut, Copy, and Paste options from the Edit menu (the drop-down menu at the top of the screen). You can simply drag one of the points that you select using the left mouse button.

SUMMARY

In this chapter, you learned many ways to give the player control in your game. Next, we will look at the details of working with images and animations in The Games Factory.

Working with Pictures and Animation in The Games Factory

IN THIS CHAPTER
• • • • • • • • • •

- Using Animation for Character Speed and Direction
- Zooming, Rotating, and Morphing
- Setting the Color Palette

In our final dealings with TGF, we are going to look at the way you create and manipulate assets for your games. Some of the most useful tools for the game developer that come with TGF are buried in the Animation and Picture Editors. These tools make it easy to import and deal with your assets in the game. They also offer animation functions such as copying, rotating, and other tedious operations that previously required you to manually work in another application like Photoshop.

THE TGF ANIMATION EDITOR
• • • • • • • • • • • • • • • • • • • •

Animation is a word that still strikes fear in the hearts of many who want to develop games, but the Animation Editor makes animation a lot easier.

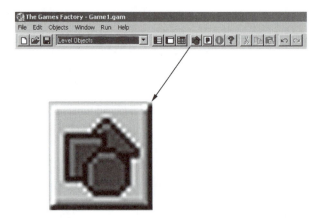

FIGURE 11.1   The pull-down menu for libraries of objects and the New Object icon.

For example, if you have an animation of a creature facing one direction and want to make it walk in the opposite direction, clicking one button in the Animation Editor will create a new animation of the creature walking in the opposite direction.

TGF gives you two methods of editing or creating an animated object (see Figure 11.1).

- You can go to the Level Editor, open a library of objects from the pull-down bar in the menu, and then pick an object from the Object Shelf on the left of the Level Editor.
- You can create a new active object using the New Object icon on the toolbar at the top of the screen.

HINT!

Only active objects can be animated from the Animation Editor.

We will open an active object that already exists to analyze how the tools have been used to animate it. As we do this, you will see the steps required to create your own animated object. An animation can often be done using one image or a few versions of one image.

1. Start by opening a new blank game, going to the Level Editor, and then opening the *Bat Flight* game library with the pull-down menu.

2. Now that the objects are on the left-hand bar, select the bat object and place it in the middle of the play area of the Level Editor screen.
3. Right-click the object; a pop-up menu opens. Move the pointer to the "Edit animation…" option and click the left mouse button.

You should now have a screen similar to Figure 11.2.

With the Animation Editor you can change the name of your animation; run a preview of what it actually looks like when all the images are run together; create a different animation, depending on the direction your character is moving in; or create a different animation for any situation your character may get into, such as climbing or running.

HINT!

To select all the frames of an animation, use the Alt+A keyboard shortcut. This will allow you to move or delete an entire sequence of animation at one time. You can also hold the Ctrl key to select multiple animation frames, and you can hold the Shift key to select all animation frames in between two selected frames.

Let's explore this screen a bit more (see Figure 11.3).

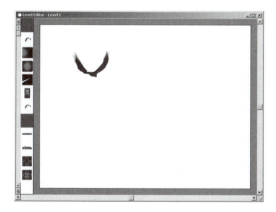

FIGURE 11.2　The Level Editor with only the bat object on it.

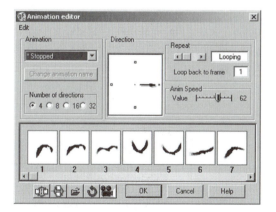

FIGURE 11.3　The main screen of the Animation Editor.

ANIMATION SPEED

At the top right of the Animation Editor are the controls for the speed of the animation, as well as the number of times it will repeat before it stops

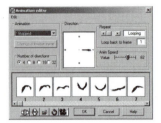

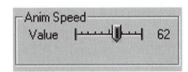

FIGURE 11.4   The animation speed control on the main
screen of the Animation Editor.

(see Figure 11.4). You can select Looping by moving the Repeat slider
below 1 with the arrow pointer. This will repeat the animation sequence
over and over.

You can also change which frame number the animation loops back to
in the "Loops Back to Frame" box. This can be used to deal with a longer
animation of which you only want to play certain parts. Say you are
working with an animation of a man getting up from a crouched position
and then running away. You may want to play only the first couple of
frames of him crouching and then loop the animation back to the running
sequence.

HINT!

For some animations, there are two sliders to control speed.
There are only two controls for an object's normal movement,
such as the walking animation of a character. If the character
was stopped, there would only be one slider that controls the
speed of the animation regardless of movement.

MINIMUM SPEED

This controls the speed when the character is not moving. Setting this to
zero halts the animation when the character is not moving. Having it set
higher makes the animation run all the time, which may look unrealistic
if your character is running frantically without moving!

MAXIMUM SPEED

This controls the maximum rate of the animation when the character is at full speed. Note that the rate of animation will be proportional to the speed of the character, in between the Minimum and Maximum settings. To create a realistic running action, you may need to change the Maximum setting to a similar value as a character's speed across the screen.

For example, if you were to set a character's movement speed high and the animation speed low, it would look like the character was being dragged across the screen. If you had the animation speed high and the actual movement speed low, it would look as though the character was trying to run fast on an icy floor.

ANIMATION DIRECTION

This is a very useful feature that can seem hidden at first. If you look at the Direction box, you will see that when you click a different direction square of the Animation Direction Clock Face, you will have the option of creating a different animation for each direction the character may move (see Figure 11.5).

For example, look at the bat animation for *Bat Flight*. Select the walking animation from the scroll list and you will see that on the clock face, the 3

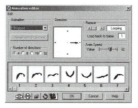

FIGURE 11.5 The Animation Direction Clock Face.

o'clock and 9 o'clock positions have smaller solid black x's, which indicate that an animation is assigned to those positions. Therefore, when the bat moves backward, a different animation will play. To add realism here, you can have the bat go slower and fly differently as it goes backward. In other words, you can have up to 32 different animated sequences for the walk direction of a character. Although 32 directions will look smooth, it will also be a real resource hog on your machine and is overkill for most purposes. A standard platform game has only four animations for walking.

HINT!

An easy way to create several different directions from one animation is to click the "Create Other Directions By Rotating This One" button. This will copy and rotate the current animation and will likely turn your objects upside down for some of the directions. However, you can correct this using the controls we discuss next.

NUMBER OF DIRECTIONS RADIO BUTTONS

You can select the total number of different directions or animations by clicking one of the buttons shown in Figure 11.6. Obviously, the higher

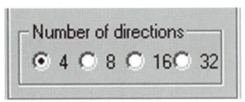

FIGURE 11.6   The Number of Directions radio buttons on the Animation Editor window.

the number of different directions, the smoother the turning effect will be. This is particularly useful for race car movement, but four different directions will be fine for a platform character.

You can manually fill the other directions using Cut, Copy, and Paste from the Edit pull-down menu (on the Animation Editor). It is recommended that you use Copy and Paste; otherwise, you will simply move one frame to another location rather than copy it.

MANIPULATION ICONS

These icons (see Figure 11.7) are used to manipulate all the frames of the animation being displayed on the Animation Editor screen. Be careful when you use them, since you may mess up your animation. The View Animation icon is safe, since it merely previews the whole sequence of images together and shows you what your animation looks like when running.

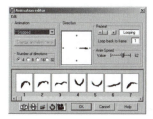

FIGURE 11.7   The Manipulation icons on the Animation Editor window.

Horizontal Flip

The Horizontal Flip function reverses all the images from left to right. This saves a lot of time and effort when you have a character going one way and you simply want to turn all the frames to face the other way. An example of this is shown in Figure 11.8.

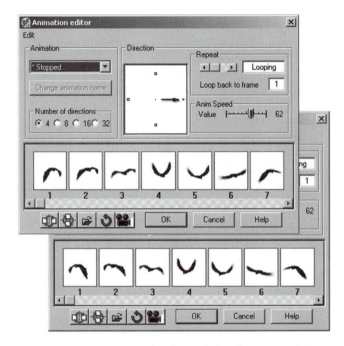

FIGURE 11.8 An example of an animated sequence being reversed using the Horizontal Flip function.

HINT!

Both the Action Point and the Hot Spot also move when you use the Horizontal Flip function.

Vertical Flip

Like the Horizontal Flip function, this function turns all the images upside down. It is useful when you have created several new directions from your original animation, and some of the sequences are the wrong way up. You can even use it to make a character walk on the ceiling. Vertical Flip also moves the Action Point and Hot Spot.

Import

Import is a very important and useful function that grabs one or more graphic images from a disk and loads them into the Animation Editor. You can then manipulate or process them in the Animation Editor.

HINT!

You can load images stored in PCX, LBM, GIF, TIF, or BMP formats. You can even load FLC and FLI files, but beware: these files are normally very large, since they contain many images—usually more than 50 separate images—and will therefore use up large amounts of memory and storage space.

Capture Style

Once you have entered the Import function, you will be asked to select a drive and the types of files to look for, which can be any of those described previously. Once you have selected the file you want, you will be asked to select a Capture style. This decides the method by which you grab one or more images from the file you are looking in.

Transparent Mode

Transparent mode will make the background color of the images that you pick transparent, rather than the actual color on the original image.

For example, if the background color of the images that you select is red, and you have Transparent mode on, instead of pasting them with a red background, TGF pastes them into the Animation Editor with a transparent background. If Transparent mode is off, then the background color for the frames you grabbed will be transferred as well. Therefore, if the background color was red, then it will be pasted into the Animation Editor as red, as shown in Figure 11.9.

FIGURE 11.9   The images in the Animation Editor with the transparent and nontransparent backgrounds.

Box Image Mode

Box Image mode imports a series of images from a disk using a single operation. Box Image mode is ideal for creating animation sequences.

HINT!

 The format and layout of this image file is important to the capture procedure. The first point in your picture should be set to the color used by your background (usually zero or transparent). The second should hold the color of your box (usually 1). A one-point-thick box should now surround each image.

Box Image mode grabs all of the images that are within boxes—the selected areas that you have defined with the mouse—and pastes each boxed image into its own animation frame, in order, from top left to bottom right.

If, for example, there are ten boxed images on the screen, and you drag a selection area that completely encloses nine of them but only half of the tenth, only nine of the images will be taken. If Box Image mode was off, one image comprising the entire contents of the selection area would be taken and pasted into only one animation frame.

Full Window Mode

Full Window mode grabs the whole area inside the Capture window (not just inside your selection area) and pastes it into your animation frame. This only produces one frame of animation, comprising the entire contents of the window.

HINT!

 If you have Box Image mode on while trying to use Full Window mode, all the boxed images in the window will be grabbed and treated as separate frames of animation.

CREATING DIFFERENT DIRECTIONS

The Animation Editor lets you quickly and easily create many different directions from only one animation direction. Be aware, though, if you have several animation frames and 32 different directions, you will be using a lot of memory space. In addition, it literally just turns your object around. Therefore, if you start with an object that faces to the right, when it is rotated to the left, it will be upside down.

Let's look at a frame of animation and then copy it to fill several frames, creating an animation.

CREATING AND EDITING A SINGLE FRAME OF ANIMATION

You should still be in our new game file and in the blank Level Editor, with only the bat object on the play field. Right-click the bat active object to bring up the pop-up menu, and then select the Edit Animation option to enter the Animation Editor.

When you are in the Animation Editor, click the middle of frame 1 with the right mouse button. This will pull down a menu. Select the "Edit Frame" option. You can also double-click the frame to pop up the Picture Editor.

Once you are in the drawing screen, or Picture Editor, for the animation, you can decide the color, size, and shape of your animation frame. We will talk more about the Picture Editor later in this chapter.

In the Picture Editor, you can modify each frame individually to suit your own requirements. To save you from laboriously copying each frame, you can return to the Animation Editor and use the following commands, which are selected from the menu produced when you right-click the frame you want to modify.

ADDING ANIMATION FRAMES

You can create most animations easily by creating several frames that are slightly different from one another, based on one original image. When they are run quickly together, they will give the impression of fluid movement. Whether you are starting from scratch or using one initial frame, it is far easier to copy each frame and then modify it as you go along than to draw each image for each frame or to modify each image by hand in a paint program.

First, click the first frame of your animation with your right mouse button, and then select the "Insert" option. This will insert an exact copy of your first frame into frame 2. You can also do the same thing using the left mouse button. Simply select the image that you want to copy with the left mouse button, hold the button down, drag the image to the frame you wish it to be copied to (in this case, frame 2), and let go of the button.

You can enter the Picture Editor for that frame and modify it slightly. When you are ready, you can insert a copy of that frame into frame 3, which you can then modify further, continuing the process until you have a finished animation. You can check on your progress at any time by using the View Animation icon.

RESIZE ZOOM

The "Resize Zoom" option allows you to create several frames of animation that will gradually shrink or grow in relation to the frame with which you start. When you select the "Resize Zoom" option, you will see a dialog box that looks like Figure 11.10.

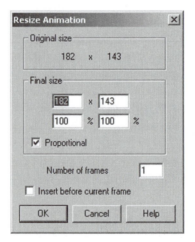

FIGURE 11.10   The Resize Zoom dialog box.

This option was used to create the fireball power-ups for *Bat Flight*. We will recreate the fireball animation here.

1. Start by opening a new and blank game file. Go to the Level Editor, click the New Object icon in the toolbar, and then select the "New Active Object" option. Now you will see the Create New Active Object Editor.

2. Double-click the first blank frame and go to the Bat Flight directory. From here, select the fireq.bmp image file, and then capture it. Click

OK, and then place a copy of the fireball on the play area. Notice that it does not move.

HINT!

You may want to create a quick backdrop object, make it solid, and choose the color black. This will give you the full effect of the animation we are creating.

3. Once you have the fireball on a black field, right-click to open the Animation Editor. Right-click the first frame and select the "Resize Zoom" option. Now you will be in the Resize Zoom dialog box, as shown in Figure 11.10.

Under the Original Size heading is the size in pixels of the frame that you are zooming from. Under the Final Size heading, you can select the size of the frame you want to end up with. You can either enter the actual size of the X and Y dimensions of the final frame (i.e., the number of pixels wide and high that the final frame will be) or you can enter a percentage ratio. For example, 50% would shrink that particular dimension by half.

If the Proportional radio button is selected and you change any of the values, the other dimension changes proportionally. For example, if you changed the width to 50%, then the height would also be changed by 50%. With the Proportional radio button deselected, you can change the dimensions independently.

The "Number of frames" option allows you to select the number of frames between the original image and the grown or shrunken final image. The higher the number, the smoother the effect will be.

The "Insert before current frame" option will grow or shrink the object before the current frame. For example, if you select the first frame of an animation to shrink by half, and you are using 10 frames to do so, which you inserted before the current frame, then when you finish the process, the first frame will be the smallest. Each of the next 10 frames will get gradually bigger until you arrive back at the original frame.

You can also perform the function both before and after an image so it appears to shrink and grow, rather than simply shrink, then reappear the same size, and then shrink again.

Rotate

The "Rotate" option can be used to insert several frames of animation that gradually rotate either clockwise or counterclockwise from the initial frame. You can choose the number of frames used to perform the rotation, ranging from 4 to 32. Obviously, the higher the number of frames used, the smoother the rotation effect will be. The rotation frames are inserted after the initial frame.

Morphing

The Morphing function allows you to change one frame into another, allowing for stunning transformations. You can use this function to make a human face morph into a monster, or a spaceship smoothly change into another spaceship, rather than simply having the images snap from one to the next. You may well have seen advanced versions of this technique in Hollywood movies. Now you can do it on your PC!

To morph an object, you simply need to set up the Animation Editor with the first image in frame one and the "morph to" image in frame two. Right-click the first image and you will be taken to the Morphing processor, as shown in Figure 11.11.

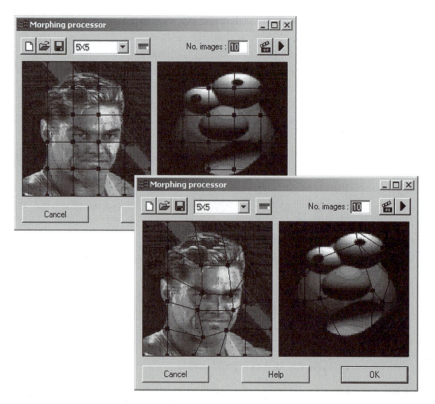

FIGURE 11.11 The Morphing processor before and after adjusting the morph points.

The easiest way to morph something is to select your second (destination) object first, enter the Animation Editor, select the frame you want, copy it using the Edit function from the Animation Editor (top left), and then exit the Animation Editor.

Now, select the first (start) object, enter the Animation Editor for that object, and paste the finishing frame after the frame you want first. You may have to enter the Edit mode and deselect the "Remove all" option, which will remove all previous animation frames if you try to paste a new frame into that animation sequence.

HINT!

The morphing function works best when there is only one frame for the original object. If there is more than one frame, delete the redundant frames so that you are left with only the start frame and the finish frame. You can leave part of the original animation if you want, but bear in mind that the morphing part of the animation will not start until the original animation has run. Also, morphing can use a lot of memory.

Using the Morphing processor, you can select the number of frames used to morph from the original frame to the final one. Clicking the "No Images" box does this. The more frames you have, the smoother and more realistic the end result will be, but it is time consuming and uses a lot of memory. By default, The Games Factory uses 10 frames, which is a compromise between smoothness of effect and speed of execution. You can also choose the definition of the change in the grid box at the top of the screen (by default, set to 5 X 5). A higher number here raises the number of fine changes that are made between each frame. Be aware that a very high definition combined with a large object will take a long time and may use up lots of memory.

The icon actually starts the whole process. When it has finished you will be presented with a whole new animation strip, morphing smoothly from the first image to the last. I used this function to give the bat wings a nice blur effect as they moved. It was easy, since I needed only two images of the bat—wings up and wings down—rather than 10 separate images.

Use of the Morph Grid

You can change the color of the Morph Grid using the icon, which you may find very useful, depending on the color of the images you are morphing.

The grid is used to define common points on the two images that you want to move. The grid is composed of a number of "elastic bands" that you can stretch to fit various strategic points on the objects you are morphing.

To morph from one face to another, you would stretch the grid so that each point corresponds to an eye, nose, edge of mouth, and so forth. Make sure that the same grid point on the other object is used to correspond to the same feature. For example, if the point one from the left and one from the top is placed on the eyebrow on the first object, the very same grid point (one from the left, one from the top) must be used on the eyebrow of the second object, even if it means stretching the point right across the image window.

HINT!

Try to ensure that you do not get grid points "crossing over" each other, since this will spoil the effect.

Setting the Hot Spot of an Object

The Hot Spot is an invisible handle, or anchor, used to drag images around on the screen. It is used as a reference for the X and Y coordinates of an object. Each image can have its own separate Hot Spot. As a default, when you create a new active object, the Hot Spot is automatically positioned at the top left corner of each image (see Figure 11.12). You can, however, move it anywhere you like.

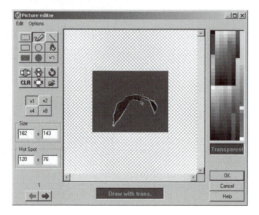

FIGURE 11.12   The Hot Spot of an object.

You can view the Hot Spot by going to the Options heading and selecting the "Show Hot Spot" option. Try to position it centrally if your object is going to have several different directions; otherwise, it will "jump" when you change direction.

Setting the Action Point of an Object

The action point is where things such as bullets are fired from objects. If, for example, you had a large spaceship with a gun mounted onboard, you would set the Action Point to the end of the barrel of the gun. This means that this is where your bullet would first appear. You can show the Action Point by going to the Options heading and selecting the "Show Action Point" option.

HINT!

The Hot Spot and Action Point can look the same, so double-check the menu to be sure the right option is selected.

The Picture Editor

The Picture Editor is used for creating your own animation, background objects, icons, and quick backdrop objects. Because many of the features are identical for all these types of objects, they are summarized in this chapter.

FIGURE 11.13   The Picture Editor window.

We have already visited the Picture Editor, but Figure 11.13 shows the Picture Editor window for your reference as we go through the specific functions of the editor.

In the center of the screen is the drawing area, where you will be drawing and editing. If the area is too large to fit in this screen, you can either scroll around it, zoom in or out using the zoom control buttons, or maximize the window using the Window Manipulation icons at the top right of the window.

ZOOM ICONS

On the left of the screen are four buttons: x1, x2, x4, and x8. These simply mean that you can view the image at its normal size, twice its normal size, and so on. The zoom function does not actually change the size of the image, only the view of the image.

THE COLOR PALETTE

To the right of the screen is the Color Palette, which allows you to choose the colors with which to draw. You can select the transparency color as well as a solid color.

You draw with any normal color by clicking a color on the palette. The selected drawing color is shown in the box immediately below the drawing area, with the letter "D" in the middle of the box. If you click the color, you will see the color of this box change.

To draw with the transparency color, click the Transparency color box below the Color Palette. When you draw on your picture, you will, in effect, be making that portion of the image clear, making it transparent in the game.

The transparent areas of an image are denoted by a specific color (see "Color Masking" in Chapter 2), which is normally green-blue, but you can change this by using the Options menu at the top of the Picture Editor.

Go to the toolbar of the Picture Editor, click the Options menu, and then select the color you like. Any color you select to be transparent will be transparent, or "show through," for the entire image. This is very useful for leafless trees, or large animated objects that have gaps in the structure. Anything in the background will be seen through the transparent areas.

THE DRAWING TOOLS

The drawing tools include the most-used feature of the digital artist—Undo. Also included here are the Pen, Fill Bucket, and solid and outlined forms and shapes.

THE PEN TOOL

The Pen tool is used to draw one pixel at a time or to draw a freehand line. Note that if you are drawing a freehand line and you move the mouse too fast, you will end up with a dotted and broken line.

To create a grainy effect, use this tool with several different colors and go over the drawing area very fast. This will lay down pixels of color spaced apart. Doing this over a gray background with brown, black, and white will give the effect of a brown stone tile.

THE LINE TOOL

The Line tool lets you draw perfectly straight lines using the mouse. Simply click the point where you want the line to start, hold down the mouse button, and as you move the mouse, it "drags" a line behind it. Move to the other end of the line (where you want to end the line), let go of the mouse button, and you will have drawn a line between the two points.

THE RECTANGLE AND FILLED RECTANGLE TOOLS

These drawing tools allow you to draw rectangles and squares more easily than constructing them out of four separate lines. After selecting the icon you want, place the pointer at the place you want the top left corner, press and hold down the mouse button, and then drag the rectangle to the shape you want.

Performing the same procedure and using the Filled Rectangle icon does exactly the same thing, except that it produces a solid rectangle of the color you have selected.

THE ELLIPSE AND FILLED ELLIPSE TOOLS

These tools allow you to create ellipses and circles, both filled and empty.

To create a circle, select the icon you want, and place the mouse pointer at the place where you want the center of the circle. Holding down the mouse button, move the pointer away from the center of the circle.

An ellipse is drawn in proportion with how far you move the pointer from the center point. Moving sideways from the center stretches the ellipse horizontally; moving it up (or down) from the center stretches it vertically.

THE FILL TOOL

The Fill tool fills an area with a solid block of color. The area to be filled should be completely enclosed. If there is a gap of even one pixel, the color will "leak" out into other areas of your frame.

THE UNDO TOOL

This tool is used to undo the last step you performed. It will only undo the last thing you did, though. Clicking it again will undo what you have undone, in effect redoing it!

THE SELECTION TOOL

The Selection tool defines a rectangular block, which can be cut or copied from your image. When it is selected, you can move the mouse to where you want the top left corner of your block and then drag a box down around the area you want. If you make a mistake, click once on another part of your image and try again.

Once you have selected a block, you can save it into memory using the following commands from the Edit menu (top left of the Picture Editor).

Cut. The original area will be cut out and replaced with a block of whatever the transparency color currently is.

Copy. This tool will do the same thing as Cut without affecting the original image.

Paste. After you have grabbed an area, you can copy it onto the image using the Paste command. This provides you with a rectangular box, which can be used to position your block over the image. You can fix it in place with a single click of the mouse button.

HORIZONTAL FLIP

This tool reverses your image from left to right, much like a mirror does.

VERTICAL FLIP

This tool turns the whole image upside down.

ROTATE

This tool allows you to rotate the whole image very finely. When you select Rotate you will be asked to select an angle by which to rotate the
image. The arrow will point to the current direction. Simply click a new
direction on the clock face, then click OK, and the image will be turned by
the angle you have specified.

CLEAR

Caution! This option clears the image window, so you can start from
scratch. If you accidentally clear all the work you wanted to save, you can
undo the Clear command from the menu, or with the Hot Key combination Ctrl Z.

SHRINK

The Shrink tool removes any unnecessary transparent border areas from
the image, reducing its size. This is very useful for conserving memory
and will speed up your game by removing overly large images, trimming
them to the minimum required.

IMPORT

This tool loads an image from a disk. It works much like the Import command works in the Animation Editor, except that in the Picture Editor
you are working with individual images.

ACTIVITIES

One of the most fun parts of this chapter was morphing. The Morph function lets you change one frame into another, allowing for stunning transformations. Go back to the section on morphing, open various images, and
experiment with morphing. If possible, import your own image into the
Morphing processor and have fun. Remember to set up the Animation

Editor with the first image in frame one, and the "morph to" image in frame two. Right-click the first image and you will be taken to the Morph Editor. This function works best when there is only one frame for the original object. If there is more than one frame, delete the redundant frames so that you are only left with the start frame and the finish frame.

SUMMARY

In this final chapter on The Games Factory, we looked at the flexible, advanced—yet easy to use—image and animation tools that will make your games really become your own. In Part Three, we will make a 3D game.

MOVING ON TO 3D

In this section, you applied many of the technologies and techniques we discussed in Part One. As you continue to work with TGF, you will discover many uses for it and many creative ways to use TGF that have simply not been thought of yet. You now have a solid foundation and will be ready to step easily into the next dimension of game development.

3D Game Creation

Introduction to the Game Creation System

IN THIS CHAPTER
················

- Using the Game Creation System
- Installation
- Functions
- Editors
- Viewing

In this part of the book, we will make a 3D game using the Pie 3D Game Creation System, referred to as GCS from here on. Pie in the Sky Software has released its software free to the readers of this book (Figure 12.1). Please visit their Web site for information on the forthcoming version of GCS.

The best thing about GCS is that it allows you to create an entire game without doing any programming. You will see how much you can do with GCS using your own imagination to make 3D games that are comparable to *Doom*. Although you will not be doing any programming, things will get a bit more complex as we start to look into the third dimension. We will learn a new set of tools and techniques, but we will use the vocabulary and processes you already learned.

From several 3D game development tools on the market, I chose the GCS package for several reasons.

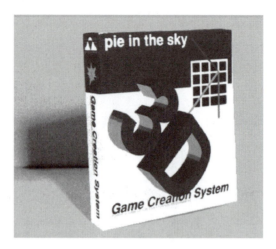

FIGURE 12.1   The Pie in the Sky logo.

- **It was FREE!** The good people at Pie in the Sky Software released GCS free only for the readers of this book. They did it partly to support the community, but also because they have a newer, more powerful version of GCS coming out. I hope you check out the screen shots on their site.
- **It has a large and helpful online support community.** Hop over to www.GCSGames.com and join the mailing list.
- **It is the easiest to use.** The last thing you need is to be overwhelmed by complexity when you are first learning the process of building a game. Once you get your feet wet with GCS, you can move to larger and more complex 3D game systems and learn them more rapidly. This product was designed with the intent of making an easy-to-use program for nonprogrammers, so the program is very much mouse and graphics based.
- **It requires a minimal system to run.** There are still many older systems in schools and in homes, and it is frustrating to use tools and games that require increasingly higher specifications to run an application. GCS has very minimal requirements since it is a DOS application: it requires a 386 or better computer with a VGA graphics card.
- **You can freely sell and distribute the products you create.** A barrier to many is the cost of an application and the cost of selling products made with a specific application. With GCS, there are no complex license agreements or royalty payment schedules.

INSTALLING GCS

To install this version of the Pie 3D GCS put the companion CD-ROM into the drive, find the GCS folder, and click on the Setup icon. The installation procedure will install everything you need and includes an uninstall option.

The first step in the installation procedure is to agree to the terms of using the software, as shown in Figure 12.2.

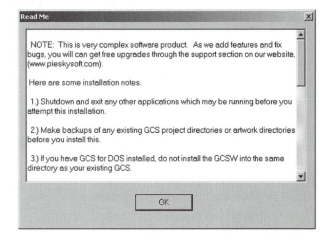

FIGURE 12.2   You must agree to the terms in order to use the software.

Next, you have to select the location in which you want the software installed. It is usually a good idea to use the default directory, since many of the examples and instructions given later in this part of the book assume a normal installation.

The last step asks you if you want to have a shortcut to GCS either in the Windows Start menu or on the desktop (Figure 12.3). It is a good idea to do this so you can find GCS later. Whatever you select here, you can later delete, move, and create shortcuts in Windows.

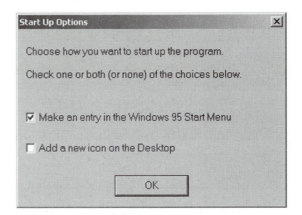

FIGURE 12.3 This option will create a shortcut on your Windows Start menu or on your desktop.

THE MAIN PARTS OF GCS

GCS consists of three main areas: the layout editor, the Paint program, and the smooth scrolling 3D game engine.

The Layout Editor

You will handle almost all aspects of game creation in the Layout Editor (commonly called the Map Editor or Mapping Utility). You will work on one game level at a time from a top view, using the toolbar icons to do the most common functions, such as copying, rotating, and placing walls. In addition, there are standard pull-down menus across the top of the screen.

HINT!

GCS has some similarities to TGF in terminology, but in GCS you are laying out a 3D world in two dimensions. Because one dimension remains unseen, you will have to visualize mentally what you are laying out, whereas with TGF, you could see exactly what was going into your game.

From the Layout Editor, you can click on "test level" to drop into the 3D world to test your layout and game play. The Layout Editor interface is shown in Figure 12.4.

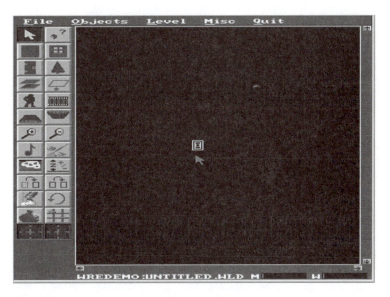

FIGURE 12.4   The Layout Editor interface.

GCS Paint

The second part of GCS is the image tool for creating or retouching images for GCS games. The GCS Paint tool has a set of features that allow the important control of image resolutions, contrast, and pixel blending. If you have trouble with these concepts, you should go back to Part One and read up on image manipulation. The GCS Paint interface is shown in Figure 12.5.

FIGURE 12.5   The GCS Paint program interface.

The Game Engine

Ironically, you can't see the most important part of GCS, the game engine, and that is what we want in a book that has "no programming required" on the cover. The term *game engine* is a rather generic term used to describe the core application that runs a game. This engine is the software that runs when the user is playing the 3D game. You never actually touch it in GCS; you simply build the levels and create the game on one end, and then the engine runs it on the other. Here are some of the things the engine does.

Visibility tests. The engine must decide which parts of the world are visible and which are hidden behind other walls or objects and are not to be displayed on the screen. Visibility testing is important for how well the game looks and operates.

If this testing were not done, you would see objects through walls and other errors. You have probably played a game where you could see an object through a wall or some such goof. If the testing was not done and objects were displayed, even if you did not see them, the speed and performance of the game would be affected. As you work with GCS, you will begin to get a feel for how to balance the amount of art you use and become more sensitive to the way the engine will handle your world.

Sounds. The engine plays sounds, controlling the volume and the way the sounds are played back. As we discussed previously, sound is very important and can make or break the "spell" of your game. A game engine typically mixes sound for depth and direction—on cue—and juggles the number of sounds, prioritizing the order in which they are played and canceling them if necessary.

Collision detection. The engine makes sure that the player and the enemies can't walk through the walls. It must detect a collision between the two and dictate the behavior of the objects that have collided.

Artificial intelligence and behavior. The engine controls all the moving objects in the game, from the burning torch to the sliding doors, to the enemy characters with their AI and very complex behavioral routine.

All of the above—and much more—must be done in "real time," or as you are playing the game. Moreover, these are just a few of the things a game engine must do and still keep a decent frame rate.

HINT!

Frame rate is the rate at which frames are created and displayed on the computer screen, just like the frames of a movie. One critical difference, however, is that when a movie's frame rate suddenly drops to half speed, the film itself is playing at half speed. When the frame rate drops in a game, the world is still moving at the same speed; you are just seeing half as many frames, so it becomes choppy.

Figure 12.6 shows traditional film frames and the frames of a computer game (if game frames could be put on film). Keep in mind that film is static, but a game's frames can be different each time. Figure 12.6 illustrates the effect of frame rate drop in a game.

FIGURE 12.6   Film frames and computer game frames during rate drop.

GCS FIRST LOOK

Once you have GCS installed and running, you need to know a few things about GCS. When you edit levels and build games using GCS, you are in a full-screen DOS window, but the game is a 100% Windows game. You need to be aware of certain things so as not to lose any work when switching between the DOS editor and the Windows engine.

Running GCS

1. Click Start on the lower left of your Windows screen.
2. Choose the Programs menu.
3. Select the GCSWE group.
4. From that group, choose GCSWE to launch GCS.
5. A DOS window will open on your Windows desktop that says, "Press a key to start DOS editor" (see Figure 12.7). At this point, the World Editor is ready to start; just press the space bar or any key to begin.

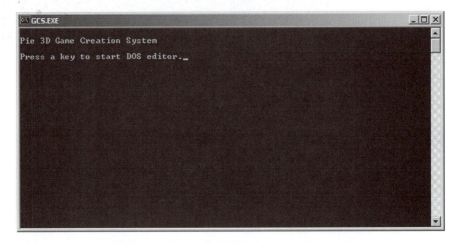

Pie 3D Game Creation System

Press a key to start DOS editor._

FIGURE 12.7 The DOS window that opens when you launch GCS.

When GCS first runs, you will be prompted to select a project file from a window, as shown in Figure 12.8. This is a good time to remind you of the distinction between a project and a level.

The Project Folder is where all the level files are stored. Once you select the WREDEMO project, you can store multiple level files within it.

Click Show List, and then click WREDEMO. Click Accept and open the WREDEMO project.

HINT!

A red box will pop up warning you that the colors are going to change on your screen. This is normal: GCS is adjusting itself to use the same colors that the WREDEMO game will use.

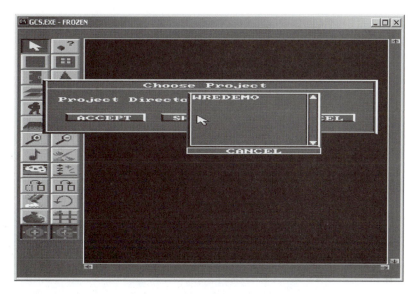

FIGURE 12.8   The Select a Project window.

THE GCS MAIN SCREEN

You should now be looking at the GCS main screen, shown in Figure 12.9. There are pull-down menus across the top of the screen, icon

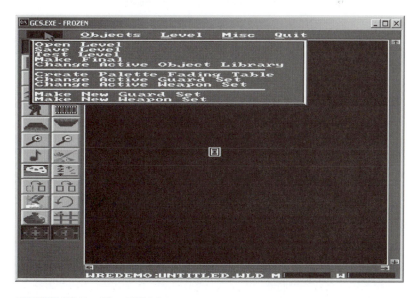

FIGURE 12.9   The GCS Main screen.

buttons on the left side of the screen, and the viewport window in the middle. There is one white-layered square in the center of the screen, an empty level named UNTITLED.

Just as a word processor usually opens a document called untitled when you start it up, GCS starts with an untitled level as well. To load the demo level we want to look at, click on the File menu in the upper left part of the screen, and then select "Open level."

Now you are back to the box labeled Choose Project. The word WRE-DEMO should already be typed for you, so just click Accept. Next, you will be asked to select a level from a scrolling list. Click Intro.wld, and then click Accept (see Figure 12.10).

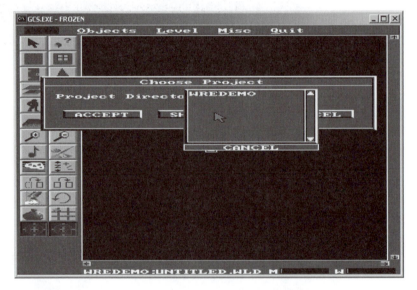

FIGURE 12.10 Opening a level that is stored in a project folder.

When the level opens, you will see in the viewport a top-down view of the level, like the plan of a house. The yellow lines are walls, and the blue squares are inventory items. The little yellow squares are enemy guards.

View Mode

If you want to see what each wall actually looks like, click on the icon in the top row that looks like a question mark and a little box (Figure 12.11). Next, move the mouse pointer around on the level. As the little white line jumps around from wall section to wall section, a picture of that wall ap-

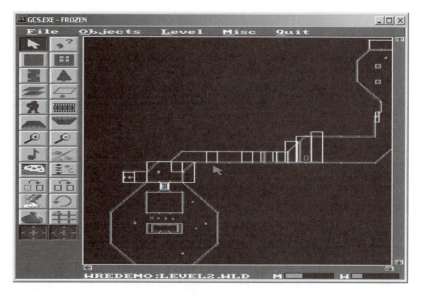

FIGURE 12.11   Looking at the walls in your level in View mode.

pears in the lower left of the screen. This is one way around the fact that you are looking down on your level and can't actually be in it to see the third dimension.

Now, click the right mouse button to get out of View mode. Notice that when you are in View mode, the question mark icon stays depressed, letting you know that you are in View mode. When you click on the right mouse button you will leave View mode and enter Selection mode. The big arrow icon is now depressed. You can use the arrow keys to scroll the top view around. The keypad + and – keys zoom in and out, respectively.

Test the Level

Before you modify the level, it would be fun to jump into the 3D world to see this level in 3D.

1. Pull down the File menu, and select "Test level."
2. A red box comes up asking if you want sound. If you have a sound card, press Yes.
3. Another box comes up that asks if you want to test the game in God mode. *God mode* is a term used to mean that the player is impervious to damage. This can be useful for testing purposes. Click either Yes or No.

The screen should now change back to the Windows desktop as the Windows game engine starts up. Since the game engine will use Microsoft's Direct X/Direct 3D, the program must select which Direct X drivers and which video mode to use. The first time you start up the game engine, the program will try to choose the drivers and best mode automatically. Sometimes it cannot, and you will be prompted to make selections. Once those are answered, you should have a dialog box on your screen with your name and address on it, as shown in Figure 12.12.

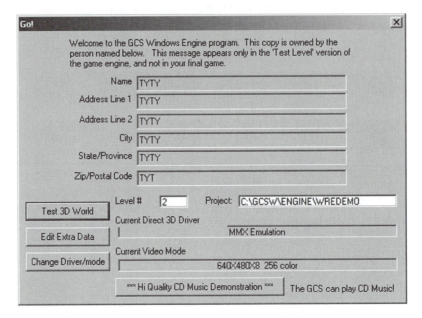

FIGURE 12.12 The options screen that you see the first time you run the 3D engine.

HINT!

In the next chapter, we will talk in greater detail about choosing drivers and screen resolutions for optimal performance.

In addition, there will be three buttons available; right now, you want to press Test 3D World. The 3D game engine will then start, and you will be in the 3D world. If you receive an error message, or something else goes wrong, the problem is probably quite easy to fix. See the troubleshooting section at the end of Chapter 18.

Entering the 3D World
HINT!

When you first run GCS, it will choose a screen resolution for you that will most likely work but may not be the best your video card can do. If the 3D world screen appears to be low resolution, don't worry. Later, we will look at how to run and fine-tune your setup.

Once you are in the 3D world, you can move around with the arrow keys or the keypad arrow keys. Press the space bar to fire your weapon, or the Esc key to exit the 3D world.

F1 brings up a help screen. The mouse can also move the pointer; move it left or right to turn, move it down to go backward. You can press the left mouse button to fire the weapon, and the right mouse button moves you forward at a fast rate. If you press Esc or are killed, the 3D world will end. Depending on how the game play ends, the game engine may exit altogether, or you may just return to the desktop, with the game engine program open on the desktop.

Returning to the Editor

When the game play ends, you can get back to the world editor by finding the DOS prompt window, which will be blank or show the words "Press a key to start DOS editor." If the title bar at the top of the window is gray, click on it with the mouse to make it the top window again, and then press the space bar to go back to the Level Editor.

WATCHOUT!

Whenever you come back to the game engine after testing a level, the Level Editor will always be waiting in a DOS prompt box. It is **very** important that you restart the Level Editor rather than launch GCS again using the Start menu (or desktop icon). If you do restart GCS, you will have two copies of the GCS Level Editor running, which will lead to a crash, and possibly the loss of your level. If you are not sure if the Level Editor is already running, look on your task bar on the bottom of your Windows desktop. If you see a GCSWE button with the MSDOS logo on the left, it means that the Level Editor is already running. Click on it to bring it up so you can press the space bar and return to the Level Editor.

ACTIVITIES

As an activity for this chapter, make sure that GCS is installed and running properly. Before we move on and start making games in GCS, it would be wise to turn off your computer, restart it, and make sure that GCS runs properly.

SUMMARY

Now that we have poked around GCS a little bit and it's installed on your system, let's look at getting it to run as efficiently as possible on your system. In the next chapter, we look at and learn more about the technology behind the GCS 3D engine and your computer.

Running the GCS Game Engine

IN THIS CHAPTER

- Using the Setup Screens
- Choosing a Drawing Device
- Using the Level Editor

We will spend this chapter exploring all the options for setting up and running the GCS 3D engine on your system. Setting up the engine to run at its best on your system can be confusing, so we will look at the various options and technologies in detail here. Don't let this chapter overwhelm you. Perhaps the best way to use this chapter is if you really need (or want) to use it to speed things up. If you are happy with the default settings of GCS and it runs well on your system, then skim this chapter and come back to it later.

HINT!

This chapter teaches you how to work with and move between the Windows and DOS environments.

As we said earlier, GCS is a Windows program; however, the rest of GCS is based in DOS. When we switch from the DOS Editor to the Windows 3D engine, we are switching operating systems—making a big move in terms of how we should work on our computer. In The Games Factory, we were always in the same territory, and no matter how complex things may have gotten, we could always do one operation to return to the main screen or exit the application. In GCS, we have to remember that we are jumping from DOS to Windows. You have to start the Level Editor from the DOS box or window and return to it the same way. If you ever close the DOS window instead of going into the editor to save your work, you will lose your work.

STARTING UP THE GCS WINDOWS ENGINE

Run GCS as we reviewed in the last chapter: Start menu | Programs | GCSWE (group) | GCSWE (see Figure 13.1).

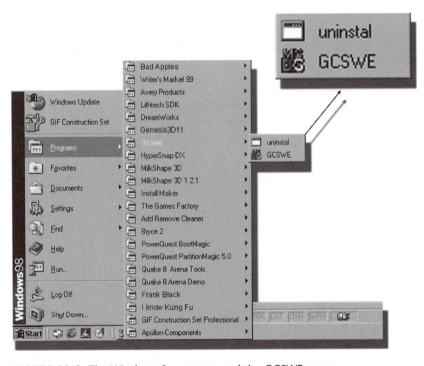

FIGURE 13.1 The Windows Start menu and the GCSWE group.

Use the Level Editor commands to open the WREDEMO project, and then open the INTRO.WLD level. Go to the File menu and select "Test level." At this point, the DOS editor will close and the GCS Windows Engine (GCSWE) will start up.

HINT!

If the Windows engine does not seem to start up after 10 seconds or so, it is possible that Windows decided to start the game engine behind your DOS prompt window. If so, you must bring the window to the top by minimizing the other windows on your desktop.

IMPORTANT DOS BOX NOTES

The DOS boxes, when running in Windows, can operate in two modes: full screen or in a window. The Level Editor always runs full screen. What we are concerned with now is how the DOS prompt box looks when the editor halts temporarily to display the message "Press a key to start the DOS editor." If your DOS prompt box is running in full-screen mode when displaying that text message, press Ctrl + Esc (hold down the Ctrl key and then press Esc) to return to the desktop. Then, right-click on the MS-DOS prompt task bar button on the bottom of the screen to change the screen properties to "Window" (see Figure 13.2).

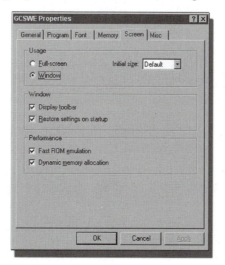

FIGURE 13.2   The GCS Properties Screen tab.

If you are still in full-screen DOS mode after selecting "Test level" and you see the message "Press any key to start level editor," you will need to change a setting in the properties of the DOS prompt box as described earlier.

FINDING THE BEST SETUP FOR THE 3D ENGINE

When you run GCS for the first time, you will see the Windows window shown in Figure 13.3.

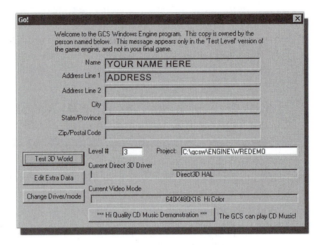

FIGURE 13.3   The Windows option window that comes up the first time you run the GCS 3D engine.

Let GCS select what it thinks is best and run the world.

Once you enter the 3D game world, you will notice a yellow number in the upper part of the screen. It appears only when testing levels, not in the final game. This is the fps number, or frames per second display. Anything over 10 fps is pretty good, and the game will play fairly well. If the fps dips below 5, it may start to get a little difficult to control your motion. We want to get this number as high as possible.

We will look at all the options available to you to make the GCS engine run as well as possible on your system. Try a variety of video modes and Direct 3D devices to find the combination that works best for you.

HINT!

A good portion of game design and development—especially level editing—is spent balancing the technology, user base machines, amount and size of the art and world geometry, and other factors to make the best game possible. Some games call for huge worlds with little geometry; others may call for small rooms with highly detailed art and models.

THE SETUP OPTIONS

The GCS game engine relies heavily on Microsoft's Direct 3D (D3D). Microsoft developed a set of prewritten code libraries with certain functions that are repeatedly used by games: drawing geometry, handling the textures and art, and so forth. When any of these redundant tasks are needed by GCS, the program calls them. Since GCS relies on D3D, we will be looking at the different modes of operation, full-screen modes, and the best setup for all of these options. The GCS Windows engine tries to make these selections for you, when you run it for the first time, based on what is most likely to work. However, in some cases, the program cannot decide which is best or you may want to experiment to get the best performance.

Selecting a DirectDraw Device

To select a DirectDraw Device:

1. Start up GCS by using the "Test level" command on the WRE-DEMO Intro level.
2. When the game engine dialog box with three buttons appears, click Change Driver/Mode. This button just makes the dialog box go away so that you can access the program's pull-down menu. You can now change the DirectDraw Device (see Figure 13.4).
3. Go to the File menu of the game engine, and choose "Select DD Device." On most computers, there is only one choice, so this should be simple. However, the selection box does let you see some of the features of your video card, such as whether it has hardware acceleration and how much video RAM Direct X thinks the card has.

On computers that have a piggyback-type hardware accelerator, there will be two choices. Some 3D accelerator cards, such as the Diamond Monster and Monster II, connect to your old video card without replacing

FIGURE 13.4 The Direct Draw Device dialog box.

it. If you have such a device, you will see more than one listing in the DD selection box. One will be your old unaccelerated card, usually called Display. The other will be the accelerated device, called 3DFX or something else. Choosing the accelerated device is usually the way to go. The only time you might want to try the Display device is if you are having trouble with the accelerated device and want to try slower software emulation to isolate a problem. You can also use this option when testing your game to see how it will run on a slower system without 3D hardware.

HINT!

When you make a change to your DD device, your options for the other choices will probably change as well. Therefore, after you change your DD device, you must then change the D3D device and the video mode.

CHOOSING A DIRECT 3D DEVICE

Microsoft's Direct 3D allows you to select from a list of 3D drivers. Even though the game engine tries to make the best decision for you automatically, you may want to change it. Go to the File menu and choose "Select D3D Device." The number of options here depends on your computer and your video card (see Figure 13.5).

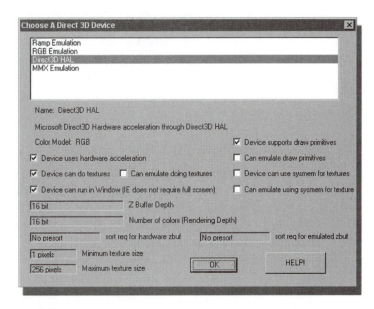

FIGURE 13.5   The Select D3D Device window.

Here are the most common choices.

HAL. This device represents your 3D acceleration hardware. It is usually (but not always!) the driver that gives you the best performance. However, it is also the most likely to suffer from incompatibilities. If something seems wrong with the graphics, try the Ramp driver. In addition, some 3D accelerators (e.g., the S3 Virge) actually run slower than the software drivers. If the software drivers mentioned here work fine, but the HAL driver messes up, send an e-mail to Pie Software with your exact video card, and they will try to resolve the incompatibility.

Ramp. If you choose this device, all of the 3D graphic computations will be done in software, and your hardware acceleration will not be used. Microsoft seems to be phasing out the Ramp driver, so if you have Direct X 6.0 or later installed on your machine, it might be better to try the MMX or RGB software drivers if your HAL driver does not run correctly.

MMX. This device uses multimedia extensions built into your CPU to accelerate the 3D graphics. If you don't have a HAL driver, try both this driver and the Ramp driver to see which one works better for you. If you have Direct X version 6.0 installed, the MMX driver may also use the 3D acceleration.

RGB. RGB is a software 3D graphics device like RAMP and MMX. Try this one and compare it to RAMP and MMX on your system.

The full-screen video modes that are possible change when you change the D3D device. Therefore, you will automatically go into the Video Mode selection box if you change your D3D device.

CHOOSING SCREEN SIZE

Your video hardware has the capability to change the resolution of your screen, as we talked about in Part One of this book. If you remember, the more dots, the sharper and larger the image, which takes more resources to display—more RAM and computer time to draw the 3D graphics. Although high-resolution screens look good, they may cause your computer to fail if it runs out of video memory or if it becomes too bogged down because there is too much information for it to handle. Low-resolution images are less refined, but they require less work from the computer. See Figure 13.6 for the screen size selection window.

You will remember that screen resolution is measured in width and height. A screen with a resolution of 640x480 has 640 dots from left to right, and 480 dots up and down; the total number of pixels being (640 × 480 = 307,200).

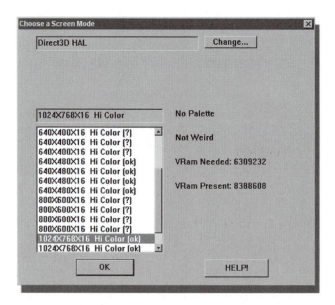

FIGURE 13.6   The screen size selection window.

We are also concerned with color depth here. The lowest number of colors that GCS can work with is 256. This is called either "256-color mode" or "8-bit color mode." GCS can work with 8-bit color, but in some cases the colors won't look exactly right. Sixteen-bit color is probably the best choice. It gives you 65,535 colors, which are plenty for excellent graphics, and it only uses twice as much video RAM as 8-bit color does.

The most common mode for using the GCS is 640x480x16, which means a 640x480 resolution screen with 16-bit color. Keep in mind the difference between art and images for the game and the display mode. We are talking about display mode here.

HINT!

There are also 32-bit color modes, which offer 16 million colors, but in practice, this looks no different from the 16-bit color modes and uses twice as much video RAM. However, this shouldn't be a problem if you have a video card with lots of RAM (12MB or more).

It is actually a bit of a mystery as to which video modes Direct X will make available. With some video cards, there are over 50 modes from which to choose; on others, there are only three. Try to stick with the most common ones at first. The most likely to work are 640x480x16 and 320x200x16.

You can experiment with the other modes if you wish, but working with the common modes should suffice.

HINT!

Although GCS runs in 8-bit color modes (256 colors), certain colors may be drawn incorrectly. The 16-bit color modes are better if you can use them. The 8-bit color modes have the advantage that they use much less video memory.

The top selection of the video mode list is the Windowed option. If this is selected, GCS will run in a window on the Windows desktop. In this case, the color depth is not adjustable from within GCS. If your Windows screen is set to 256 colors, GCS will have to run in 256-color mode. If you really want to run in a window on the desktop, you can change the resolution and color depth by exiting GCS and the Level Editor, and then right-clicking on the desktop and choosing Properties. From there, you can go to the Settings tab to change the main screen resolution and color depth (see Figure 13.7).

FIGURE 13.7   The Settings tab in the Windows Properties dialog box.

HINT!

Using the Windowed screen mode with 256 colors is not recommended. Direct 3D does not appear to do such a great job with palette management, and most of your colors will be inaccurate. This appears to be a Direct X weakness, because Microsoft's own demos exhibit this behavior when running windowed in 256 colors.

If Performance Is Terrible in All Modes

Since Pie in the Sky has made sure that the frame rate is decent on an old 120MHz Pentium with no hardware acceleration, you may have a problem with your system ID if it is a better one than this and still runs poorly or you over designed your game. The next suggested step is to consider a new computer or 3D hardware card; the best bet is probably a new 3D card. If you are running an older Pentium class computer without a 3D card, getting one will greatly improve your performance. Of course, more RAM will help as well, as we discussed in the beginning of the book.

HINT!

For a list of video cards that work well with GCS, see www.pieskysoft.com.

WINDOWS ENGINE GAME OPTIONS

When you test your level and the Windows engine starts, you have access to an Options menu that allows you to make changes affecting control of the game and the graphics quality.

To use these options during 3D game play, press and release the Alt key, and then use the mouse or arrow keys to choose the option you want. When you press Enter or click on the desired option, you will automatically return to 3D game play. See Figure 13.8 for the pull-down menu of options.

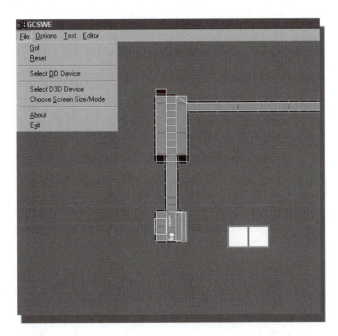

FIGURE 13.8   The pull-down menu of options for the Windows engine.

HINT!

 Some menu options, including changing screen size or driver, will not operate unless you pause the 3D game first by selecting Reset from the File menu. To resume your game, select Go from the File menu after you are finished using the menu.

Horizon Bitmap

The game engine can display a bitmap horizon or sky bitmap in the distance when you start using the Extra Features Editor. This option can enable or disable the horizon you have set. Turning it off can increase performance.

Wall Bumping (Collision Detection)

Ordinarily, walls are treated as solid by the game engine; in other words, you cannot pass through them. However, with this option you can make the walls so that you are able to walk through them. Even though in the game you will probably want most walls solid, during the testing of your level it is convenient to turn off wall bumping so you can go directly through walls to get from place to place quickly.

FPS Display (Frames Per Second)

This turns the Frames Per Second display on and off (the yellow number in the upper left of your screen). Some people find the number very distracting when trying to see how the game will look to the end user.

Correct Orientation

Leave this off! This option was for the DOS game engine.

Bilinear Filtering

This option performs a smoothing operation on the pixels in your screen's image. Although bilinear filtering can make a level look much nicer, on some video cards it can cost you significant performance, and on many others it has no measurable effect. Moreover, on some video cards it tends to make dark outlines around the enemies and other shaped objects. You will have to experiment to see what works best on your card.

Bilinear filtering can be turned on and off before or during 3D game play.

Dithering Enable

As with bilinear filtering, Dithering Enable can change the quality of your graphics, but at a potential price. Try turning it on and off to see which effect you prefer.

Object Presort

Some video cards (i.e., some hardware accelerated ones) draw black rectangles around enemies, objects, door frames, and other objects that use transparency. Turning on Object Presort should eliminate the problem if it arises.

Brightness

If your monitor is too dark to show walls and textures very well, you can use this option as a last resort. It only works when you change the setting *before* you start up the 3D world. Many video cards today come with their own utilities for boosting brightness that work very well, so use the GCS option only as a last resort. It increases brightness, but at a price, as your colors become washed out.

Joystick

This option allows you to select or enable a joystick device. To calibrate your joystick, use the Windows control panel, and adjust the properties.

Mouse

This option allows you to select or enable mouse control. In the unlikely event that there are two or more mice on your system, you can select the one you want to use with the Select option. You can also change the sensitivity in the x and y directions. You can hold down the right mouse button for forward motion, which is more convenient than walking forward by pushing the mouse forward.

STARTING UP THE 3D WORLD

After you have selected your devices, video mode, and the options that work best for you, start up the 3D world by going to the File menu and selecting Go. You will do this many times in the process of making all these choices.

Returning to the Level Editor

The Esc key exits the game engine when you want to return to the Level Editor. If you are using a nonstandard mode (not 320x200 or 640x480), you may be asked if the video mode worked well or not. This is so GCS can keep track of which modes don't work well on your system and remind you if you try to use them again.

When you exit the game engine, Windows should return you to a DOS prompt box, and there should be a message that reads "Press any key to start the DOS editor." Now that you are returning from using the Windows game engine, press the space bar to restart the editor.

If you exit from the Windows game engine and you don't return to the Level Editor as you would expect, and you don't see the Level Editor window on the desktop, check the task bar that runs along the bottom of your screen. Each program that runs in Windows has a little block on the task bar, as shown in Figure 13.9.

One of those blocks should be your Level Editor, which is still running, but is halted until you restore it to full screen by pressing the space bar.

HINT!

If the window with the message "Press a key to start DOS editor" is on the screen, but it ignores your key presses, then probably that window is not the active window. Click on the title of the window once with the mouse to make sure the window title is blue, not gray. Then, try pressing the space bar again.

FIGURE 13.9   The Windows task bar and the running applications.

WATCHOUT!

Whatever you do, *do not* go to the Start menu to restart GCS if you still have a copy of the Level Editor running! This will crash your computer, and you may lose your level design! Make sure the Level Editor isn't running by looking at your task bar at the bottom of the screen before you try to start a new one from the Start menu!

ACCESSING THE MENU WHEN THE GAME IS RUNNING

If you are running the game engine in a full screen mode, there is no mouse pointer. However, if you would like to access the menu, you can press and release the Alt key. The game play will halt and a menu will appear. After you make your selection, the menu will disappear, and the 3D game play will continue.

HINT!

Some menu commands require that the 3D game be paused first by selecting Reset in the File menu.

GETTING BACK TO THE DESKTOP TEMPORARILY

If you are in full-screen mode, you can go back to the desktop while halting the GCS by pressing and releasing the Alt key, and then selecting Reset from the File menu. When you wish to return to game play, select Go in the File menu. Sometimes this fails, because Direct X cannot regain control of the keyboard.

CHANGING SCREEN MODE DURING GAME PLAY

It is possible to change the screen mode during game play.

1. Press Alt and release it to bring up the menu.
2. Next, select Reset from the File menu. This stops GCS.
3. Choose Screen Size/Mode from the File menu. Select a new video mode, and then press OK. At this point, you can then select Go from the File menu to restart the 3D world where you left it.

ACTIVITIES

For this chapter, your activity will be to make sure that GCS is installed and running properly—again. In this chapter, we took further steps in setting up and running GCS, and before we move on and start making a game, it would be wise to turn off your computer, restart it, and make sure that GCS runs properly. Review the sections of this chapter and be sure you understand them.

SUMMARY

Well, that was the whirlwind tour of probably the most tedious part of GCS, and we can now focus more on making the game world. While these aspects are a bit tedious, they are very important to the overall quality of your game—how well it looks and runs. The effort spent here will ensure that you can make a game that pushes the limits in terms of quality and performance. Moreover, knowing all the terms and technology described in this chapter will be very useful if you plan to move up to a more complex development environment in the future.

In the next chapter, we look closer at the 3D Game World Editor.

Looking Deeper into the 3D Editor

IN THIS CHAPTER
• • • • • • • • • • • • • • •

- Creating Special Effects, such as Fog
- Adding Music
- Creating "Project Files"

In this chapter, we look at the various options of the Level Editor in greater depth. Although there are figures that illustrate what you can do, you may want to start playing with the icons and changing a level. This is often the best way to learn. If you do this, be sure to make a copy of the level first by selecting the Save option in the File menu. However, instead of just accepting the name level, you can save it as another name by selecting Save As… . Now you are free to modify a level without the worry of losing the original level.

HINT!
• •

In general, the right mouse click should get you out of most active functions.

THE SELECT AND VIEW ICONS

The Select icon is the arrow button (Figure 14.1). When you choose it, you are ready to select objects from the viewport to move, copy, elevate, rotate, and so forth. This is the "top level" of GCS, which means that on completion or cancellation of most commands, you automatically return to this "select"mode.

The next icon with the question mark is the View icon. When you click on this, you go into View mode. Then, as you move around on the viewport, you can see what the walls look like by watching the lower left corner of the screen (see Figure 14.2).

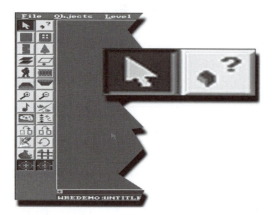

FIGURE 14.1   The main screen of the Level Editor, and the Select and View icons.

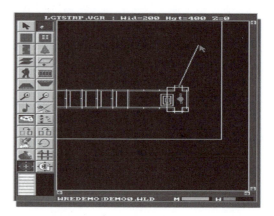

FIGURE 14.2   The Level Editor View mode.

OBJECT PLACING ICONS

You click on these icons when you want to add a new object to your 3D level. The Object Placing icons are shown in Figure 14.3.

- The **Brick Wall** icons add walls to your levels.
- The **Windowed Wall** icon is for walls that have black pixels; the black will be treated as clear or invisible in the 3D world (color masking). If you make a wall with a black rectangle in the middle, the wall will have a window cut out through which the player can see.
- The **Door** icon is not really a placing icon; it operates on walls you have already placed. If you select a wall and then click this icon, it

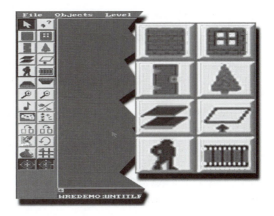

FIGURE 14.3   The Object Placing icons.

will assign to that wall the properties of a door. We look at doors in detail in a later chapter.

- The **Tree** icon is for placing stand-up objects such as trees or lamps in your level. These are taken from a library.
- The **Flat Squares** icon is for solid-color floor/ceiling polygons.
- The **Wire Frame** square icon is for placing platforms.
- The **Person** icon is for placing enemies chosen from a library.
- The **Film** icon is for placing animated objects that you have already created and put into your library.

We go into greater detail about these icons in a later chapter. Each one has further options and properties that allow design control in your game.

MAGNIFY ICONS

The Magnify icons (Figure 14.4) are for zooming in and out on your top-view layout. The + magnifying glass zooms in, and the – magnifying glass zooms out. When you click on one of these icons, you enter Magnify mode. Each left-click zooms you in (or out) again. The location of your mouse pointer, when you click the button, is where the new screen center will be.

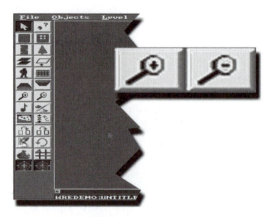

FIGURE 14.4 The Magnify icons.

FADING TABLE ICON (FOG)

First, the bad news: you must choose the color black.

Normally you would click on this icon (Figure 14.5) to set the fading color for this level, a color that your level will fade to as the light recedes. Choosing white would look like fog, and choosing red would not look right, but currently, you have to choose black. With the DOS game engine it was possible to change the color that the level faded to with distance, but this is not possible with the Windows game engine because of limitations of Microsoft's Direct X/Direct 3D 5.0.

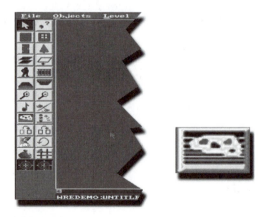

FIGURE 14.5 The Fading Table icon—you must choose black.

EDITING ICONS

The Editing icons all perform their operations on items that you have se-lected while in Select mode (see Figure 14.6).

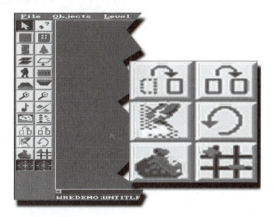

FIGURE 14.6   The Editing icons. Objects must be selected to be affected.

- The top icon is the Set Elevation icon. This is for moving your walls up and down.
- The Move icon is for moving groups of objects.
- The Copy icon is for copying objects. It works the same as the Move icon, except that it leaves the original objects where they were and makes a copy somewhere else.
- The Eraser icon is for removing objects.
- The Circular Arrow icon is for rotating groups of objects by 90-de-gree increments.
- The Bag icon is not really an Editing icon; it belongs with the Placing icons and is used for placing inventory items. As for why it isn't in with the Placing icons, when asked, Pie in the Sky defers to Ralph Waldo Emerson: "A foolish consistency is the hobgoblin of little minds." We will talk more about Editing icons and inventory items later in the book.

FLOOR/CEILING ICONS

Do not use these! These icons were for creating a floor or ceiling in the GCS DOS version (see Figure 14.7). The floor/ceiling capabilities of GCS

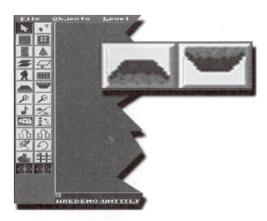

FIGURE 14.7 The Floor/Ceiling icons. Do not use these in the DOS Editor.

have been greatly improved and extended, and these buttons are now obsolete. We will look at how to put down floors and ceilings in Chapter 17, "The Extra Features Editor."

GRID ICONS

The grid is covered in more detail later. The icon that looks like a tic-tac-toe board (Figure 14.8) sets the grid spacing, usually 100, 200, or 400. This setting doesn't affect wall-placing grids, but it does affect grids for placing trees and other stand-up objects. It sets the grid for the editing commands.

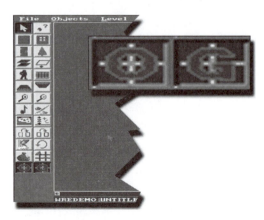

FIGURE 14.8 The Grid icons.

- The O icon toggles the snap-to-object features.
- The G icon toggles the snap-to-grid features.

MUSIC ICON

You can add music to your level by clicking on the Music icon (Figure 14.9). You can specify a suitable midi file that exists in a directory, or play midi music from a CD. We will talk about making sound later.

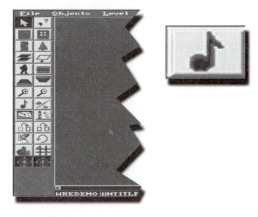

FIGURE 14.9   The Music icon.

Now that you have been introduced to and looked around GCS (you even entered a 3D game world and then came back to the editor), we can move on to the next step, creating game project files. You will avoid many problems if you set up your game files correctly.

CREATING GAME PROJECT FILES

New games in GCS are kept in separate directories called project directories. Each project is an entire game and can have multiple levels. For example, you might have a project or game that features a haunted house and call it "HAUNTED," and then have many levels such as "cemetery," "floor-1," "dungeon," and "attic."

The first thing you do when you create a new game is to tell GCS the name of your project or game. A project directory then created for you. To start a new project, start from the DOS command line and run GCS.

The first dialog box asks you to select a project. If you want to make a new one, just click on the Name box, and make up a name for your new project that is eight or fewer characters. Then, either press Enter, or click Accept.

HINT!

For those of you not familiar with DOS, you are limited to eight or fewer letters or numbers in all filenames.

When you press Accept, GCS then creates a directory on your hard drive filled with files that the 3D engine needs for the 3D world you are about to detail. This directory has the same name as your project. For example, if you made a project called myproj, then a new directory would be created. Assuming you installed GCS in the directory c:\p3dgcs, this would be the full name of the project directory: c:\gcsw\engine\myproj.

Many files are put in this project directory. These include the picture files for your game's background, the damage indicator artwork, and so on. At the beginning, these files are stock or default entities. Once you create your directory, you may edit these files to customize the game. We will do this in a later chapter.

Next, GCS asks you to pick a palette for your new game. A palette is a set of colors. $rp9a.pal is the general-purpose palette. $rp9a will probably suit your needs for most applications.

In GCS, each set of artwork is kept in a separate directory on your hard drive. All the object libraries and enemy directories are specific to certain palettes, or color sets. If you try to mix images from different palettes, the colors will be wrong, and the enemies, walls, or whatever will come out looking like fluorescent soup. This is because GCS uses 256-color artwork for efficiency.

We discussed the various color palettes in Part One, and this is where you will need that knowledge the most. The images in GCS are not only limited to 256 colors, they are limited to the same 256 colors for the entire level—pretty limiting, but it helps the engine run faster. Although you are limited to 256 colors, the engine actually uses thousands of colors because it creates shades of the colors you have selected.

You may want to think about your palette a bit before building all the artwork. Since you are limited in colors and shades of colors, you should decide whether to use a lot of reds and oranges for a volcano, blacks and browns for a haunted house, or blues and whites for an icy level. This sort of planning and color scheming allows your artwork to have a great deal of subtle variation in color.

To keep together artwork that uses the same palette, there is a separate master directory for each palette. The enemy directories and object libraries are all kept in directories that are inside the master palette directory on your hard drive. Once you choose a palette for a project, there is no way to change it. Since you cannot change a palette without re-matching every piece of artwork in your game, it is always easier to start a new project.

Your new palette directory name should appear when you click the Show List button when choosing a palette. Since your palette file has nothing in it, the first thing you must do is create a new weapon set, a new guard set, and a new library directory. All these sets must be in your palette directory in order for you to make a game that uses your new palette. Your new palette directory has no artwork in it, so you will have to either copy some .VGR files into your newly created library file and import them, or palette match some from the other palette directories and import those.

Once you have selected which palette to use for your project, you are asked to choose an object library. Unlike the palette choice, you can switch libraries at any time. Object libraries are just what they sound like: directories filled with artwork images. Object libraries also have a system for storing the sizes of an object.

Choose any library from the list. You can browse through the libraries in your palette directory easily, adding a wall from one library and then switching to another. After selecting the library, you are left facing a blank world from the top view. The little box in the middle of the screen is the default player starting position, in the exact middle of the level.

GCS rejects a project with no levels. Therefore, when it creates a new project, it creates an empty level named "untitled." You can start editing right away. When you've created something you want to keep, click Save to save the level with a real name. You cannot save your level with the name "untitled."

PUTTING WALLS AND OBJECTS IN A LEVEL

All the trees, enemies, and wall pieces that make up the 3D world are called *objects*. Rooms and hallways must be made from fixed-length sections of textured wall. It is easy to predefine the sizes of textured walls or other objects, but that will be discussed later. The point is that doing your

3D layout is simply a matter of selecting the object you want to place and then placing it.

WATCHOUT!

You must have at least one solid wall in your level, or you will receive an error message when you "Test level." Be sure to place at least one wall section before attempting to run the game engine.

Putting Walls into Your Layout

Now we are ready to lay out a test room. To get started right away, just click on the Solid Brick Wall icon. Then, select a wall texture from the scrolling list. As you move the mouse over the items on the list (without clicking), pictures of walls will appear to the right of the scroll box. When you find one you like, click on the name in the scrolling list. When you click on the name, you are then in Place mode. The menu bar at the top of the screen goes away, and a text message appears telling you to choose an anchor point for your wall. In addition, a grid appears in the viewport to help you align your walls. As you move your mouse around on the viewport, you are dragging your wall around. See Figure 14.10 for the Wall Selection menu.

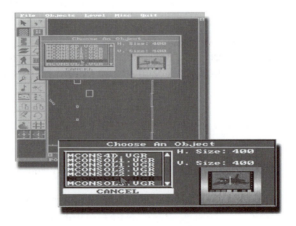

FIGURE 14.10 The Wall Selection menu. Notice the wall in the lower left.

HINT!

 Unlike other programs, you do not hold the mouse button down to drag things. As you drag the wall around, it always hangs in an east-facing orientation. You first must left-click to fasten the lower end of the wall to the grid. Now you will see another wall section following the mouse and attached to the first wall you put down.

After placing a wall, you have three options.

- Get out of Wall-Placing mode with two right-clicks. This leaves your first wall but cancels the second one that is pending placement.
- Detach the new wall section with one right-click. Then, you can drag it around, ready to place a new wall somewhere else in your level.
- Choose a direction for the new wall, and left-click to make it permanent. After doing this, you should have two walls that are attached.

When starting a new layout, you should make big rooms and hallways that all have the same wall type. Thus, you would choose the third option. You can always go back later, delete a wall here and there, and replace it with another type for variation and customization.

Move Around in Zoom Mode

A thing to remember about Place mode is that you can scroll up, down, or side to side by clicking on either of the Magnifying Glass icons. If you want to move your view of your level, click on one of the Magnifying Glass icon; the cursor turns into a cross. Clicking the left mouse button zooms you in or out, depending on which icon you selected. The + icon zooms you in, and the – icon zooms you out. When you are in Magnify mode, the magnify buttons remain down. You can also use the cursor keys or the keypad + and – keys to zoom in and out. You can exit Magnify mode by right-clicking on the mouse, which puts you back in Place mode.

Putting Up Trees and Other Stand-up Items

The other icon is a brick wall with a window on it. It is used for walls that have holes in them, such as a wall with a window or a fence with a rough top. Placing these objects in your level is the same as placing the solid walls.

The third tool icon in GCS is for drawing stand-up objects, such as trees, floor lamps, and so forth. These are shaped objects that look the same from every direction. When you click on the icon, you are presented with a list of object names (see Figure 14.11). Moving the mouse pointer across the list shows the images in the lower left-hand corner of the screen. Choosing one item puts you in Place mode.

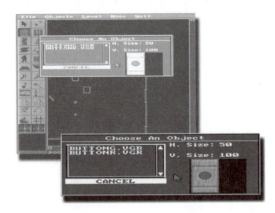

FIGURE 14.11   The Object Placement window.

This Place mode is a little different, though. The direction doesn't matter for these stand-up items since they always rotate to face you. Therefore, there is no reason to anchor one end first and then swing it to the proper direction. These are called *anchored sprites*.

To place the stand-up objects, drag the square to the place you want, and left-click to place it. The square shows a rough representation of the horizontal width of the stand-up object so you can judge its distance from walls. Once you left-click to place the stand-up, another potential stand-up square appears attached to your mouse pointer. You can drag and place this one, or you can right-click to exit Place mode.

HINT!

Usually you should turn off the grid before you decide to click on the Tree icon. When placing things such as floor lamps, wastebaskets, and so forth, the grid is usually more of a hindrance than a help. You can click on the Grid icon to toggle the snap-to-grid feature on and off.

Solid Color Horizontal Panels

3D GCS can have texture-mapped floors and ceilings, which we will discuss when we talk about the Extra Features Editor in Chapter 17. Use this button when you want to make a horizontal surface that is not a floor or a ceiling (e.g., a table top).

Click on the Tool icon that looks like two purple sheets suspended in the air. Choose a color from the color box that pops up. Click twice to specify the corners of the rectangular floor areas that you want covered. You can also adjust the elevation of this surface.

Platforms

Platforms are rectangular areas in the 3D world that sense the presence of the player. One of the most common uses of a platform is to raise the player when he or she steps on one. Another function is to use the platform as a trigger for a teleport device to another level. In fact, this is how most level switches are implemented with GCS.

HINT!

The rectangular platforms are, by default, not drawn; they are invisible. Usually they are placed right in front of tunnels or staircases. When the player walks up to the staircase, the game switches levels as if he or she had traversed the staircase.

As mentioned earlier, another common use is to raise the player. Let's say you create a box out of wall panels, and you want the player to be able to jump up on the box and stand there. Without a platform, the player would sink right down into the box instead of standing on top of it. The box must have a platform over it so that when the player is within the platform's boundary, his or her feet are lifted to the height of the platform's z value.

CREATING A PLATFORM

To create and place a platform object, click on the Tool icon that looks like a suspended square wire frame (see Figure 14.12).

A dialog box appears with some options (Figure 14.13). You can set the platform to be visible; this puts a floor polygon in the same place as

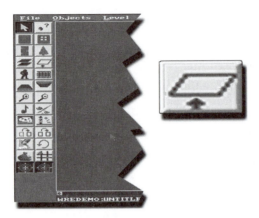

FIGURE 14.12   The Platform icon.

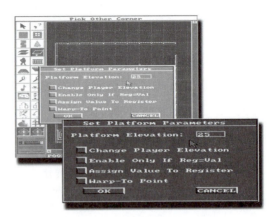

FIGURE 14.13   The Platform Options dialog box.

the platform. If you choose to do this, you will be asked to pick a color and choose the function of the platform. Warping to a different level is a common one. If you select this, you must know the entry point number of the destination level. Don't worry if you don't know what an entry point is; we discuss it later.

Putting In the Bad Guys

Placing enemy characters is as easy as placing stand-up objects. You get a dialog box of options for each enemy, and when you are finished, you click OK and are put into Place mode. You are then asked to choose a direction for the enemy to face (north is toward the top of the screen). After you decide on the facing direction, click where you want your enemy to be in your level.

HINT!

You should usually turn the grid off before placing enemies. Otherwise, the Layout Editor may place your enemies in the middle of walls when attempting to align your enemy with the grid.

After you place them, the enemies can be copied, moved, and rotated like any other object using the normal Copy, Move, and Rotate icons. However, there is a maximum number of 32 enemies on any one level.

As you learn more about the characters in GCS you will be able to control how the enemies patrol (randomly or centered in one spot) and other behaviors by setting their parameters. You can also change their appearance by editing their artwork files. We look at all these options in a later chapter.

ACTIVITIES

One of the most significant and fun things in this level is putting walls into your layout, and you should explore that more as an exercise. Load GCS and start laying out walls, as detailed in the section "Putting Walls into Your Layout." Remember, to get started right away, just click on the Solid Brick Wall icon in the Level Editor and then select a wall texture from the scrolling list. As you move the mouse over the items in the list (without clicking), pictures of walls appear to the right of the scroll box. When you find one you like, click on the name in the scrolling list. When you click on the name, you are then in Place mode. The menu bar at the top of the screen goes away, and a text message appears telling you to choose an anchor point for your wall. In addition, a grid appears in the viewport to help you align your walls. As you move your mouse around on the viewport, you drag your wall around. See Figure 14.10 for the Wall Selection menu. Have fun dragging out a game level in minutes.

SUMMARY

We learned how to place walls and objects in our game. If you have not done so already, you may want to run a test on a level. Drag out a few walls, select one wall, and click the Door icon to assign the door properties to it. Go with all of the default settings and then run your world. If you are unable to get your test level running, you may need to go back and try the options for running the 3D engine again; it may not be set up properly on your system.

Once you are comfortable with that, turn to the next chapter, where we start laying out a game level.

Making a 3D Game Level

IN THIS CHAPTER
· · · · · · · · · · · · · ·

- Creating Different Levels
- Evaluating Memory Capabilities
- Choosing and Moving Objects
- Creating Enemy Characters

Laying out a good game level is simple with GCS; in fact, you can drag them out in minutes. This chapter takes you through your first basic game level.

In this chapter, we lay down the most basic of game levels. We begin by placing the player's starting point. Then we set up the walls that make up the hallways and chambers of our level, adding a door or two. Finally, we populate the level with the enemies. Once you have gone through this basic process, you will be able to make larger and more complex game levels that you can attach to each other for a more complex game.

DESIGNING THE LEVEL

We start with a basic level, in which you enter through the front door (which is sealed behind you) and then proceed through the level, kill a few guards, and open a few doors to get to the last room.

PLACING THE FIRST WALL

Select the Wall icon. This brings up the menu from which we choose the art that goes on the wall we are about to place (see Figure 15.1).

We will use this first selected wall for the outer walls of the level. Most of the level will have the same walls. I selected a mossy rock wall, because it will make the level look as if it has been hewn out of solid rock on the outer walls. I selected a brownish brick wall for the inside walls so the player will get the feeling that the base was cut out of rock and the interior walls were finished in stone. This is also a design device to help the player feel oriented when wandering the level. I use these two basic walls for most of the level, and you can start filling in the floor plan by laying out walls when you are comfortable (see Figure 15.2).

Using grid snap, we will be able to make our level very quickly and all the walls will line up and close beautifully.

HINT!

Each level can contain a maximum number of 700 objects.

You can see that our level has a few twists and turns and can seem complicated, but the first thing that was done was simple. One huge

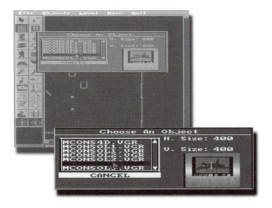

FIGURE 15.1   The menu for choosing the art for a wall.

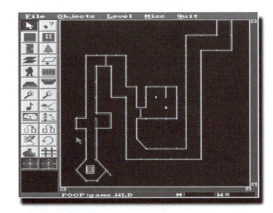

FIGURE 15.2   The floor plan of our test level.

room was built and the complexity was added after the second (finished stone) wall was selected.

WORKING WITH RAM LIMITS AND NUMBER OF OBJECT LIMITS

At the bottom of the Level Editor screen are two horizontal bars representing the M and W meters. These meters monitor the limits of your level size in two ways.

The RAM limitation while working with GCS is that all your artwork must fit into the video memory of the hardware accelerated video card that may be used. The more pixels in your artwork, the quicker your texture RAM is used up. The M bar meter at the bottom of the GCS screen shows how much texture RAM you have left. Note that the amount of texture RAM left is based on a typical customer with a 4MB HAL card; it does not reflect your own video card, since you'll want your game to run on all computers, not just your own.

THE M METER

Each time you add a new wall, the M meter increases. When the meter increases to the end, you cannot add any more different objects to your game without hearing warning beeps. Due to technical issues, the M meter is most accurate right after you come back from a test. If you have been adding and removing many objects, it can become inaccurate, thus requiring another "test" command.

HINT!

If GCS starts beeping at you, it is trying to warn you that you may have loaded too many unique pieces of artwork. You may ignore these warnings if your target machine has more than 4MB of video RAM. Currently, there is no way to turn this beeping off.

THE W METER

The W meter measures the number of objects you have placed in your 3D world. It is very different from the M meter because the W meter doesn't care whether you are placing a wall you have used before on that level. Any object placed into a 3D world counts as one object. A tiny key on the floor or a huge wall panel each count as one object. Adding an enemy, a platform, or a solid-color floor panel also counts as one object.

You cannot have more than 700 total objects on a level. When your W meter reaches its limit, you cannot add any more objects to your 3D world without removing another object.

EDITING YOUR 3D LEVELS

Once you have started laying out the walls of your level, you will undoubtedly want to start manipulating and editing the level to a greater degree. Here you will learn how to place walls and other objects and how to edit your layouts.

GRID SNAP

In making a room, it is very important to get your wall panels to butt up against each other perfectly. Gaps even 1 cm wide can result in unsightly bright lines between walls. This is the reason for grid snap. When using grid snap, your walls naturally line up along the grid; you don't have to worry about misalignment.

The only problem with grid snap is placing a wall halfway between the grid lines. Here, you need to go to the MISC pull-down menu and choose the command that aligns the grid to an object. This is very useful when working with walls of different sizes. Sometimes it is better to turn the grid off, and use object snap, as described next.

HINT!

When using very fine grids (50 units or smaller), you must turn off object snap, or the two effects will interfere with each other.

OBJECT SNAP

Object snap is very similar to grid snap, but it snaps new objects to existing walls rather than to a fixed grid. This is very handy when you need to join walls not aligned along a grid snap line. This may seem to make grid snap extraneous, but in reality, grid snap is better because it always lets you close rooms and hallways. If you mix different-sized wall sections, you can still manage to connect the walls with no gaps by using object snap instead of grid snap. However, you may have a problem when it comes time to close a room. When you mix wall sizes, you may find that there is no wall section that fits nicely in the leftover gap. If you use walls of 400 cm width and 400 cm grid spacing, you will never have this problem.

WATCHOUT!

You can always turn off both grid snap and object snap, and place your walls free form. You can actually get quite close by operating all the way zoomed in. If you try to make rooms and hallways this way, however, your errors will pile up as you place long strings of walls. Eventually, you will be faced with many nasty gaps between your walls that are next to impossible to repair.

SELECTING OBJECTS

It is very common to put down walls that you decide to remove later. The process of refining what you originally created is sometimes called *tweaking*. All the pros tweak their work, or pay attention to the details, and that is why their work looks so good. There are several things you can do to walls that have already been placed. These include moving, deleting, copying, rotating, raising, and lowering. Like many Windows programs you may have used, these functions are implemented in a two-step process. First, you select the objects on which to operate, and then you press the tool icon to make the action happen.

The Big Arrow icon in the upper left corner of the screen is the Selection tool. If you are not in the middle of placing a wall or some other action, then you are probably already in Selection mode. When you click on existing walls or objects while you are in Selection mode, red x's appear on those items. The little red x means that an object is selected. If you want to select many objects at once, you can either click on the center of each object, and "x" them one by one, or you can click where there is no object and "rubber-band" a rectangle around a whole region. See Figure 15.3 for selected and unselected objects.

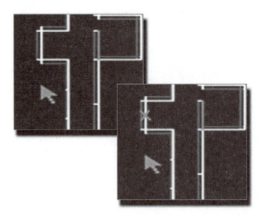

FIGURE 15.3   Selected and unselected objects
in the Level Editor View window.

HINT!

Object selection in GCS works differently than in other graphical programs you may have used. In other programs, clicking
on a second object after selecting a first causes the first one to
become deselected. In GCS, the more objects you click, the
more are selected. In addition, in many other programs, you
hold the left button down and drag the mouse while holding
the button down to make your selection rectangle. This is *not*
the way GCS works. To get the rectangle in GCS, you simply
left-click *once* in a spot where there are no objects nearby. A
rectangle is started. Then click again at the opposite corner of
the selection rectangle.

The real beauty of this selection system becomes evident when you
want to choose a few items that you *don't* want selected. If you left-click
again on an object that already has a red x on it, the red x vanishes, thus
deselecting the object. To move or copy nearly all the objects in a room,
draw a box around the entire room to select everything. Then, simply go
through and deselect the few objects that you don't want to include.

A right click cancels all the selected items. Most of the editing tools
leave the items selected. The right mouse button is great for quickly deselecting in case you don't have any further editing to do on those items.
The tools that need selected items are the icons in the bottom third of the
icon bar. The most commonly used icons are Move, Copy, Delete, and
Rotate.

MOVING WALLS OR ENTIRE ROOMS

To move some objects from one spot to another, first select the things you want to move and then click the Move icon. You will then be asked to pick a reference point. Pick an endpoint of one wall that you have selected. The point you pick will be the *drag p*oint of the cluster of objects you selected. When you then click on the new grid position, the drag point will be put exactly where the mouse is.

Take, for example, the layout of a secretary's cubicle in a large office room. To move the secretary's cubicle 400 cm down the wall, use the Selection tool to draw a box around the desk, plant, partition, and wastebasket. Click the Move icon. Form a reference point and click at the place where the partition meets the office room wall. Next, move the mouse pointer down 400 cm. Click on a different spot on the same wall. GCS moves all the objects down and puts them in just the right spot relative to where the partition meets the wall.

If in the preceding example I had chosen the center of the desk as a reference point, it would have been harder to click in the right spot when choosing the move destination. I would be looking at the layout, trying to figure out where the center of the desk would have to be to get the partition to butt up against the office wall perfectly. I could easily misjudge and end up with the partition sticking through the wall or leaving a gap between the wall and the partition. One problem you may encounter is that the grid does not let you move your objects exactly where you want them to go. You can easily make the grid spacing finer with the Grid icon tool. You can also turn grid snap off, but that might be undesirable when trying to match up walls. Of course, if you are just moving symmetrical objects, the grid is not really needed. If the grid is really preventing you from putting a wall just where you want it, the object snap feature should allow you to join walls perfectly even with the grid snap turned off.

COPYING GROUPS OF OBJECTS

The copy function is identical to the move function, except that the original objects stay in their original positions. A copy is placed at the new position.

ERASING GROUPS OF OBJECTS

The delete function should be obvious. Select whatever objects you want to discard. Click the Erase icon. All the objects with little red x's on them are gone forever.

ROTATING GROUPS OF OBJECTS AROUND A POINT

The rotate function is really fun to use. Select your objects and click on the Rotate icon. Once you pick a rotation point, all the objects rotate counterclockwise 90 degrees. If you want a different rotation angle, just click again to go another 90 degrees. To exit Rotate mode, just click on the Selection tool, or right-click once. The objects remain selected after a rotation because you frequently want to move them after rotating.

HINT!

You can't rotate in 45-degree increments because that would involve changing the sizes of the wall sections. If you zoom in and measure the wall lengths on your screen, you will notice that the diagonal sections of your walls are longer than the right angle sections.

ADJUSTING ALTITUDE

The Elevation Adjustment tool also operates on selected objects. You can raise an entire cluster of objects by a certain amount, or you can move them all to the same new elevation. Those may sound the same when you read the sentence, but they're not.

If you want to raise a cluster of many objects by 50 cm, select all the objects and then click the Elevation Adjust icon. Put a 50 in the text box, and click OK. If you don't click the Absolute button, the objects would just move up 50 cm from their initial heights. This raising function maintains one object at a higher elevation than another. To move the objects back down, you would do the same steps, but you would type in an elevation of –50 cm. The negative number moves them back down.

Do the same steps as in the preceding example, only this time click the Absolute button—every object will move to the same height. All the objects, no matter what their original elevation, will be placed at the level entered in the Options box (see Figure 15.4). Note that Figure 15.4 is not from GCS but is only an illustration of the concept.

CHANGING A PLACED WALL INTO A DOOR

To turn a wall panel into an opening door, select the wall, and then press the Door icon. You can actually make multiple doors at once by selecting

Group moved up

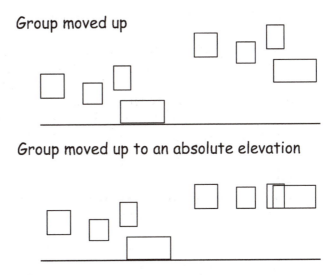

Group moved up to an absolute elevation

FIGURE 15.4 The difference between Elevation Adjust with and without the Absolute option selected.

several walls. Usually, though, your doors open in different directions, have different keys, and so forth. We go into the details of making doors later in this chapter.

THE FIND ALL FUNCTION

When using GCS, sometimes you need to eliminate all instances of a particular wall. Instead of having to find them individually, the GCS can whip through your level, find all instances of a particular wall, and select them for you. To use this, just select one wall object, and click on the Find All menu command in the Object pull-down menu. All objects of that type will be selected.

HINT!

An idiosyncrasy of this feature is that it finds only up/down copies of the object, or only diagonals, but not both at the same time. Therefore, to delete all instances of a wall, you generally need to first find all of the up/down and side-to-side walls and then delete them. Then you must find all the diagonal versions, and delete those.

INVERT

Frequently it is necessary to flip a wall 180 degrees. Although you can do this with each wall individually with the rotate function, it is more convenient to select a number of walls, and press Ctrl + I. The usefulness of this feature is illustrated in the following section.

EDITING OBJECT ATTRIBUTES

Each wall in your level has various attributes. These attributes alter the way the wall is drawn by the 3D engine and how the wall interacts with both the player and enemies. First, select a wall. Then, select "Edit Attributes" from the Objects pull-down menu. You will see a list of settings for the wall (see Figure 15.5). All these settings are turned off by default.

FIGURE 15.5 The Wall Settings menu.

WATCHOUT!

It is not advisable to set the attributes for groups of selected objects; this practice leads to serious errors. Select objects, set their attributes one at a time, and test your level frequently. Although this is tedious and makes level building seem to go slower, you will save yourself a lot of frustration and time in the long run.

DON'T DRAW BACKSIDES

Each wall has a front and a back, which is great for a room within a room, where you want to see both sides of the wall. It makes level design easier.

However, the 3D engine doing 3D calculations to draw both sides of a wall can be a waste if the player will never see the back of the wall, such as the outer wall of our dungeon level. Thus, the Don't Draw Backsides option speeds up the frame rate because the 3D engine does not have to draw the backs of walls that are not seen.

HINT!

Pay attention to your walls and which side is front and back. Since both sides are drawn, the walls appear normal when you test your level. However, when you turn on the Don't Draw Backsides attribute, walls will be invisible when looked at from the back. The walls are still there; you just can't see them from the back.

If you are using this feature and a wall seems invisible, select the wall and use the invert command (Ctrl + I) to flip the wall. Now the front of the wall will be facing you and it will reappear.

WATCHOUT!

Use the Don't Draw Backsides attribute *only* with walls! You will make critical errors if you use this feature with any other type of object.

DON'T FADE WITH DISTANCE (FULL BRIGHT)

Full Bright is used with lights, torches, glowing keys, and other objects that seem to have their own light sources. This attribute turns off fading and shading for the particular object that you select.

DON'T DRAW IF FAR AWAY

You can speed up the frame rate of your level by setting this attribute with small objects. Why slow down your computer by having it do the calculations necessary to draw objects that are too far away for you to see? This also applies to objects inside buildings or rooms that are way on the other side of your layout. Use this feature to tweak your finished level to make it run at the optimal frame rate by not drawing objects you can't see.

CAN'T BUMP INTO OBJECT (COLLISION DETECTION OFF)

By setting this attribute, you allow the player to pass through the object as if it were a ghost or hologram. It is great for making curtains, for example. You will need to use this attribute when making door frames; otherwise, you won't be able to get through your doorways. You might also want to use it to cut down the frustration level of players who become stuck in dense areas of foliage or in crowded rooms.

SET WALL LIGHTING BY ANGLE

You can enhance the 3D look of your level with this feature. Walls with a north/south orientation are shaded differently than walls with an east/west orientation. You'll see that corners look especially good.

OBJECT WON'T SHOW UP ON RADAR

The name for this attribute is a holdover from a previous attribute. Originally, GCS had a radar device, and the radar data were used for wall bumping and detection of guards. The radar was not very popular so it was removed when the Windows version came out, but the name lingers on. Now this attribute simply controls whether enemies can walk through the wall.

You have to use this feature when constructing door frames through which you want enemy characters to walk and shoot.

SET FTC (FLOOR-TO-CEILING) ON SOLID WALLS

This attribute is used to create a barrier that tells the 3D engine to forget about drawing any object that would normally appear behind the selected wall, because the wall extends from floor to ceiling and is not transparent. It maximizes the frame rate. You should be careful when using this feature, and it should be used when your level is complete and final.

WATCHOUT!

Never use this attribute with a windowed wall, fence, or any other wall panel through which the player can see, since everything behind the wall would be invisible. For best performance, make sure you set this attribute on every solid wall that goes from floor to ceiling.

ADDING DOORS TO YOUR GAME

Doors add so much to a game—interactivity, the feeling of suspense, the opportunity for exploration. Doors are a great tool for the designer—*The player will need the green key card to get through this door, but the green key card is beyond a room full of sleeping guards, suspended over a pit of lava, and behind an electrical force field (hehehehehehe, evil designer laugh)*. Locked doors force players to look carefully at every texture you created while searching for the key.

Doors are extremely easy to make. The whole process consists of selecting a normal wall section, clicking the Door icon, and then setting a few parameters.

Look at your layout and decide where you might want to place a door. Then, click on the Brick Wall icon and place a wall section where you want your door. It doesn't have to look like a door; you are free to make "secret" doors out of any solid wall. You can make a secret door part of a continuous stone wall or a bookcase.

HINT!

You cannot make doors out of symmetrical objects such as trees—only walls.

After placing the object, return to selection mode by right-clicking, or by left-clicking on the Selection tool icon. Then left-click once on the center of the door-to-be. When the little red x is on the door, click on the Door icon in the toolbar.

A Door menu appears with some text boxes and push buttons. Fill in the numbers, or use the defaults. Push the buttons to choose the sliding direction, and then click OK. Your door should now be functional (see Figure 15.6).

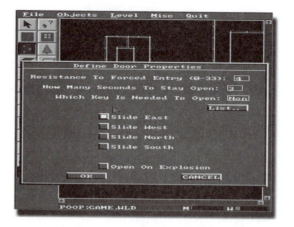

FIGURE 15.6 The Door Properties menu that pops up after you click the Door icon.

WATCHOUT!

Doors will fail if you make them too wide. Walls greater than 600 cm wide may fail, and walls 1200 cm or wider will certainly fail when you test your level.

DOOR PARAMETERS

- **Resistance to forced entry**. This number determines how hard it is to open or break the door.
  - **0.** A value of 0 means that merely bumping the door breaks it, and it then stays open forever.
  - **1.** Putting a 1 in here makes it open by shooting or kicking. Increasing this number increases the difficulty of breaking the door.
  - **2–8.** If the player bumps the door while shooting his or her weapon, the door will only be weakened by repeated attacks if the resistance is lower than eight.
  - **Up to 31.** If the door is set to resistance 31, the door is only damageable by jump-kicking. This takes some practice by the player, but it is a fun action to master. Please note that on levels where you have a texture-mapped ceiling, the player cannot jump for technical reasons. Therefore, it is best to leave doors like that for outside areas or for indoor areas with high ceilings.

Resistance set higher than 31 units? May as well be a wall. The player will not affect doors with resistance set higher than 31.

- **Number of seconds to stay open.** When the door is opened by enemies or by the player, it stays open for a while before automatically closing. Doors do not close on the player; they stay open until the player gets about 800 cm away.

- **Key value.** The key value number selects the key that unlocks a door. The player must have this key in his or her inventory to get through. If the player does not have the right key, an icon of the needed key shows up in an inventory window on the game play screen. The keys are coded by color.

WATCHOUT!

If you have changed the default inventory item pictures, these colors might not be accurate. If you are modifying the picture images for the keys, it is up to you to keep track of which color keys you have modified.

- **Open on explosion.** The button on the Door dialog box labeled "Open on Explosion" makes the door open if an explosion from a hand grenade or other source occurs close to the door.

TIPS FOR PLACING DOOR FRAMES

Doors are important in game design because they create intrigue, apprehension, and suspense (e.g., as secret passages or hidden positions). You need to set certain object attributes to make your door frames operate properly.

1. Select the wall your door frame is on.
2. Select the Edit Attributes option from the Object pull-down menu.
3. Click the Can't Bump into Object button. This allows the player to pass through the wall the door frame is on.
4. Next, click the Object Won't Show Up on Radar button. This allows enemy characters to pass through doors and shoot through doorways.
5. Finally, select the Don't Draw Backsides option. This improves 3D engine performance. Once you set this option and the door frame is gone in your game, the wall object it is on may be reversed. You

must go back to the Level Editor and flip the wall so the door frame is visible.

HOW TO AVOID GRAPHICAL PROBLEMS WITH DOORS

The normal door movement is to slide sideways into the wall on either side of it. This can cause problems if you aren't careful. When the door and the artwork slides to the left or right, the wall section that is moving does not stop at the door frame; it remains the same size and passes through space and walls without discretion. In other words, the wall or door panel comes through the side of a wall when it opens, and you, as game designer, are responsible for making sure the door panel is hidden when it slides sideways.

The easiest way to deal with doors is to put your doors in hallways. Make sure that the hallway has some inaccessible space on the side into which the door panel slides (see Figure 15.7). Otherwise, the player may be in a room when an enemy unit opens the door, and when it slides through the supposedly solid wall of the room, the game atmosphere is ruined.

Another problem is the door sliding out along another wall panel lengthwise and becoming partially visible through the wall. Here, the door and the wall panel are exactly overlaid in the 3D world and are fighting to be displayed because they are both in the same location. The graphics then break down and a shimmering mess of vertical strips appears.

Recessing your door slightly into a door frame avoids this problem. By door frame, we mean that you build a square of dead space on either side

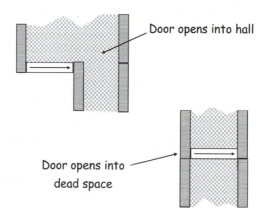

FIGURE 15.7 Proper and improper placement of a sliding door.

of the door and place your door at the entrance. However, if you set the object to be a door and leave it here, you run into the same effect described previously. Offset the door 200 cm, so it will not be aligned with any other walls when the panel opens. The snap-to-grid option makes this offsetting impossible if the grid is set to the standard 400 cm. You will have to change the resolution of the grid or turn the grid feature off.

Click on the Grid tool and change the grid setting to 200 cm. Then, select the door with the Selection tool, and click on the Move icon. Move the door back one 200-cm grid line, so that the door is now centered in the frame. Now when the door opens, the panel slides safely into the dead space. Of course, you can set your grid spacing to as little as 50 cm to inset the door just enough to keep the "scalloping" from occurring. It's best to be zoomed in before setting your grid to such a fine spacing.

HINT!

If you make a door, but you can't go through it when you test your level, read "Tips for Placing Door Frames," the previous section. Likewise, if enemies can't walk through or shoot through your door, that section explains the attributes that must be set to make the door function properly.

ADDING ENEMY CHARACTERS TO YOUR GAME

No 3D action game is complete without enemies. You can place up to 32 enemies in a level. Placing them is as easy as placing trees, but you have more options. To place an enemy, click on the Person icon. This creates an enemy in your game level. The type of enemy created is controlled by the selection of the Active Guard Set in the File menu.

After clicking the Person icon, a big dialog box appears filled with options, as shown in Figure 15.8.

First, you must determine the properties of the enemy unit. The following parameters adjust their strength and behavior.

- **Quickness**. Determines the quickness of the enemy's movements.
- **Step Size**. Determines how fast the enemy moves by adjusting the distance traveled in each walking step.
- **Resistance**. Sets how much damage the enemy can sustain before succumbing.
- **Attack Strength**. Controls how much damage is inflicted on the player when the enemy strikes or fires upon the player.

FIGURE 15.8   The Guard Options menu.

- **Attack Accuracy**. Sets how often the enemy will hit you with his weapon.
- **Range**. Controls how close an enemy must be before his attacks harm the player.

ENEMY CHARACTER BEHAVIOR

Here are some different types of enemy characters.

- **Sentry, then hunt**. The enemy stands still until he sees the player and then chases after the player in Attack mode.
- **Random patrol.** The enemy walks about at random and then chases the player when he or she is finally seen.
- **Stand and shoot**. The enemy stands still, but if he sees the player, he remains in his current positionand shoots.

ENEMY INTELLIGENCE

We can assign different levels of intelligence to the enemy.

- **Einstein with an Attitude**. The enemy is highly alert.
- **Average but armed**. The enemy is somewhat alert.
- **Dufus**. The enemy is not very alert.
- **What was the question?** The enemy is so oblivious that he almost never attacks a nonshooting player.

The basic behavior of enemies is always the same: they ignore the player until alarmed, and then they hunt the player down relentlessly. What causes them to become alarmed is a complex calculation.

WHAT ALERTS AN ENEMY?

Initially, all enemies are in a casual state. The only event that can cause enemies to become alarmed is seeing the player. However, not all enemies become alarmed as soon as they sight the player. Whether they recognize the player as hostile depends on the intelligence setting, the viewing angle, and what the player is doing.

The most intelligent enemy units recognize the player on sight from any angle, and become alarmed. The least intelligent do not become alarmed even if the player is standing in front of him, blasting his pal. All enemy units become alarmed if they take a hit from the player.

The view angle is very important in being recognized. If the player is directly behind an enemy, the chance of alarm is much less. Moreover, for the most part the enemies can't see through walls.

If an enemy comes near a slain fellow enemy, alertness can also be raised.

What the player is doing affects the chance of being detected. Certainly, if the player is running around shooting weapons, he is much more likely to be spotted than if he is standing still. All this information about the player's running, jumping, or shooting is boiled down into one number called the *profile*.

The bigger the profile, the easier the player is to spot. Running or moving quickly raises the profile. Shooting a weapon raises the profile drastically. Being wounded also raises the profile.

HOW ENEMIES BEHAVE

Enemies shoot when they are alarmed. If the player is out of range, enemies do not continue shooting but make their way toward the player. At the halfway point, enemies stop and take at least one shot. If within range, enemies shoot repeatedly before venturing closer.

These steps repeat until the enemies are so close that there is no point in coming any closer. Then they just stand and attack continuously.

If the player's weapon hits an enemy, the enemy's shooting is interrupted for a moment. How much damage is done to the enemy depends on many factors. The range and accuracy of the player's weapon are very important. These parameters are adjustable by editing the text file weapons.txt in the engine directory.

In addition, the Resistance to Damage setting determines how much damage the enemy unit sustains when hit by the player's weapons. If the enemy is damaged enough, he attempts a retreat. If he runs into a wall as he flees, he turns and fights to the death.

If the enemy actually gets very far away from the player after running away, he may return to the non-alarmed mode, but this is very infrequent.

ACTIVITIES

We discussed adding doors to your game in this chapter. Doors add so much to a game: interactivity, a feeling of suspense, the opportunity for exploration. Practice placing doors and playing with their values. Remember that although doors are extremely easy to make (the entire process basically consists of selecting a normal wall section, clicking the door icon, and then setting a few parameters), getting them to look and function properly in your game can take time. First, look at your layout and decide where you might want to place a door. Then, click on the brick wall icon and place a wall section where you want your door. It doesn't have to look like a door—you can make "secret" doors out of any solid wall or make a secret door part of a continuous stonewall or a bookcase. Remember that doors will fail if you make them too wide. The main door parameters to play with are "Resistance to forced entry" and "Number of Seconds to Stay Open." Have fun!

SUMMARY

After you lay out the basics of a level and run a test, you should be able to play in your own 3D first-person shooter—however, it is not yet your own, really. In the next chapter, we use the paint program that comes with GCS (GCS Paint) and start learning how to use the tool that will allow you to customize and change the objects in order to make your own game.

GCSPaint and Artwork in Your Game

IN THIS CHAPTER
••••••••••••••••

- Using the Paint Program for Importing and Editing Images
- Learning about Image Dimensions
- Mastering Special Effects

We will now leave the Level Editor for a while to look at the paint program that comes with GCS and absorb some technical facts about dealing with images in GCS. The paint program is called GCSPaint. With GCSPaint, you can import and edit images for use in the Level Editor and in your game.

GCSPaint is automatically installed when you install GCS. You can access it from the Level Editor, as seen in Figure 16.1, or you can run it by finding the icon to launch it from Windows.

To find the icon for GCSPaint outside of the Level Editor, do the following.

1. Go to My Computer and look on your C drive.
2. Assuming you have performed a standard installation, the EXE for GCSPaint will be in the folder called GCSW.
3. Click on the EXE to launch GCSPaint.

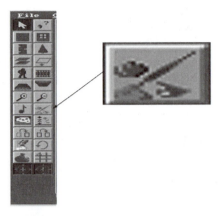

FIGURE 16.1   The Icon in the Level
Editor to launch GCSPaint.

HINT!

GCS has two different color depths. One is the color depth of
the original artwork. In GCS, all the artwork for your game
must be in 256-color VGA files. However, you can run the
game engine with the color depth of your system set to 16- or
24-bit color. Although all the artwork on the walls and floors
are 256 colors, the fading to black with distance requires thousands of new colors to represent the continuous fade to black.
Thus, there is a graphical advantage to using a 16- or 24-bit
color video mode even though all the original artwork is 256
color. This is because the engine is taking every color—pure
red, for example—and then creating hundreds of colors to
fade from red to black. Therefore, to fade red (RGB 255,0,0)
to black (RGB 0,0,0), the engine must display colors such as
RGB 255,0,0
RGB 254,0,0
RGB 253,0,0
RGB 252,0,0
Notice that the amount of red decreases as it approaches black.

It should be mentioned here that in the upcoming version of GCS, you
can use 24-bit color artwork in your levels, as well as colored light
sources and colored fog effects. In fact, the next version of GCS is going to
be a major jump forward.

MEMORY AND IMAGE RESOLUTION CONCERNS

You remember that each pixel of a 256-color piece of artwork takes up one pixel's worth of RAM. Each pixel can take 1, 2, or 4 bytes of texture RAM, depending on the video mode that a user has chosen.

- 256-color mode requires 1 byte per pixel of storage.
- 16-bit color requires 2 bytes per pixel.
- 24- or 32-bit color requires 4 bytes per pixel.

Therefore, a 64x64 picture for a wall section would take 4096 4K pixels, and that would take up 8192 bytes of texture RAM when running in 16-bit color mode. If you wanted to make a game with no weapons, inventory items, or enemies you could probably have 290 different wall images in your levels. This is because 290 8K-wall panels will use up approximately 2.5MB.

In your real game, you will want inventory items, enemy characters, trees, and weapons. This all takes up space. In a GCS game level, you will most likely have at least 20 or 30 unique wall sections in a given level. You can see that managing your resources is important.

Let's say that you wanted high-resolution artwork for your wall panels. The engine can't take any image that has a dimension bigger than 256. The largest image that could work is 200x200. This image contains 40,000 pixels, or 10 times more than our 64x64 image. This means 10 times less unique art for the wall panels in your levels. In practice, you should never go higher than 128x128 for most games, but with the speed of computers today, you may want to push the limit. Just be aware of how the engine works and what the limit is so you don't waste time creating a game that no one can play.

GETTING IMAGE FILES INTO THE 3D WORLD

Levels in GCS are made out of objects; trees, enemies, ammo, and walls are all objects. In fact, as you have seen, the walls are built panel by panel, just like modular construction. Erecting another wall is nearly the same process as placing a tree or a health-pack. These objects are the 3D portions of the 3D world. Objects are geometry.

Almost every type of object has an image file associated with it. These images are the artwork called *textures* or *texture maps* that are placed on the surfaces of the objects.

In GCS, all images have to be either VGR or VGA files. If you want to use one of your GIF, PCX, or BMP images, load those pictures into GCSPaint one by one, and save them in the VGR format.

HINT!
. . . .

 You don't need to know this, but for those of you who are curious, the VGA file format is the format of MVPPAINT, which was written by David Johndrow years ago and is the format that GCS uses. VGR is simply a rotated VGA file. This is true because of programming issues that cause images to draw faster in different situations depending on how they are oriented.

IMAGES AND OBJECTS WORKING TOGETHER TO MAKE A BETTER WORLD

The 3D world is empty at first and, other than the need for at least one wall, you can literally test an empty level with one wall in it and wander around in oblivion. In the Level Editor, you fill this void with walls and objects.

Each object has an image stretched over it by the 3D game engine. This stretching of the artwork or images you assign to the objects to fit the geometry is often called *texture mapping a polygon*, or *adding art to your geometry*.

When using the 3D game editor, it is as if you are building a world constructed entirely of white wall panels. Each time you select a blank wall, you assign the image that will be stretched over it. The wall object is usually larger than the image, so in order to get the image to fit the wall, the engine must stretch it out. Since we are working with a digital image, you will see the pixels as the image increases in size.

The game engine stretches and compresses images to fit the objects they are on. If you assign a square image of, say, a person to a very tall thin wall, you will have a sideways-compressed image of a person on that wall, much like a fun-house mirror reflection.

Therefore, you can't just tell the game engine to put an image into the game; you must tell it how much to stretch the image. For a brick wall section, this is fairly straightforward. Most typical walls are 400x400 units in size.

BITMAP IMAGE RESOLUTION VS. 3D WORLD SIZE

Distances inside the virtual 3D game world are measured in centimeters, but the unit of measure really doesn't have any impact on world design.

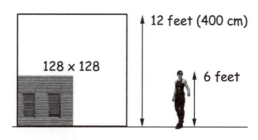

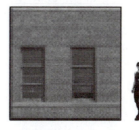

FIGURE 16.2   The average game wall is 400 cm long (about 12 feet). The typical 128x128 image is stretched across it

The bottom line is that wall panels that are 400 units long in the 3D world look about 12 feet long. However, the length of the wall has nothing to do with the resolution (or size) of the picture that the engine paints on this 12x12 wall panel. We could stretch a 32x32 pixel image on it (it would appear blocky, though), or we could put a 64x64 pixel image on it, or maybe even a 104x64 (see Figure 16.2).

HINT!

The typical wall is 400x400 cm big in the 3D world, and the art on it is usually 128x128 pixels or smaller. The 128x128-pixel limit is for the image artwork only.

WATCHOUT!

You can make the game engine stretch a tiny image, such as an 8x8 pixel image, across a huge 800x800 cm wall panel; however, it will look terrible (see "Pixel Rip" in Part One). You may also cause a *numerical overflow* in the 3D calculations if you try to do a stretch or compression that is this extreme.

TYPICAL DIMENSIONS

The typical wall panel is about 400x400 cm and contains 64x64 image. In general, stick to these dimensions:

- Images with horizontal or vertical dimensions of about 32 to 104 pixels.
- Walls should be between 50 and 600 units wide.

You will not encounter critical errors or overflows with these safe dimensions. You might experience trouble when making very short, wide walls, say 800x50. Therefore, be careful when making steps or guardrails.

HINT!

Having random wall dimensions such as 477x613 cm makes it hard for you to match up the walls of adjacent rooms when laying out a level. The odd numbers do not affect the speed or smoothness of the game engine. On the other hand, there is no reason to keep these strict dimensions in your image files, as they are stretched to the wall size and do not affect the layout of the level.

WATCHOUT!

The preceding note does *not* apply to floor and ceiling panel artwork, which must be 64x64, 128x28, or 256x256 pixels in size.

WALLS WITH SHAPES AND HOLES—WINDOWED WALLS

Walls are not limited to rectangular shapes. In fact, you can have walls with a few large cutouts. Examples are walls with windows, doors with rounded tops, a prison cell wall made of bars, or fences with gaps you can see through. All these are as easy to make as solid walls.

Simply make the invisible parts black. If you want a brick wall with a big round hole in it, load your brick wall image in the paint program. Use the Circle tool to paint a big, solid black circle on the image of the wall. The trick is that the black you use must be the first color of the palette. In GCSPaint, the first color is color 0. You can read the color numbers on the bottom of the screen when in GCSPaint. Choose your black from the upper left corner of the palette grid.

When the game engine draws this kind of wall object, it stretches the image exactly like a solid textured wall. The only difference is that it never paints the color 0 (black). So whatever was behind the wall shows through (color transparency again).

WHY BOTHER HAVING TWO TYPES OF WALLS?

Two reasons:

- You will want to be able to use black as a color on many occasions in your game without it always being treated as clear.
- Windowed walls take more computer time to draw because there are more computations involved. It is much more efficient to have two types of walls.

HINT!

You can use many windowed walls in your levels; there is no real limit. In fact, you can define all your walls as windowed walls, but you might find that it hurts performance—the fps rate drops off and the game does not appear as smooth.

Objects

Symmetrical objects are things such as trees, floor lamps, and chairs. Unlike walls, which are stationary and can be looked at from various angles, symmetrical objects always look the same. The viewing direction does not matter because they always rotate to face you. These stand-up objects are also called *anchored sprites* and will always turn to face the player (see Figure 16.3).

To make a tree, you draw a tree on a black background. You put the size at 400x600 cm in the 3D world. The engine draws that wall facing the player. It doesn't draw any of the black background between the leaves and around the outside edge of the image.

The important thing to remember about these objects is that they are stretched over a rectangle, just like the images on the regular solid textured walls. The panels on which these images are stretched have horizontal and vertical size in centimeters, just as the other walls do.

Top Down View

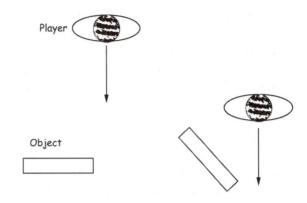

FIGURE 16.3   An object will always rotate to face a player.

Just like the shaped walls, the images you make are subject to the same hole restrictions. If you want to make your own shrub, don't try to have see-through areas between each leaf—you may have trouble. Most trees, chairs, and other objects will be nowhere near this limit. The transparent portion should be limited and not very complex.

CEILING AND FLOOR IMAGES

Typically, you will use floor sections in tile patterns that repeat in the north, south, east and west directions.

Because your image repeats on the floor, the patterns you put on your image will be discontinuous as you go from one panel to the next. Sometimes this effect is desired, such as when you are making floor tiles that look like square tiles. With a dirt floor, though, you don't want the user to see the tile boundaries. This means blending the color on the top of the image with the pixels on the bottom and blending the left with the right side.

HINT!

GCSPaint can handle blending for you in the f/x submenu. You can smooth the edges of your image to improve their appearance in your 3D world.

VGA VS. VGR IMAGE FILES

Note that the 3D game engine can read two types of image files: VGA and VGR. Typically, all your walls and other objects are VGR files, and all the big things, such as the backdrop, are VGA files.

The file types are so close in format that they are interchangeable for the most part without a problem. For example, if you used the DOS copy command to copy a 64x64-pixel WALLVGR file to WALLVGA, you could still read it in as a VGA with GCSPaint. However, the image will be rotated 90 degrees.

In fact, that's what a VGR file is: a rotated VGA image. The 3D game engine can read artwork more efficiently if the images are rotated 90 degrees. Therefore, the VGR file format has the pixel data rotated 90 degrees internally. You never know this when you bring up your images with GCSPaint because GCSPaint puts them up on the screen right side up, although the image is on its side in the VGR file.

The only files that need to be rotated with the game engine are those in the 3D game play world. Pictures of the hit point guys (HTPT0VGA), the game play screen (BACKDROPVGA), and the weapons identification "fat" files (GUNNONEVGA) all are put on the screen as regular flat pictures, not in the 3D viewport. That is why they are VGA files.

The wall panel artwork, however, needs to be rotated 90 degrees. You could do this by saving your artwork as a VGA file, but make sure that you rotate the picture onto its side before saving. Then rename the VGA file as a VGR file, so that GCS will let you import it.

There is really no reason to do this except to illustrate the difference between VGR and VGA files. This is necessary because when using GCSPaint, you must keep aware of which file type you want to load or save.

HINT!

An idiosyncrasy of GCSPaint is that it never asks you whether you want to save as VGR or VGA. If you call GCSPaint from the icon in the GCS program, you will always be saving as VGR, although you can read both VGR and VGA files. If you quit GCS, and run GCSPaint from the DOS command line, then all images you save are written to VGA files. This is good because some bigger files that you might like to edit, such as BACK-DROPVGA or BACKG40VGA, are too wide to be saved as VGR files. Therefore, to change these large VGA image files, you need to exit GCS and run GCSPaint from the DOS command line.

GCSPAINT

With GCSPaint, you don't need to hire an artist to create and edit graphics for your 3D project. GCSPaint is an image workshop containing all the tools and special effects you'll need to create original artwork or to manipulate existing images. At the beginning of this chapter we looked at how to start GCSPaint. If you are in the Level Editor, click on the GCSPaint icon. The Level Editor will suspend operation and the GCSPaint screen will appear.

The main menu for GCSPaint is located on the lower right side of the screen. The current palette of 256 colors is located on the lower portion of the screen as shown in Figure 16.4.

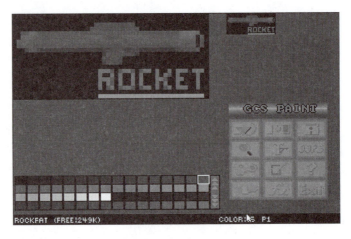

FIGURE 16.4   The GCSPaint main screen.

GCSPAINT HELP

Click on the **?** icon for an introduction to GCSPaint's many features. The Help screens explain how to use each tool and special effect as you click the various buttons on the main menu.

DISK COMMANDS

Click on the main menu's Disk icon. You are presented with several options: Create New Image, Load Image, Save Image, Merge Image, View as Tile. We will look at all these next.

Create New Image

Create a new image by dragging the size box to the desired dimensions. Please note that the maximum image size in GCSPaint is 192x150. If you want to work on larger images, exit GCS and run GCSPaint from the DOS command line. Now you can work on full-screen 320x200 images.

Save Image

GCSPaint saves your images in the VGR format. Limit your filenames to eight characters because of the DOS naming convention.

If you need to save your image in the VGA format, you will have to run GCSPaint from the DOS prompt: c:\gcsw\GCSPaint.exe.

This enables you to save large images such as title screens and background images. Conserve RAM memory at game time by keeping your images small. Typical walls should be 64x64, and typical characters should be about 60 pixels tall. You can scale down large images with the resize command. Try to maintain a reasonable balance between appearance and size when saving your images.

You should also avoid leaving a lot of unused black background in your images. Use the move command to put your images in the upper left corner of the screen. Then, use the resize command to crop the excess black background.

WATCHOUT!

You should also test images that will later become shaped and symmetrical objects to make sure that they don't have too many holes. The 3D game engine does not draw color 0; thus, those areas are transparent. An abundance of see-through holes can sometimes cause critical errors when you test your levels. An easy way of testing for this pitfall is to use the color replacement feature to change areas drawn with color 0 to a bright color. Then, you can clearly see how many invisible holes are in your image. Use color replacement again to refill those unintentional holes with a color other than color 0.

Merge Image

This command lets you combine two separate images. A problem arises when you try to import an image that is larger than your current image.

A warning flashes momentarily at the bottom of the screen and the operation fails. Use the resize command, without scaling, to make your current image big enough to accommodate the imported image.

View as Tile

You will undoubtedly be working on wall, fence, or foliage artwork for your project. A common problem with artwork repeated or stacked in your 3D world is that distracting patterns appear. Edges look harsh and ill fitting. This command gives you a preview of what your image will look like when the artwork is placed side by side or stacked in your 3D world.

Hidden Main Menu

Large images sometimes cover up the main menu so you can't see it. To view the hidden main menu, move your mouse pointer to where the main menu normally appears and press the space bar. Once you select a command, the main menu disappears and your image fills the entire screen.

Palette

GCS works with one palette of 256 colors. All the images that you use in your game must use this palette. Each color has a number from 0 to 255.

The palette box displays 64 of the 256 colors on the lower portion of the screen. To see the other 192 colors, simply click on the arrows on the right side of the palette box.

Select a Color

Move your mouse pointer over the desired color in the palette box. Click the left mouse button to select a color. You can also pick up a color from your image. Move your mouse pointer to a pixel in your image. Click the right mouse button to select that color from your image.

Hidden Palette Box

Large images sometimes cover up the palette box so you can't see it. To view the hidden palette box, move the mouse pointer to where the palette box normally appears and press the space bar. Once you select a color, the palette disappears again and the image fills the entire screen.

Load a Palette

Images do not always come with their own palettes. These images appear in wild colors when you load them because they are drawn using a default palette. Remember that GCS uses only one palette of 256 colors at a time, so make sure that you are loading the same palette that will be used throughout your game.

Modify Palette

It is possible to customize your own palette. You can adjust each color by adjusting its red, green, and blue components. You can also work on several colors at once with the Trend option.

Match Palettes

GCSPaint gives you the option of matching the palettes of imported images to the palette currently in use. This is particularly helpful when you are using scanned images for your game. This feature enables you to make all types of artwork compatible with the palette you are using for your game.

Save Palette

You should always save the palettes of images before you try to match them to the master palette of your game. If the palette matching operation doesn't turn out well, reload the image with its original palette and try again.

WATCHOUT!

If you don't save the original palette, the original image will be ruined forever and you won't have a second chance.

Draw Tools

GCSPaint equips you with many powerful drawing tools: lines, rectangles, circles, ellipses, and polygons.

Interpolation

This command creates a morphing effect between two polygons. You can specify the number of intermediary shapes in the morph. You can also set the number of colors involved in the morph.

WATCHOUT!

Be aware that interpolation will fail if original polygons have too many sides.

Settings

You can set preferences for GCSPaint. Choose this command to specify the brush size. You can even design brush patterns. In addition, you can set prompt delays to suit your needs. Memory settings are also adjustable.

Text

Two CHR files come with GCSPaint, although you can put public domain BGI files in the same directory as well. Select the size and style of the text to put in your image. If your text operation fails, it's probably because the text was too big for your image. Try again with smaller letters, a more compact font, or a larger image.

Color Tools

GCSPaint also comes with color manipulation tools.

Fill You can fill areas of color with either solid colors or patterns.

Color Replacement This tool lets you switch colors in your image. It is a big time saver, since you don't have to add the new color to your image pixel by pixel.

Random Replacement This handy tool lets you replace a percentage of a color in your image with a new color. This is especially useful when doing artwork that requires a haphazard pattern, such as dirt floors or carpeting.

Color Phase This tool fills an area with a gradient. Pick a color and start the phase on that color.

Color Sunburst This is similar to the Color Phase tool, except that it makes gradient fills in rounded areas. Pick a color, and then start the sunburst on that color.

SPECIAL EFFECTS

Special effects can enhance the look of your game's images, and include anti-aliasing, blending, brightening, and smoothing the graphics.

Outline

Trying to draw borders around areas by hand can be tedious at best. Select this tool and your border is done in a flash! Your outline can be done with or without filled-in corners. Pick the color that you want to outline, and then start the outline on that color.

Anti-Aliasing

This tool helps prevent the optical illusion that often occurs when two highly contrasting colors are butted up against each other. This tool also helps to eliminate the sawtooth effect appearance of diagonal lines in low-resolution graphics.

Merge/Blend

This tool allows you to superimpose another image over your current image. You can control the transparency of the image that you are importing. Be sure that the image you are importing is smaller than your current image. If you try to import an image that is too big, the operation will fail.

Brighten/Darken

You can use this tool to brighten or darken lines or rectangles in your image.

WATCHOUT!

Be sure to say no to the prompt that asks you if you want the operation to affect the whole image and its palette. You never want to change the palette, since this would make the image incompatible with all of the other images in your game.

Smooth Image

This is one of the best special effects that GCSPaint has to offer. You can smooth all the pixels in your image, or you can apply the tool to the edges of your image. You can control the intensity of the operation: light, medium, heavy, and extremely blurred. Other stunning effects include negative image, grainy glass, and double image. The pixel wraparound feature is especially useful when working on wall panels.

Contrast

There are times when you want to adjust the contrast of your image. This tool is just about as easy as fine-tuning the contrast button on your TV!

Rectangle tools

These tools include Copy, Move, Overlay, and Erase. In addition, you can flip, rotate, and resize your image.

Zoom

There are times when you need to move in close to work on the details of your image. Zoom makes this possible.

The best thing about Zoom is that most GCSPaint's features can be applied while in Zoom mode. It is also possible to save the zoomed-in part of your image as a separate file.

WATCHOUT!

A prompt warns you not to save the zoomed section under the same filename as your original image, so you don't overwrite it.

OOPS

You can cancel just about any operation in GCSPaint by selecting the OOPS icon on the main menu. Usually prompts warn you that certain operations can't be undone. Another way to cancel an operation is to click the right mouse button.

ACTIVITIES

Plan the art for your level: wall, ceiling, doors, and items. All these are covered in this chapter under "Memory and Image Resolution Concerns." Now that we have looked at some of the technical aspects of adding art to your game, you are ready to plan some of the art for your game. As we discussed in the first part of this book, each pixel of a an image takes up resources, so you have to plan your work. For example, a 64x64 picture for a wall section would take 4096 4K pixels, which would take up 8192 bytes of texture RAM when running in 16-bit color mode. If you wanted to make a game with no weapons, inventory items, or enemies, you could probably have 290 different wall images in your levels. This is because 290 8K-wall panels use up approximately 2.5MB. In your real game, you will want inventory items, enemy characters, trees, and weapons. This all takes up space. In a GCS game level you will most likely have at least 20 or 30 unique wall sections in a given level. You can see that managing your resources is important. For this exercise, you can design your level (a castle, for example) and then decide what 20 or so types of wall you want in the castle—plain stone, stone with a picture on it, stone with a crack in it. If you decide you want high-resolution artwork for your wall panels, remember that the engine can't take any image that has a dimension bigger than 256. An image this big contains 40,000 pixels, or 10 times more than our 64x64 image. This means 10 times less unique art for the wall panels in your levels. In practice, you should never go higher than 128x128 for most games, but with the speed of computers today, you may want to push the limit. Just be aware of how the engine works and what the limit is, so you don't waste time creating a game that no one can play. Have fun creating walls.

SUMMARY

Now that you understand the graphic formats, how they fit into the game, and how to use GCSPaint, you are ready to move on to the Advanced Features Editor, which is an extension of the DOS Level Editor in many ways. You will learn some of the additional effects and features of the Windows-based engine to further tweak your game level.

The Extra Features Editor

IN THIS CHAPTER
. . . .

- Working with Floors and Ceilings
- Adjusting Lighting and Fading
- Modifying the Background

Why are we forced to do all this jumping around from DOS to Windows, and now into the Extra Features Editor? The engine that runs the game, the Game Editor, and the paint program are all separate programs. To develop even one of these applications is a great deal of work, so when the game engine was rewritten and upgraded, several concessions were made so that the original DOS editor would not have to be totally rewritten.

The original GCS engine was a DOS-based engine and was replaced by the aptly named Windows Replacement Engine. This new Windows-based engine was a great improvement on the original DOS engine. However, in order to take advantage of the many features added to extend the capabilities of the game engine, an intermediary editor had to be written. This was called the Extra Features Editor, because it edits the extra features of the new engine. Since these features are not available in the DOS editor, we have to deal with them while we are out of the DOS editor and not yet into the Windows engine. This section shows you how to access these features.

THE GCS EXTRA FEATURES EDITOR

In addition to the increases in graphics technology, some new features were added to the game engine. These features dramatically increase the visual impact of your game levels, as well as your ability to control the appearance of your games. You can use these new features by using a part of the Windows game engine called the Extra Features Editor. This editor makes changes to the EXTRA??.TXT file in your project directory—a simple text file containing information about floor and ceiling tiles, lighting effects, and other things.

HINT!

EXTRA??.TXT is a filename in which the question marks are replaced with a level number. In the real game, the file would be named something like EXTRA001.TXT.

HOW TO LAUNCH THE EXTRA FEATURES EDITOR

When we test a level, the first thing we see is the dialog box in Windows with your name on it and the three buttons: Test 3D World, Edit Extra Data, and Change Driver Mode (see Figure 17.1).

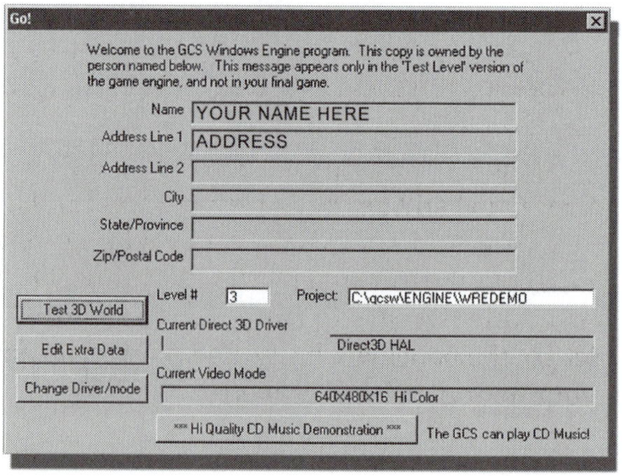

FIGURE 17.1 The Windows dialog box with the Edit Extra Data button.

We already looked at two of the buttons in detail. Here we will look at the Edit Extra Data button, which takes us to the Extra Features Editor (EFE). Click the Edit Extra Data button.

After you click the EFE button, the client area shows a top view of your game level, similar to that of the DOS Level Editor. You will not be able to move or place walls or objects with this editor; they are on the screen only for reference. Once the editor is running, you will be able to place floor and ceiling panels and change various settings.

You can zoom in and out using the + and – keys on your keypad, and you can use the scroll bars to move around on the image.

HINT!

If the + and – keys do not appear to work, make sure that the main window is selected rather than the little dialog box. The main window's title bar must be blue (or the active color), and the little dialog box's title bar gray for the + and – keys to function. You can make this happen by clicking on the title of the main window.

PLACING FLOOR PANELS

The floor and ceiling panels in GCS are based on a 400x400 grid of squares. You may control the size of the panels you put down, but the size must be an even multiple of 400 units. The bitmap artwork that covers the panel will repeat over and over again to fill in panels that are larger than 400 units. It is more efficient to use large panels than many smaller panels to fill in space.

To make a floor panel, just click once on your level. A small 400x400 floor panel will be created in your level at the default height of 0.

To make larger panels, click and hold down the mouse button, and then drag the mouse while holding down the button. The panel will grow or shrink to its maximum dimension as you move the mouse. When you let go, the panel will be created. When you enter the 3D world next time, your floor panel will be there.

WATCHOUT!

You must exit the Windows game engine and restart it in order for your changes to appear in the 3D world. If you go directly from the Extra Features to the 3D world via the Go menu item, your most recent changes will not appear in the 3D world, even though you saved them.

DELETING FLOOR PANELS

To remove a floor panel, click on a panel that you already placed. An X appears in the middle of the panel, which indicates that it is selected. Then, go to the Editor menu and select Delete Panel. The panel disappears, and is deleted.

CHOOSING THE FLOOR IMAGE FILE

Just as you do when placing a wall, you must choose the artwork file to use for the current floor panel. You choose the image from a list before you create the panel. To choose your image, go to the Editor menu, and select the Set Texture option. A dialog box appears with a list of image files for floor or ceiling panels. Select the one you want and click OK. All the images on this list are loaded into memory when your level loads, regardless of whether they are actually used. If you would like to add to this list, press the button labeled "Add more textures to list" that is located below the list of available textures.

ADDING TO THE LIST OF AVAILABLE FLOOR AND CEILING TEXTURES

Clicking the "Add more textures to list" button in the Set Texture dialog box brings up another dialog box with two lists of image files.

On the left is a list of .VGA files in the FLCL_LIB (Floor Ceiling Library) object library directory. As you select different files in the list, the preview window in the center of the dialog box shows you what the artwork looks like. When you find a piece of artwork that you would like to add to the level's floor or ceilings, click on the arrow underneath the preview picture. This adds the image to the level. You can add more images if you like. You can also remove images from the right-hand list with the button below the list (see Figure 17.2).

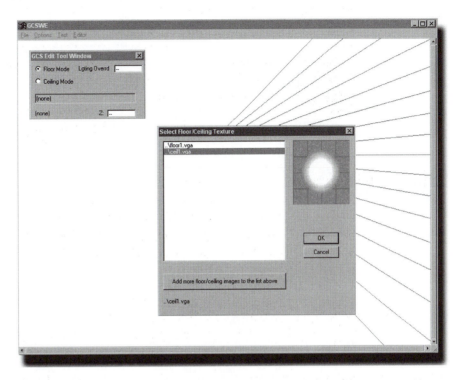

FIGURE 17.2   The window for adding more floor and ceiling images to the library.

HINT!

A quirk of the EFE requires you to save your changes and exit the GCSWE after making changes to the texture list. When you return to the EFE, the list will be updated with your changes.

MAKING CEILING PANELS

Making ceiling panels is the same as making floor panels; it's just a matter of switching from Floor mode to Ceiling mode. The Editor menu has two items labeled Floor Mode and Ceiling Mode. If you wish to place ceiling panels, click Ceiling Mode. When you do, the level is redrawn without the floor panels, and you are ready to place ceiling tiles. Ceiling tiles are created at a default height of 400 units above 0.

HINT!

Floor panels are not drawn on the screen when you are in Ceiling mode.

GRAY AND WHITE PANELS

You will notice that some panels in the drawing are white and some are gray. The panels with the same texture as the current drawing texture are white. The panels with a texture other than the currently selected texture are gray. For example, when you use the Set Texture menu item to set the current texture to Floor1.vga, all the Floor1.vga panels in your level panels turn white, and all those that are something else becomes gray (see Figure 17.3).

Another method for changing the floor/ceiling mode is to use the modeless dialog box (Figure 17.4) that is constantly on the screen when you are using the EFE. The two radio buttons—Floor Mode and Ceiling Mode—allow you to switch between floor and ceiling modes.

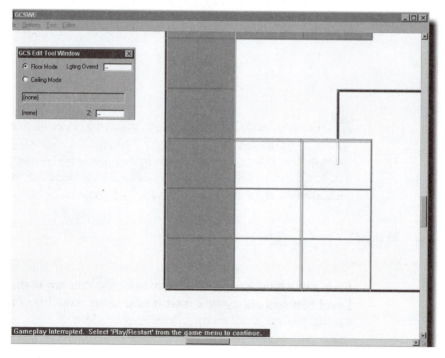

FIGURE 17.3   The white and gray floor panels.

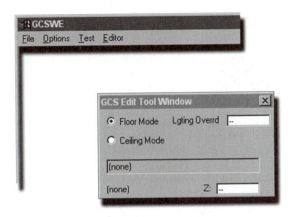

FIGURE 17.4   The modeless dialog box used to switch between Floor and Ceiling mode.

This dialog box is useful in other ways. To get information about a floor panel, click on a panel to select it. An X appears on the panel. As soon as the panel is selected, the name of the image file appears in the dialog box and the height appears in the Z: box. You can even select multiple panels by clicking on several at a time. If all the panels you select have the same height, the Z: box displays the height; otherwise, it indicates Various.

ADJUSTING THE HEIGHT OF FLOOR OR CEILING PANELS

To adjust the height of a floor or ceiling panel, select it, and then use your mouse to select the height in the Z: box in the GCS Edit Tool window. Type in a new height, and all the panels you selected move to the specified height. To deselect the panels after you change the height, just right-click anywhere on the layout, and all selected panels become unselected.

LEVEL SETTINGS

Each game level can have its own settings. You can make changes in the Level Settings dialog box, and if you select Save Extra from the Editor menu, your settings stay set (see Figure 17.5).

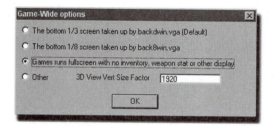

FIGURE 17.5   The Game Level Settings dialog box.

FADE START DISTANCE AND TOTAL DARKNESS DISTANCE

If you wish, you can have the walls and floors fade to black as they recede from the player's perspective. The walls will be shown at maximum brightness until the distance from the observer is equal to the Fade Start Distance. This distance is in regular GCS units, where one typical wall section is 400 units. Total Darkness Distance is the distance at which the brightness has faded all the way to zero. Entirely darkened sections are not drawn.

For example, say the Fade Start Distance is set to 1000 units, and there is only one wall in your level. If you are close to the wall, it appears at full brightness. As you back away, it stays at full brightness until it is 1000 units away, at which point it starts to darken as you move farther away.

Now assume the Fade End Distance is set to 3000 units. If you keep moving away from that wall section, it continues to darken until you get to 3000 units away, at which point it fades to black.

Sometimes you want to set the Fade Start Distance to a negative value, which causes a wall to be somewhat faded even when you are right up against it. This is desirable when using special lighting effects that "wash out" when you get close.

HINT!

In order for the fading with distance to work, the "Fade to blk with distance" check box must be checked. However, even if it is *not* checked, Fade Start and Total Darkness distances still set the Zero Point darkness. If you want the walls to be at maximum brightness, make sure you make the Fade Start Distance a positive value.

WALL FADE CODE 0 POINT SETTING

"Wall Fade Code 0 pt" sets the zero point for walls with lighting over-rides. The GCS editor sets lighting overrides according to the section on lighting effects. You can change the bias on lighting effects globally with this value.

OTHER LEVEL OPTIONS

Working with level design as it relates to a realistic look is important. In this section, we discuss ceiling heights and horizon backgrounds.

FADE LIGHTS WITH DISTANCE

"Fade Lights with Distance" lets you choose whether to have lighting effects diminish with distance. Sometimes this is desirable when you don't want faraway lights to "show through" when surrounding walls are not drawn because they have faded to pure blackness. If this is not an issue, leave this option off for better realism.

Z-BUFFER OPTION

If you plan to have floors and ceiling panels at varying heights, you must turn this on, even though it hurts animation speed. If all your floor and ceiling panels are the same height, you can get a performance boost by turning this off for the current level.

BACKGROUND OPTIONS

Now let's look at some of the options you have when creating your background.

RED, GREEN, AND BLUE

These boxes set the color of the background of the 3D viewport, the color that shows through the gaps of the walls and floor panels. You can set this color using the RGB numerical mixtures we discussed previously.

Most of the time, you will want the background of the 3D world to be black, which would be:

Black = R0, G0, B0
White = R255, G255, B255
Dark Blue = R0, G0, B64

HORIZON TEXTURE

You have the option of using a horizon texture bitmap, such as a wide mountain scene that moves as you turn in the 3D world. It is drawn behind all walls and objects and looks like it is far away because of its movement. This movement is called *parallax movement*.

The image must be a 256-color VGA file, and it is usually very large, maybe 1024 units wide or larger.

The XSCL and YSCL buttons allow you to stretch a horizon horizontally and vertically. The left/right speed allows you to fine-tune how much the image moves when you turn in the 3D world.

You will have to tweak the horizon so it does not appear to spin faster than the walls in your 3D world. The same goes for the up/down speed, which is for when the user uses the A or Z keys to look up or down.

GAME-WIDE OPTIONS

Another dialog box allows you to change settings that affect the entire game, not just one level. At present, there is only one game-wide option, as shown in Figure 17.6.

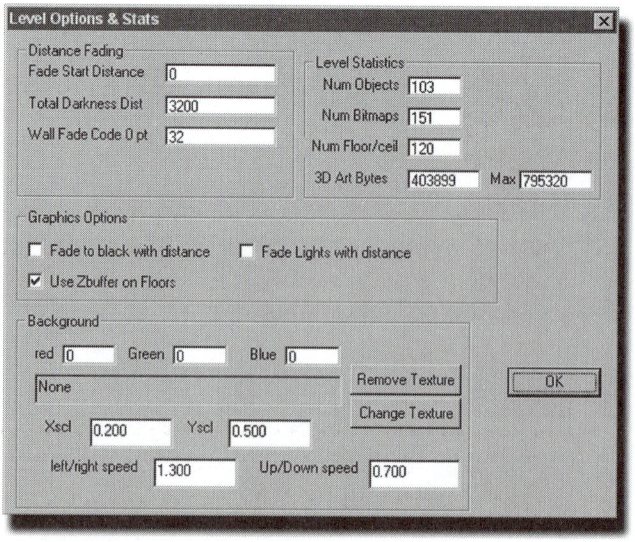

FIGURE 17.6   The Level Options and Stats dialog box.

3D VIEW VERTICAL SIZE FACTOR

Originally, one-third of the screen was covered in the DOS GCS engine. Here you get to choose the amount of the screen as n/1920ths. For example, if you want the 3D view to use one-half of the vertical size of the screen, you would enter the number 960, because 1920/2 = 960. If you want the entire screen to be used for the 3D view, enter 1920.

The .VGA file called backgwin.vga is stretched into the remaining portion of the screen. You may change the size of backgwin.vga as desired.

SPECIAL EFFECTS WITH THE DOS LEVEL EDITOR

Special effects include a number of game enhancements, including the cheat keys.

ADDING LIGHT SOURCES

You can make stunning visual effects by adding light sources to your levels. A light source is an invisible object in the 3D world that emits light in all directions. In GCS, you can make rectangular light sources of any size and put them anywhere in the 3D world. This is accomplished in the DOS GCS Editor.

HINT!

A light source is really just a new kind of platform object, and it is created using the Platform icon in the GCS Level Editor.

Light sources are flat rectangles when viewed from the top. The area within the rectangle is illuminated at maximum intensity, and as you move away from the edges, the light falls off steadily with distance when it gets outside the rectangle.

HINT!

You will probably want to turn off "Snap to grid" when you make a light source. Usually, you do not want the edge of a light source to be on the edge of a wall; rather, you want your wall corners to be either decisively in the light rectangle or in the falloff area.

Adding lights to the 3D world is relatively easy using the DOS GCS Editor. To add a light source, do the following.

1. Make a platform object.
2. Specify that it is *not* visible.
3. Select the function "Assign Value to Register." Press OK.
4. A new dialog box appears, asking you for the univ register and the value you want to assign. Here you must place a number between 192 and 223. For a light source of maximum brightness, put the value 223 in the top box where the univ reg number goes.
5. In addition to selecting the brightness of a light, you also need to specify how far from the platform's edges the light travels before fading out. After you decide on a fadeout distance, divide the desired range by 10, and put that number in the bottom box where the value goes.

For example, if I wanted a light source to reach 1100 units, I would put the value 110 in there. The maximum range is either 1280 units or 2550 units, depending on if the GCS DOS Editor can accept byte values greater than 127.

HINT!

You can also add negative light sources, which take light away. Any value less than 208 in the top box takes away light instead of adding it.

WATCHOUT!

The lighting effects are calculated only at the wall and floor panel corners. Therefore to get smooth lighting effects, the range has to cover all four corners of a wall panel. Small lights that only include one corner of a wall panel don't produce a very nice effect. Make your light sources large, unless you have small wall panels.

There can be up to 32 light sources on a game level; having more than 32 sources makes some of them nonfunctional.

LIGHTING EFFECTS

You can modify the lighting on a wall panel to make it darker or lighter and make it pulse or flash. To modify lighting, do the following.

1. Place the wall in your level with the DOS Level Editor.
2. Select Edit Attributes in the Object menu. A dialog box appears showing options for that wall object (see Figure 17.7).

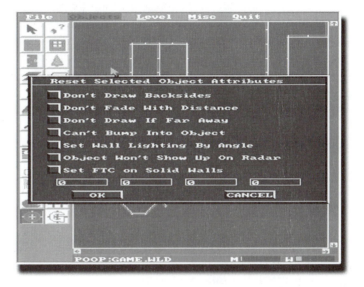

FIGURE 17.7   The Wall Options dialog box.

3. If you have only one wall section selected, four red boxes are displayed along the bottom of the dialog box. To make a wall object have special lighting effects, you must enter a number in the *third* red box. To modify the constant illumination on the wall section, enter a number between 1 and 63 in the red box.
4. Enter 63 in the third red box to brighten the wall by the maximum amount possible.
5. Enter 1 in the third red box to darken the panel by the maximum amount.

The number that represents the zero point of illumination is a variable that you can set in the Level Options dialog box. This is called the Wall Fade Code 0 Point setting. All lighting effect values greater than this number lighten the wall section; all values below this number darken the wall section.

For example, if the Wall Fade Code 0 point is set to 48, any value greater than 48 brightens the wall section, and values less than 48 will darken the wall section.

In addition, you can make a wall pulsate or flash intermittently. To do this, you calculate a number based on a command code and an intensity value.

1. First, choose one of the following commands:

   - **Command 2**. Pulsate phase 1
   - **Command 3**. Pulsate phase 2
   - **Command 4**. Pulsate phase 3
   - **Command 5**. Flash intermittently

2. Multiply the command number by 32.
3. Add an intensity value from 1 to 31. Most of the time you would leave the intensity at 31 for the maximum effect, but you can adjust this for milder effects.

Here are some examples of numbers to put in the third red box of a wall section.

   - **63**. For constant brightness added to a wall section's illumination.
   - **95**. For pulsate effect using phase 1.
   - **127**. For pulsate effect using phase 2.
   - **159**. For pulsate effect using phase 3.
   - **191**. For intermittent effect.

USING SPECIAL LIGHTING EFFECTS IN LIGHT SOURCES

You can also apply these pulsating and intermittent effects to lighting sources.

1. Make your light source according to the instructions given earlier.
2. Select that platform object with the DOS Level Editor.
3. Go into the Edit Attributes dialog box.
4. Put a value in the *fourth* little red box. Calculate the value as we did in the section "Lighting Effects."

HINT!

When applying these effects to a light source (platform object), make sure to put the number in the *fourth* (last) little red box instead of the third, as you would for a wall section. If you put it in the wrong box, the lighting source will not work.

USING CHEAT KEYS IN YOUR GAME

GCS has five cheat functions you can invoke during a game using the following codes:

- **kill all**. Kills all enemies on a level.
- **invincible**. Turns on God mode.
- **magic heal**. Brings the player to 100% health.
- **open doors**. Opens all doors on the level for a few seconds.
- **Teleport n**. Teleports the user to entry point n.

To use a cheat code, do the following

1. Hold down the left Shift key.
2. Press the "c" key.
3. You will be prompted to enter the cheat code.
4. After entering the cheat code, press Enter.

ACTIVITIES

For this exercise, play with one of the most powerful effects in the image—Fade Start Distance and Total Darkness Distance. It does two powerful things: speeds up rendering of the world and adds atmosphere. If you wish, you can have the walls and floors fade to black as they recede from the viewpoint. The walls display at maximum brightness until they reach a distance from the observer equal to the Fade Start Distance. Distance is given in regular GCS units, in which one typical wall section is 400 units. Total Darkness Distance is the distance at which the brightness fades to zero. No wall sections will be drawn that are entirely darkened.

Say the Fade Start Distance is set to 1000 units, and assume there is only one wall in your level. If you are close to the wall, it will be drawn at full brightness. As you back away, it stays at full brightness until it is 1000 units away, at which point it darkens as you move away. Now assume the Fade End Distance is set to 3000 units. If you keep moving away from that wall section, it continues to darken until you get to 3000 units away and it is black.

Sometimes you want to set the Fade Start Distance to a negative value, which causes a wall to be somewhat faded even when you are right up against it. This is desirable when using special lighting effects because otherwise, the lighting effects "wash out" when you get close. In order for the Fading with Distance to work, the check box called "Fade to blk with distance" must be checked. However, even if it is NOT checked, the Fade Start Distance and total darkness still set the "Zero Point" darkness. If you want the walls to be all at maximum brightness, make sure you make the Fade Start Distance a positive value.

SUMMARY

Now that you can take advantage of the special features in the Extra Features Editor, we are ready to complete our 3D game.

Assembling the Final Game

IN THIS CHAPTER
• • • • • • • • • • • • • •

- Connecting All the Levels
- Testing to See If It Works
- Adding the "Start the Game" Device
- Dealing with Common Problems

Now that you know how to lay out a 3D level, operate the paint program, and even enhance your level with the Extra Features Editor, you are ready to make all those 3D levels into a game. The final step is to hook them all together with stairwells, transporters, or other devices, and then click Make Final to create the game.

WATCHOUT!
• •

Please read this chapter carefully. If you don't do these steps just right, your final game will not function properly.

CONNECTING THE LEVELS

To make your final game, each of your levels must have a unique level number. In general, it makes sense to set the level at which the player starts as level 0, the next level as 1, and so on until the last level. Level connections do not have to be linear, however. For example, you might have level 0 connected to levels 3, 5, and 10, which isn't a sequential progression of levels, since the user is going all over the place. Basically, each level needs to have a unique level number before you can make your final compiled game, and a linear progression is easiest for your first few games.

WARP-TO POINTS

Traveling between game levels is done through *warp-to* points. A warp-to point is merely the place where the player appears in a level. These points are set using the Warp-To Point Manager from the Level pull-down menu. You can put as many warp-to points in a level as you like. You assign a name to each warp-to point after you set it with the mouse (see Figures 18.1 and 18.2).

Once a warp-to point is defined, you can make the player travel to that level and position at any time by using platforms, or by having an animated object execute the "warp-to point" command. Normally, the passageways between levels are done with a simple invisible platform placed around a stairwell wall piece. When the player walks within the invisible boundary of the platform object, he or she is whisked to a different level and position.

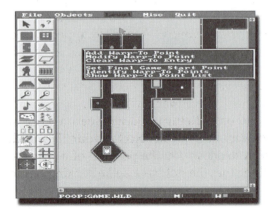

FIGURE 18.1   The Warp-To Point Manager.

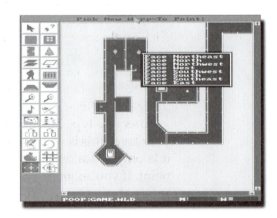

FIGURE 18.2   Selecting a warp-to point and direction selector.

HINT!

The warp-to point is only a destination; the platform makes the level switch happen. To make a connection between two levels, you must set both a warp-to point in the destination level and a platform in the original level.

WATCHOUT!

This does *not* work in test mode. All warp-to platforms or animated object commands will be ignored in test mode. These will work only in final game that you start with the GO.BAT batch file.

It is very important to keep track of all the connections between levels on pencil and paper. Do not try to keep the level numbers and the warp-to point names in your head. List each of your level names, and write down the name and level number. When you have assigned each level a number and written it down on paper, it is time to assign connections between the levels.

Internally, the GCS makes a table when you use the Warp-To Manager from the Level menu. You must enter a name for each warp-to point. Warp-to points specify a level number and a position.

Say you want the user to start at level 0, walk up to a staircase, and then switch to level 7. Assuming that you have already set a current level number for each of your levels, you can go about setting warp-to points.

To do so, open level 7 of your game, then click on the Warp-to Point Manager menu choice in the Level menu. Next, choose Add, and then click on the spot you want the player to appear. A text box appears, asking you to choose which direction the player should end up facing (north is toward the top of the screen). It then asks you to type in a reference name of your choice. Choose a descriptive name, such as "Back into the lobby from stairs," so you will know which warp-to is what.

After you type in the name and press Return, you will see a red dot in your level; this is your warp-to point. It is not an object in your 3D world, it is only a marker on the screen to show you the position of a warp-to point. If you zoom in, you will see that the dot has a spike sticking out to show which direction you are facing.

HINT!

Because a warp-to point is not a really 3D object, the Box and Question Mark icon do not identify it. If you would like to see which warp-to point it is, bring up the Warp-To Manager and click on "Identify warp-to."

Thus, if a platform is set to warp the player to the lobby, he or she is warped to level 7 in the final game and appears at the place you clicked.

Now you have set one warp-to point. To make it a functional passageway between levels, you must make a platform object in level 0, and place it right in front of the staircase wall. Make sure that the platform sticks out at least 150 cm from the wall. When you make the platform, click on the Warp-To box. Then when you click OK, you will be given a list of the warp-to points to choose from. Select the one you just made. You have formed the connection between level 0 and level 7 of your game.

WATCHOUT!

Platforms can perform only one function at a time, so press only the Warp-To button, not any of the others. If you click on more than one function for your platform, the platform might not work.

If you want the connection between levels 0 and 7 to be a two-way connection so the user can come back the same way, you must make another level 0 warp-to point. You must make a platform in your level 7 that sends the user there. To set a warp-to point in level 0, you need to open level 0, click the Warp-To Manager from the Level menu, and assign a name to your new warp-to point.

WATCHOUT!

A design challenge here is to make sure that you don't put the platform in level 7 where the user lands in the exact same spot as where he or she is teleported in from level 0. This mistake causes an endless loop, and the user bounces back and forth between the two levels indefinitely.

IMPORTANT CONSIDERATIONS

We're almost there! Let's create the "Start Game" Device and make sure everything works.

No Level Switches in Test Mode

The only way to test your interlevel connections is to click Make Final, exit GCS, and run the game from the target directory. Level switch platforms and animated objects that give the level switch command are ignored in test mode.

Make Final does *not* work unless you have specified a game start position.

Bring up the Warp-To Manager, and click on the command to set the final game start position. Don't confuse this with the Set Player Position command in the Level menu; that command is only for testing the 3D world.

After you specify and name the game start position, it appears as a yellow dot with a spike. You can only have one game start position. The starting point can be on any of your levels; the player does not have to start on level 0.

SETTING THE GAME START POSITION

The Set Player Position command in the Level menu is used only with the test command; it does *not* set where the player starts in the final game. These positions are ignored in the final game. To set the starting position for the player in the final game, you *must* use the Set Final Game Start Point command from the Warp-To Manager menu. This sets the location of the player when he or she starts the final game using the GO.BAT batch file.

Make Final will *not* work unless you have tested all your levels.

When you click on "Test level" to try out your level, several files are created in the project directory on your hard drive. The Make Final feature uses these files to compile all your .VGR files and other files into compressed binary files. The upshot is that unless you have clicked on "Test level" for each level, the Make Final command will fail.

When you make changes in any level in your project, you must test the level in the 3D world. Otherwise, when you click on Make Final, your changes will not be reflected in the final product.

If you change the level number of a level using the Set Current Level Number command, you must click on "Test level," enter the 3D world, and come back. Otherwise, that level will not be stored correctly. If you make a mistake and give two of your levels the same number, only one of the two levels will make it to the final game. The level that you tested last is included, and its twin is bypassed. Then, in your final product, any warp-to points that were meant for the missing level would take the player to inappropriate spots, since the warp-to points weren't meant for that level.

When you click on Make Final, only levels that have warp-to points assigned to them will be included in the final product. This makes sense because if there is no way for the player to get to that level, there is no reason to include that level in the final product.

PREPARING FOR MAKE FINAL

1. Go through all your levels and figure out where you want players to enter the levels.
2. Set the warp-to points, and write them down!
3. Go through all the levels and put in the level-switching platforms. Use your list to get the *correct* warp-to point names.

WATCHOUT!

If you set a platform to a nonexistent warp-to point, you will get a critical error message when you go over that platform in the final game.

Don't forget to click on "Test level" after setting each warp-to point. If you don't test each level in the 3D world after changing it in any way, the changes will not be included your final product!

Don't forget to set the final game starting point from the Warp-To menu. If you do, GCS will refuse to obey the Make Final command.

After this, you are ready to make your final game. Open any of your game levels, and select Make Final from the File menu. The GCS game engine starts up, but instead of the normal dialog box, a different one appears. All the levels in your game are listed in the dialog box. Select the first one, so it is highlighted in blue. Then, click Compile this Level (see Figure 18.3).

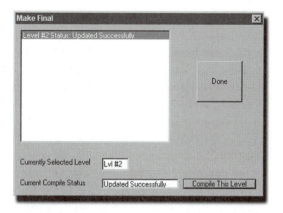

FIGURE 18.3   The Levels dialog box during the Make Final operation.

After this is done, exit the game engine and go back to the Level Editor. Repeat this process for your other levels. When your game level has been "made final," your game is ready for testing.

TRYING OUT YOUR FINAL GAME

To try out your final product, do the following

1. Exit GCS.
2. Change directory to the target game directory. The target directory should be in the root of your hard drive and have the same name as your project. For example, if your project is named "Blaster," and your GCS is installed on drive C:, your final game target directory is named "C:\Blaster."
3. Run the game by opening a DOS prompt box and changing directory to your final game directory, typing one of the following Go.bat command lines:

   go. (for no sound)

   go s1. (for sound; letter "s" and number one, *not* letter "s" and letter "L")

   go s1 j. (for sound, and joystick control)

   go s1 m. (for sound, and mouse control)

   go s1 m g. (for sound, mouse control, and God mode)

You will notice that the game loads much faster than it does in "Test level."

WHAT TO DO IF THERE ARE PROBLEMS

Make sure you typed an "s one" (s1), not "s" and the letter "L" (sl). This mistake is the most often made.

Don't put slashes or dashes in front of the command-line options, as you might for other DOS applications.

If the level-to-level connections aren't working, you can always redo them. Use the Box and Question Mark icon to tell you what each platform is set to do, and examine your warp-to points. You can overwrite their current values by erasing and replacing platforms, and using the Warp-To Manager to reset your warp-to points.

HINT!

If you feel that your warp-to points are beyond repair, or if you are simply confused and want to start with a clean slate (perhaps because you didn't write them down), exit GCS, delete the WARP_TO.DAT and GAMESTRT.DAT files, and start putting in your warp-to points from scratch.

WATCHOUT!

If you remove a warp-to point, you must also remember to remove any platforms that direct the player to the now-absent warp-to point. Warping to a deleted warp-to can cause unexpected results, or a critical error.

COMMON PROBLEMS IN THE FINAL GAME

You might find it helpful to print the THEATERS.TXT file from your target data\ subdirectory. The first column is the warp-to point number. The third column is the level number. The next three numbers are the x, y, and z coordinates of the point in the 3D world where the player appears.

If strange things are happening, such as levels missing in your final game, or if you are appearing in totally unexpected places, a common mistake is that you have given two levels the same level number. GCS will not complain about this, but the final game will never work correctly. This type of error does not normally generate critical errors, but it can cause level switches to unpredictable places.

MAKING AN INSTALLATION FOR YOUR FINAL GAME

ON THE CD

Once the final game is running the way you want on your system, you'll want to distribute the final product for others to try. To do this, I suggest you use Install Maker by Clickteam, which is included on the companion CD-ROM. Install it and follow the wizard through the process of building a professional installation routine. Install Maker allows you to create custom bitmaps, README files, install directories and, best of all, an uninstall routine.

TROUBLESHOOTING

We may have missed something along the way—it's okay. Here are some common troubleshooting tips to get you back on track.

WHAT TO DO IF THE GAME ENGINE WON'T GO INTO THE 3D WORLD

First, to isolate your problem, always try the original and unchanged WREDEMO level (remember I suggested that you make a copy if you altered it). If that fails, you know the problem isn't with the level itself; it must be with the driver or mode selection. If the demo levels work fine, but your level won't, the problem must be with your new level.

If the WREDEMO level will not run, how does it fail? Normally, when you press the Enter 3D World button, text messages flash in the lower left-hand part of the screen as the game engine loads the various components of your game level. When all the data is complete, the video should blank for a split second while it changes to the new full-screen mode. The game engine should then start.

HINT!

If the level fails before the screen blanks, the problem is probably with the installation or something that is preventing the level data from loading correctly. If there is a critical error or a *seterror*, write the numbers down and contact Pie in the Sky at their Web site for assistance. In addition, look in the ENGINE directory for a file called "error.txt," which is written when an error occurs, and send that along.

If the error or crash occurs directly after the screen blanks, it could be a Direct X graphics type of error; in which case, switching the DirectDraw Device, the D3D Device, or video mode might solve the problem. The most reliable settings are a DD Device of "Display," a D3D Device of "RAMP," and a video mode of "320x200x16." To change your settings, start the game engine, and press the Change Device/Mode button instead of the Enter 3D World button. Then, use the items in the File menu to change your settings to the following.

DD Device: Display—Use Select DD Device from the File menu to set this.

D3D Device: RAMP—Use Select D3D Device from the File menu to set this.

Display Mode: 320x200x16 Hi Color—Use Choose Screen Size/Mode from the File menu to set this.

If these settings fail, you'll have to contact Pie in the Sky at their Web site for assistance. Check the Web site www.pieskysoft.com for the latest support info. Your problem may have been experienced by others, and there may be a solution on the site.

If these settings *do* work, you'll have to do some experimentation to find out whether it was the video mode, the HAL driver, or some setting that caused the problem. Make sure you do your testing on the unmodified WREDEMO level, since that is known to be a functioning game level.

DEBUGGING YOUR GAME LEVEL

If the WREDEMO levels work fine in the 3D world, but your level does not, first find out if all your levels fail, or just that particular one. If you only have one level so far in your project, try adding a new level with just a few walls in it that are close to the start position. Try setting the objdef library to "Basiclib," the active guard set to "def_enem," and the level number to 30 or something you aren't using in your other level(s). If the WREDEMO levels test fine but even this very simple level does not run in the GCS Windows engine, there must be something wrong with the entire project. Write down any error numbers and print out the error.txt file that is created in the ENGINE directory when the game gets an unrecoverable error. Contact Pie in the Sky at their Web site for assistance, or check out www.pieskysoft.com to see if others have experienced your problem—there may be a solution there for you.

TROUBLESHOOTING QUESTIONS AND ANSWERS

Q. *I put platforms and warp-to points in my level, but it never works. I go there and stand right in the middle of the platform, but nothing happens.*

Level switching cannot occur when testing an individual level. You need to "Make Final," and then run the final game.

In addition, make sure that you "Test level" after setting any platform. If you forget to test your level after making changes, the platform will not be in your final game.

Use the ? icon to check that your platforms are in the right place and are set correctly. If in doubt, delete your platform and replace it with a new one, but don't forget to "Test level" before making final again!

Q. *How can I put more than one type of enemy on a level?*

The Level Editor assumes that you have just one type of enemy on your game level. However, you may have several different types of enemies on your level. To add more types of enemies, you need to use the Extra Features Editor, not the DOS Editor.

Q. *When I save my files in GCSPaint, they aren't saved, or they are saved as the wrong file type.*

A few things could be happening.

If you want to save your images as a .VGR file, you must launch GCSPaint from the icon on the GCS Layout Editor screen.

If you launched the paint program by typing "GCSPAINT," your files will be saved as .VGA files.

If you save your .VGR file in the proper directory, it may not show up in your Import list in the Library Manager dialog box. Be advised that although things you add to the list usually appear at the end, this is not always so. This is dependent on DOS file order on the hard drives, which is unpredictable. Look through the list carefully, and you can probably find your files.

Q. *How do I change the damage indicator guy for my game?*

Exit the GCS, and bring up GCSPaint from the command line. You need to load the .VGA file called htpt.vga from your project directory. You will see that this image file is a tiled repeat of the damage indicator with varying degrees of damage in each picture. Feel free to change your damage images.

WATCHOUT!

Do not try to change the dimensions of the damage boxes or the size of the ENTIRE htpt.vga image. If you do, the engine may crash.

Q. *Why doesn't sound work in my final game? Why doesn't my joystick work?*

The joystick cannot be used when testing levels. You need to add "s1" to the Go command line: go s1. (Make sure you use a one ["1"] character, not ["L"] in your "s1" option!)

You must also add a "j" if you want joystick support. When you actually finish your game, you will probably want to use GCS-MENU to create a way for your customers to choose sound on/off, joystick on/off, and so forth.

Q. *When I try to define written text for memos and animated objects to use, it never works.*

You need to edit the file pstr.txt in your project directory, and then you must run the program pstr.exe on it to actually make new text messages available for your game. The Help file on "Text Messages" explains how to do this. Be very careful not to ignore the two periods and the backslash when you type PSTR! In addition, make sure you understand how to give each message in your pstr.txt file a different number when you are editing the file.

Q. *When I try to load my .GIF, .PCX, or .BMP file into GCSPaint, the screen flashes, and it refuses to load my picture.*

The most common cause of this problem is that you are trying to import a picture that has too many pixels in it. The largest image that GCSPaint can handle is 200x200 pixels. If an image is more than 200 pixels high *or* 200 pixels wide, the image will refuse to load. A 200x200 object is too big for a practical object in a GCS game.

If you are absolutely sure that your image is small enough, but the image is still being rejected, then perhaps your .PCX or .BMP file is not the right type. Since GCS artwork must be 256 colors, all .PCX or .BMP files that you import must be 256 colors as well. Sixteen-color files are not accepted, and neither are 16-million-color versions of these files.

Q. *Why is the computer beeping at me whenever I do anything with my level?*
You are close to, or have already added, too much artwork to your level, and memory is full. See the explanation of the M and W meters in Chapter 15, "Making a 3D Game Level."

A LEGAL NOTICE OF WHAT YOU MAY DISTRIBUTE

When you use the Make Final command, GCS makes a directory on your hard drive with the same name as your project. You may distribute all the files in this directory and the data\ subdirectory. These files comprise *your* game. The .EXE files in that directory are copyrighted by Pie in the Sky Software, but as with shareware programs, you have implicit permission to distribute them in unmodified form. The same goes for all the other files that the unmodified GCS puts in that directory when you "Make Final."

When the user copies the game files from your floppies to his or her hard drive, make sure the user preserves the directory structure. This means that the data\ subdirectory and its contents must be contained within the main game directory when the user types the go.bat command line to start the game.

ACTIVITIES

For this final exercise of the book, have a party. That's right, if you have created several games using this book and want to show them off, invite friends and family to come over and check them out. Have fun making games and creating worlds.

THE END

Well, this brings us to the end of the Pie 3D Game Creation System, and the end of this book. I hope this book was a fun and effective introduction to game design and development. Please keep in touch.

Looking Ahead to Career Possibilities

The development of a computer game is a unique production, combining a wide range of elements into what should be enjoyable experience for the end user. A typical game project involves programmers, artists, musicians, designers, and countless others who are necessary components of a successful venture. If you enjoyed creating and using the games in this book, you might want to think about a career in the game development industry.

Note: The salaries listed next to each category vary dramatically according to game genre, the game publisher or software developer, and level of experience. Consider most of the salaries "entry level," or with a year or two of experience.

THE KEY POSITIONS IN A DEVELOPMENT TEAM

A development project requires several key positions, without any one of which the project would not be successful. Depending on the size of a team, a single person may be forced to wear many hats, or in the case of

SOURCE   This section has been modified from Chapter 1 of *3D Game Programming Using Direct X8* by Clayton Crooks II © 2001, Charles River Media).

the lone developer, *all* the hats. Because the game industry is still in its infancy, it's sometimes difficult to discuss the positions that make up a team.

DESIGNERS

Game Designer (~$50K/yr)
Level Designer (~$45K/yr)

The designer makes many of the decisions related to the creation of important aspects of the game, such as puzzles or the levels in a first-person shooter. Like a screenwriter, a designer is responsible for the overall feel of the game. Communication is a very important aspect of this job, as the designer works with the other team members for the duration of a project.

In the beginning stages of making a game, designers spend most of their time focusing on writing short scripts and working on the beginning storyboard sketches. A typical storyboard displays the action of a game in a very simple manner. Depending on their talents, designers may even include stick figures and basic shapes to convey their messages. (A storyboard is a rough draft that will later be transformed into the game itself.)

After the decisions are made on the game concepts, the designer begins working on a blueprint for the game called a *design document*. Simply put, the document details every aspect of a game, and it evolves as the game is being developed.

PROGRAMMER (~$60–$90K/YR)

Game programmers are software developers who take the ideas, level designs, art, and music and combine them into a software project. Programmers write the code for the game, but they may have several additional responsibilities. For example, if an artist is designing graphics for the game, the lead programmer could be responsible for the development of a custom set of tools for creation of the graphics. It is also the programmer's job to keep everything running smoothly and figure out a way to satisfy everyone, from the producer to the artists.

Programmers are responsible for combining the vast number of elements to form the executable program. They decide how fast players can run or how high they can jump. They are responsible for accounting for everything inside the virtual world. While doing all this, they often attempt to create software that is reusable for other projects, and they spend a great deal of time optimizing the computer code to make it as fast as possible.

A project may have several programmers who specialize in one key area, such as graphics, sound, or artificial intelligence (AI). The following list details the various types of programmers and their primary responsibilities.

- **Engine or graphics programmers** create the software that controls how graphics and animations are stored and ultimately displayed on the screen.
- **AI programmers** create a series of rules that determine how enemies or characters react to game situations and make them act as realistically as possible.
- **Sound programmers** work with the audio personnel to create a realistic-sounding environment.
- **Tool programmers** often write software for artists, designers, and sound designers to use in the development studio.

AUDIO-RELATED POSITIONS ($50K–$75K/YR)

High-quality music and sound effects are an integral part of any gaming project, but this is one area in which many teams simply cannot afford to invest a great deal of money. Having superb audio components for music, sound, and voice can greatly enhance the total experience for the consumer. The opposite is also true, however, and music that is done poorly can be enough to keep people away from your product regardless of its other qualities. Several individual positions are usually filled with key audio personnel, perhaps a programmer, or other team members as needed.

MUSICIAN

Musicians usually have the lightest workload compared to other development team members. They usually are responsible only for the music for a game, and although it is an important job, it does not typically take a great deal of time. Because of the relatively short production times, musicians often have secondary work outside of the gaming industry.

SOUND EFFECTS TECHNICIAN

Depending on the team, a musician could also be involved with creation of sound effects. Often this work makes up for their lack of work opportunities on the project and helps to reduce the overall budget. Another route that many teams choose to follow is the purchase of preexisting sound effects. Many sound effects companies distribute their work on CD-ROMs or via the Internet, and many teams choose to modify these sound effects to their liking rather than hire in-house personnel.

ARTISTS (~$45–$75K/YR)

The artists are responsible for the graphics elements that make up a project. They often specialize in one area within a project, such as 3D graphics or 2D artwork-like textures. The artists usually have a set of specifications from the programmer for creating graphics. Unfortunately, artists and programmers may disagree on these specifications. For example, an artist might want to increase the polygon counts on a 3D model so that his or her work will *look* better on screen, whereas a programmer may want to decrease these counts to make the program run faster and more smoothly.

Game artists must work with a variety of technical constraints imposed by the limitations of the hardware. Although hardware continues to increase in speed and decrease in cost, there is never enough power to satisfy a game development project. Therefore, the artists are often given the responsibility to create objects that work within the constraints.

Depending on the development team, there are three types of artists: a *character artist* (or *animator*, as some prefer to be called), *3D modelers*, and *texture artists*.

CHARACTER ARTISTS

Character artists have one of the most demanding jobs on the team. They create all of the movable objects in a game, such as the main character, a spaceship, or a vehicle. It is their job to turn the preliminary sketches into a believable object on a computer screen.

Using 3D modeling tools such 3ds max, TrueSpace, Maya, or Light-Wave, the character artists use basic shapes and combine them to form the character. If you have never used a 3D modeling program, you can think of it as a type of digital clay. Once created, the character is then skinned with a 2D graphic image that is made in another application program.

The character artists are also responsible for animation of objects. They may be required to animate a horse, a human being, or a creature from another world. Character artists often look at real-world examples to get their ideas on how a character should move in certain situations. Depending on the type of game, they may have to create facial expressions or emotion as well.

It is often the responsibility of a character artist to implement cut scenes in a game. Many artists enjoy creating the cut screens more than characters. They have much greater freedom and are not restricted as to the number of polygons a certain object can have or the size of the object.

3D MODELER

The 3D modeler usually works on a game's setting, such as a basketball arena or a Wild West wasteland. Background artists work hand in hand with the designer to create believable environments that work within the constraints of a game. As with character artists, background artists use a wide range of tools, including both 2D and 3D graphics tools, although they usually model static objects.

TEXTURE ARTIST

Texture artists might be the best friends of the other artists. It is their job to take the work created by the modeler or character artist and add detail. For example, they could create a brick texture that, when added to a 3D box created by the modeler, creates the illusion of a pile of bricks. On the other hand, they could create a texture that looks like cheese, turning this same box into a block of cheese.

PRODUCER ($65K/YR)

A producer oversees the entire project and keeps everything moving as smoothly as possible. Planning, scheduling personnel and equipment, hiring and firing, and general knowledge of the industry and competition are all the responsibilities of the producer. Producers often act as arbitrators to help resolve any problems between team members. For example, if an artist wants to increase the color palette, and a programmer wants to decrease it, the producer often makes the final decision.

MISCELLANEOUS POSITIONS ($25K–$40K/YR)

Several secondary positions can be important to the game development cycle. Depending on the budget, these positions may or may not exist or may be filled by other members of the team.

QUALITY ASSURANCE/BETA TESTERS

The beta tester tests the "playability" of a game and looks for bugs that may occur when the game is executed. It is one of the most undervalued positions and should never be completed by the person responsible for programming the game. In reality, because of tight budgets and deadlines, beta testing is one of the steps that is often cut before it is completed because due dates take precedence over most decisions. If adequate beta testing is performed, a development team can save a tremendous amount of time and resources without having to produce unnecessary patches later.

PLAY TESTERS

The play testers are often confused with beta testers. Play testers test the playability of a game and critique areas such as movement or graphic elements. Again, these positions are often filled with individuals who perform other tasks on the team. Unlike beta testers, the play testers do not actually attempt to find or report bugs.

Game Development Resources

T his list of resources is biased toward Web sites and companies that
have active Web pages because the Internet is probably the best and
most up-to-date source of information for game development and related
topics. Keep in mind that these resources are far from the only available
resources, however. In fact, there is a mountain of information out there,
and I encourage you to always be on the lookout for new information.

Usually, I chose a link or resource because it contained a large list of
other resources such as *3D Links*, *The Game Development Search Engine*,
and the various game news sites. The sum of online resources is vast and
extensive—far too vast for one book. In addition, the fact that the Web is
fluid and changing would make any extensive cataloging effort a waste.
It is suggested that you browse these links and bookmark those that are
the most useful to you, then check them at least once a week. You will
find that the online communities are very supportive and knowledge-
able. Most have various forums for communicating.

THE WEB SITE
· · · · · · · · · · ·

Web sites for a company can range from a few pages containing an online
brochure to a huge and constantly changing source of information. The
more vibrant Web sites offer mailing lists, forums, and chat rooms. Take
advantage of all this wealth of information!

THE MAILING LIST

A mailing list works just as you'd think: You get on a list and are e-mailed updates and announcements. Mailing lists function in many ways. You can get e-mail from every individual who mails to the list address. Because this method can amount to a huge number of e-mails for an active list, you can usually also get moderated lists, in which only e-mails approved by the list master are sent out to the entire list. You can also get the e-mail list digest. This is one big e-mail that contains all the e-mails from the list.

THE MESSAGE FORUM

A message forum is a place online where you can post messages under topics and discussion threads. The typical forum has many topic headings under which you can start a message thread with a post that has to do with the topic. Then people will usually respond to your post. It is advised that you search the forums and get to know them before posting. There is nothing more aggravating than to have the same questions asked 10 times a day because people don't bother looking at the messages to see if their question has already been answered. Most message boards also have search utilities and other tools to help you navigate them.

NEWSGROUPS

Newsgroups are similar to message forums in that you find a newsgroup dedicated to your topic of interest and then you can post questions and answers. There are thousands of newsgroups, with topics ranging from certain products, subject areas, or people.

ICQ

ICQ, from the term "I seek you," shows you when others using ICQ are online if they are in your list. With ICQ, you can chat; send messages, files, and URLs; or play games.

GENESIS 3D–RELATED RESOURCES

The Genesis 3D Home Page

www.genesis3d.com
Contains links and all the updated information you will need.

MilkShape3D

www.swissquake.ch/chumbalum-soft/
A low-polygon-count 3D package that can import and export many game model formats, including the Genesis format.

WOG: World of Genesis

www.gameznet.com/genesis
The best source for Genesis-related information for newbie and professional alike.

Rabid Games: The Reality Factory

www.rabidgames.com
The Reality Factory is covered in Part II of this book.

vxEdit

http://members.xoom.com/edgarapoe321/quixotic.htm
vxEdit (rfEdit) is covered in Part II of this book.

3D Sector

www.gen3d.de
Tutorials and more.

GENESIS GAMES

AI Wars

www.aiwars.com

Below Zero

Developer: PcFire Interactive
Contact: Matthew Butlar

Henchman

http://henchman.homestead.com/
Features an outdoor area in the beginning of the game. The goal of *Henchman* wasn't to develop a commercial game, but to build a programming tutorial out of it.

The Heir

www.ourfun.com

Heroes for Hire

www.peanutco.com

TrilobiteShell

www.trilobiteworks.com
Trilobite is a game shell based on the Genesis 3D rendering engine. A game shell is the code that organizes the capabilities of the rendering engine into a cohesive application—a game.

Cheese Frenzy

www.gametitan.com
In this action game, the player gets the incredible perspective of a mouse that is on the hunt for his captured friend while collecting cheese bits. Avoiding enemies such as mouse traps, cats, and household dangers, the player has to scurry like a boy or girl mouse through everyday household obstacles, collect cheese for points, and power-up for more chances and speed boosts to exit before the timer goes off. The game play is simplistic, with the player having the option to concentrate on the score or to finish the plot. There are numerous animated sequences explaining the story before the beginning of each stage and at the end of game play. Each stage has its own levels, or rooms of the house. Current stages are Suburban House, Country House, City House, Laboratory House, and, the grand finale, Moon Base House, with Boss Monster Ratto. The game features a bright and stylized look that is appealing to children as well as adults. The content is mainly slapstick, nongory, and child safe.

PAN: Ground Zero

www.gekido.bc.ca/index.htm.
The Prison Arena Network (PAN) is multiplayer online combat, fast and furious. Combining all the classic death-match and traditional online variations, PAN throws the player into a life-or-death existence as an in-

mate in the most sadistic prison network ever conceived. Inmates of PAN are subjected to brutal hand-to-hand combat, forced to fight other inmates to survive.

PIG: Politically Incorrect Game

www.cybertag.com
Due to the rising of unhealthy ideologies in the developers' country (France), they decided to use Genesis 3D to contribute to the struggle against all fascism by investing all their time and financial power in the development of PIG.

SpaceBlast!

by Nitroheads
www.gfxspace.com/spaceblast/
SpaceBlast is a fast and furious arcade-style multiplayer space combat game that will bring you and your friends many sleepless nights.

G-Sector

G-Sector is the boldest step in freeware: a full 3D game using the Genesis 3D engine. It supports Glide and Direct3D for 3D acceleration. G-Sector is developed "in-house" by Freeform Interactive LLC, the owners of Ingava.com, FreeGamesWeb.com, GamesHEAD.com, and the FvF -franchise.

G-Sector is a 3D action game based around hoverboard combat—a hybrid between an "extreme game" and a third-person shooter. Players control the heroine Cyra as she hoverboards through futuristic cities and arenas. Game play is based on using ramps and tricks to build velocity and avoid opponents' shots. Using a chase-cam and customizable mouse/keyboard interface, *G-Sector* should be familiar to players of the 3D shooter genre. Its features include 3D graphics, a third-person view, and extreme hoverboard combat action.

Gangsters

www.crosswinds.net/~nightwood/index2.html
Gangsters is a first-person shooter, developed by Nightwood using the Genesis 3D engine. It sports a huge arsenal of weapons and some of the best levels made with Genesis.

Pack Rat

www.roguestudios.com

Crystal Interactive picked up the limited license to *Pack Rat* in August 2000. The game is getting enhancements to the engine and the levels. Look for *Pack Rat* at a computer software store near you after October 31, 2000.

SOTA: Survivor of the Ages

www.alien-logic.com

Survivor of the Ages is a third-person RPG with some fighter game elements. It features a fully 3D world populated by creatures of all virtues and kinds. SOTA also features rich textures and scenes along with original soundtracks. SOTA has some of the most advanced collision detection seen in games today. Each character has multiple damage areas distributed at key points. These points allow for precise control of the kind of damage the player wants to inflict on an enemy. There are many more fun and startling features in SOTA. The recommended system is a PII-class processor or better, 64MB or more of RAM, and a 3DFX card such as the VooDoo2 and VooDoo3 or better.

MISCELLANEOUS RESOURCES

Fonts 'n' Things

www.fontsnthings.com

Fonts are very useful for texture creation. You can find many free fonts and links to more sources of fonts at this site.

3D RAPH

www.raph.com/3dartists

Lots of interviews with artists and tutorials.

Free Textures

www.freetextures.com

Loads of free textures of all kinds.

The 3D Studio

www.the3dstudio.com

Free pretextured MAX models, free seamless textures, and free MAX tutorials.

DESIGN RESOURCES

Game Developer Search Engine

www.game-developer.com

A very full site containing much of the information you will need on game development.

Gamasutra

www.gamasutra.com

The mother of all game development sites! You can find articles and resources on all aspects of game development and design here.

GIG News

www.gignews.com

Game Dev Net

www.gamedev.net

Another great source of development resources, with an online glossary of terms as well.

Game Center

www.gamecenter.com/Features/Exclusives/Design/ss01.html

This is a great article on game design.

Lupine Games

www.lupinegames.com

A must-visit link for wannabe developers.

The Inspiracy

www.theinspiracy.com

Noah Falstein maintains this site and has some great articles and information here.

International Game Developer Network (IGDN)

www.igdn.com

IGDN is an unincorporated membership association for the game developer community.

G.O.D. Games

www.godgames.com
Very cool guys. Especially read the Commandments and the Oracle.

GAME NEWS RESOURCES

The following sites have up-to-the-minute news on many areas of game development and the industry.

Game Spy

www.gamespy.com

3D Action Planet

www.3dactionplanet.com

Looney Games

www.loonygames.com

Blues News

www.bluesnews.com

Game Spot

www.gamespot.com

Game Center

www.gamecenter.com

Adrenaline Vault

www.avault.com

Classic Gaming

www.classicgaming.com

Game-Jobs.com

www.game-jobs.com
A European job recruiter for the game and entertainment industry.

Happy Puppy

www.happypuppy.com

SOFTWARE AND DEVELOPMENT ENGINE RESOURCES

Rabid Games

www.rabidgames.com
Improvement on Genesis 3D.

Genesis 3D

www.genesis3d.com
Open source 3D engine.

The Gimp

www.gimp.org
Free GNU Photoshop-like application.

MilkShape 3D

www.swissquake.ch/chumbalum-soft

Paint Shop Pro

www.jasc.com

Photoshop

www.adobe.com

BOOK AND MAGAZINE RESOURCES

Charles River Media

www.charlesriver.com

Game Architecture and Design

Andrew Rollings and Dave Morris

Game Developer's Marketplace

Ben Sawyer, Tor Berg, Alex Dunne

Game Design: Secrets of the Sages
Marc Saltzman

Awesome Game Creation
Luke Ahearn

Game Developer Magazine
www.gdmag.com
A must-visit site.

3D Design Magazine
www.3d-design.com
Great magazine and Web site.

Computer Graphics World
www.cgw.com
A great magazine and Web site. Check out their bookstore.

CONFERENCES AND CONVENTIONS

The Computer Game Developers Conference
www.cgdc.com

E3
www.e3expo.com

SIGGRAPH
www.siggraph.org

MODELING RESOURCES

3D Cafe
www.3dcafe.com

3D Palette
www.3dpalette.com

3D Links
www.3dlinks.com

Turbo Squid
www.turbosquid.com

GAME DEVELOPMENT TOOLS AND ENGINES

The Crystal Space Engine
http://crystal.linuxgames.com

The 3D Engines List
http://cg.cs.tu-berlin.de/~ki/engines.html

Rabid Games
www.rabidgames.com

Genesis 3D
www.genesis3d.com

GAME DEVELOPMENT ASSOCIATIONS

Academy of Interactive Arts & Sciences
www.vectorg.com

Computer Game Artists
www.vectorg.com

Computer Game Developers Association
www.cgda.org

Interactive Digital Software Association
www.idsa.com

International Game Developers Network
www.igdn.com

What's on the CD-ROM

The CyberRookies companion CD-ROM is packed with everything you need to make all of the fully interactive games in this book—and more! Each of the folders includes useful tools for you to learn game creation!

> **General Minimum System Requirements**: You will need a computer that can run Windows 95 with a CD-ROM drive, sound card, and mouse to complete *all* of the tutorials and play all of the games in this book.

THE GAMES FACTORY AND INSTALL MAKER BY CLICKTEAM

(www.clickteam.com)

There are two folders on the ROM (TGF FINAL 16 and TGF FINAL 32) and each includes either the 16 Bit (Win 3.1 and NT) or the 32 Bit (Windows 95/98/2000) install files for the respective version of The Games Factory. The proper file will install everything you need to run *The Games Factory*. As long as you can run Windows or Windows NT, you can run *The Games Factory* and *The Install Maker*.

This version of *The Games Factory* is a special demo version for the book and is *not* time limited. It is a fully functional shareware demo and is only limited in the following ways:

- You will see a Games Factory screen at start up
- You will *not* be able to save stand-alone games, screen savers, or Internet games. But you can save the .GAM data files created and when you upgrade to the registered version your files will be fully compatible. Please got to www.clickteam.com for the upgrade price - it is a bargain!

THE PIE 3D GAME CREATION SYSTEM BY PIE IN THE SKY SOFTWARE

(www.pieskysoft.com)

With The PIECGS you can make your own stand-alone 3D games with no programming (the 'PieGCS' folder on the ROM). Simply run the installer and you are in business. This application was designed to run on a 386 or better computer with a VGA graphics card. The best part of the PIEGCS is that it is free! The only limit being that there is no technical support, but on the Web site (www.pieskysoft.com) there is technical support files and information. You can also join the mailing list at www.gcsgames.com and get all the help you need.

SAMPLE GAME FILES

In the 'sample games' folder of the ROM are all the files and assets used in the exercises in the book in part 2. Please note that all needed assets are within the GAM files.

1. Cosmic Battle
   battle.gam
2. Bat Flight
   bat.ga.
3. Dood Hunter
   DoodHunter.gam
4. tgflibs
   battle.gam
   bat.gam
   DoodHunter.gam

Glossary

3D Three Dimensions, which are height, width, and depth.

3D Accelerator Card This is a special graphics card that takes the burden of processing the intense calculations of the 3D process off the main processor of the computer.

2 & 1/2-D Two and a half DEE is a term for the older 3D engines that fake a lot of the 3D look of their games. They used a 3D engine but most of what was seen was 2D graphics.

Algorithm An algorithm is a series of instructions for performing a programming task.

Aliasing This is the "jaggy edges" produced on low-resolution images due to pixelation.

Alpha Blending By controlling the translucency of each pixel you can get effects such as fog, glass, and see-through surfaces.

Alpha Channel An alpha channel is used to determine each pixel's translucency. For example, the bitmap is the actual graphic you wish to use and the alpha channel determines the transparency of each pixel in the bitmap. Each pixel in the alpha effects the corresponding pixel in the bitmap. The alpha is a shade of gray, and the closer to black the more transparent the alpha map and the more of the main bitmap will show, with black (0, 0, 0) being totally transparent while a color value of white (255, 255, 55) makes the corresponding pixel on the main image solid. A color value of (128, 128, 128) will make the pixel 50% transparent.

Animation Creating motion or activity using frames of imagery. Animation can be done with 2D images as in traditional animation, or with 3D objects that are either rendered as 2D stills or animated in real time.

Anti-aliasing This is the process that gets rid of the "jaggy edges" from aliasing. It simply removes the edges by blending them together.

Artificial Intelligence (A.I) Traditionally AI is the attempt to try and make a computer think, act or reason like a human, but in gaming it is mostly the effort to create the appearance that the computer is thinking.

Aspect Ratio The aspect ratio of an image is the ratio of its width to its height.

Avatar Avatar is another word for the player or character representing the user.

Bitmap A rectangular block of pixels that is broken down into data and stored in a certain format.

Byte A byte is 8 bits of data and is the equivalent of 256 different combinations (0 to 255). A single character on a computer screen is usually stored as a byte.

Cartesian Coordinate System The Cartesian Coordinate System uses three dimensions which are x, y, and z to represent a point in 3D space.

Clipping Pane The Clipping Pane is a barrier that tells the computer to stop drawing or rendering objects in the game world at a certain distance. The farther away the Clipping Plane is from the player the more he can see of the world.

Design Document This is the document that the designers create that contains everything a game should include. The design document should list every aspect from art, sound, music and character details, to storyline and gameplay.

Dithering Dithering creates the illusion that there are more colors in an image than are really present by arranging individual pixel patterns to fool the eye.

FMV Full Motion Video.

FPS First Person Shooter. A popular type of game in which the player sees all of the game's actions from the shooter's perspective (e.g. *Doom*).

FPS Frames Per Second. Games are often measured in frames per second. The computer must do all calculations and rendering in as short a time as possible, and the end result is how many frames per second the game will run.

Genre Just like the categories of fiction and movies, games are divided into genres such as First Person Shooter (FPS), Role Playing Game (RPG), and simulation.

GUI Graphical User Interface.

LAN Local Area Network. A network that covers an immediate area and is a mode of multiplayer gaming.

LOD Level of Detail. Many games support LOD, which makes 3D models less complex. For example, increasing LOD decreases the game's processing speed, whereas decreasing the LOD increases processing speed.

Massively Multiplayer A multiplayer game where the number of simultaneous players is in the hundreds or even thousands.

Mesh A 3D model. The wire frame version of a model looks like a mesh of wires.

MIDI Musical Instrument Digital Interface.

Mip Mapping This process breaks down textures or images into smaller versions. A texture may have various versions ranging from half size down to very small versions. This helps the texture retain its quality and helps the computer with rendering.

Motion Capture Motion Capture is the process where the motion (usually of a human) is captured, using various techniques and technologies, and converted into data the computer can use. Human movements such as walking and running often have such subtle and unique variations that motion capture is a great way to capture them.

Newbie A term for a player who is new to an area.

Parallax Scrolling This is a technique where several images are scrolled or moved at different rates of speed to give the sense of depth to the world. The background may move slower than the foreground, just as when you are driving a car on the highway and the roadside whips by while the buildings in the distance seem to move slower.

Pixel Picture Element. A small colored dot that makes up graphical images.

Real-Time When the game proceeds constantly in "real time" the player must respond in real time. This also refers to the distinction between real time 3D in which the world is generated as you move through it, and pre rendered 3D where you are essentially watching a movie.

RGB Red, Green, Blue. The 3 primary colors from which all other colors are made by having pixels displayed at different intensities next to each other on the screen.

Texel Texture Element. A texel is an individual pixel that is part of a texture.

Texture A texture is a 2D image that covers a polygonal face or set of faces like wallpaper. Textures can make a blank wall look like a brick wall, a flat ground look muddy, etc.

Texturing The act of applying images to 3D objects.

Translucent The process of alpha-blending two pixels together so there is the appearance of admitting and diffusing light, so that the objects beyond cannot be clearly distinguished (i.e. partly transparent).

Transparency The process of blending two pixels together so that they create a new pixel. In other words, collectively creating a new image that appears to be the two images together at various degrees of transparency.

Index